SAARC PERSPECTIVE

SAARC PERSPECTIVE

Edited by

Anil Bhuimali

Department of Economics, University of North Bengal

&

Chandan Kumar Mukhopadhyay

Department of Economics, University of North Bengal

SERIALS PUBLICATIONS

NEW DELHI

First Published - 2008

ISBN: 978-81-8387-168-6

Published by

SERIALS PUBLICATIONS
4830/24, Prahlad Street, Ansari Road
Darya Ganj, New Delhi-110002 (India)
Phone : 23245225 Fax : 91-11-23272135
E-mail: serials@satyam.net.in

CONTENTS

CONTRIBUTORS

Prof. Chandan Kumar, Mukhopadhyay, Faculty, Department of Economics, North Bengal University.

Tamash Ranjan Majumdar, Faculty, Department of Economics, North Bengal University.

Govinda Choudhuri, Faculty, Department of Economics, North Bengal University.

Biplab Chakraborty, Project Fellow, SAP(DRS), Department of Economics, North Bengal University.

Prof. Anil Bhuimali, Faculty, Department of Economics, North Bengal, University.

Mr. Biswajit Maitra, Faculty, Department of Commerce, AC College of Commerce, Jalpaiguri.

Mr. Nilanjan Biswa, Faculty (Part Time), P.D. Women's College, Jalpaiguri.

Prof. Kanak Kanti Begchi, Faculty, Department of Economics, North Bengal University.

Mr. Subhobrata Chakraborty, Faculty, Department of Economics, Sikkim Government College.

Mr. Sidharha Sankar Laha, Senior Research Fellow, Department of Economics, North Bengal University.

Md. Gholam Kibria, Faculty, Department of Management, Pabna Government College, Bangladesh.

Mr. Shyam Charan Barma, Research Fellow, Department of Economics, North Bengal University.

Mr. Kamananda Dev., SAARC Fellow, Department of Economics, North Bengal University.

Mr. Sankar Prasad Acharya, Staff to Nepal Restra Bank, Nepal.

Mr. Arjun Baral, Faculty, Department of Economics, Tribhuban University, Nepal.

Mr. Kanchan Dutta, Faculty, St. Joseph's College, Darjeeling.

Mr. Anil Kumar Biswas, Faculty, P.D. Women's College, Jalpaiguri.

INTRODUCTORY OVERVIEW

INTRODUCTION

During the Middle Ages Asia (including the South Asia region) was the most developed region of the world. India, for example, was famous for the delicacy of its cottons and exported clothes, spices and craft goods substantially to abroad. The South Asia region had a glorious past in its culture and heritage (e.g., the Indus Valley Civilization of northern India). Today, however, all the South Asia nations are part of the developing world. The nations have not shared in the Industrial Revolution and the higher standard of living that industrialization has had provided to the western world. Reform process initiatives in South Asia economies especially since 1990s has helped achieving healthy GDP and export growth rates, improved creditworthiness indicators and enhanced foreign investment. In spite of all such efforts the region's contribution in world trade is far less than two percent and almost forty percent of its population is afflicted with abject poverty, malnutrition and illiteracy. The poor are mostly located in the rural areas depending on subsistence agriculture and low-skill wage employed for their livelihood.

The present volume titled *Some Regional Issues in South Asia Perspective* is the out-come of a collectively effort of the Department of Economics, University of North Bengal. The financial support comes from the University Grant Cormnission (SAP-DRS scheme). The researchers have studied different socio-economic aspects such as education, literacy, trade, tourism, finance and some specific problems of small tea planters- jute industry and so on. Thirteen research papers including one on Investment in Education, one on small tea gardens, one on female literacy, three on tourism, one on structural change, four on finance, one on jute industry and one on trade. All the papers cover the whole of South Asia nations excepting Sri Lanka.

Tribal people lag for behind the non-tribals in terms of social, economic and political persuasion. This is equally true for their educational development. There remains wide variations in many respects among different tribal groups (e.g. between the Santhals and Bodos in Duars of North Bengal). In his paper Chandan Kumar Mukhopadhyay deals with investment motivation of a tribal community in duars on education. The author tries to derive the benefits from investment in education over time by the santhal community living in the duars region. To that end, present value of a stream of yearly benefits over time has been calculated and so also the cost involved of going to school have been clearly identified and estimated. In the course of discussion some important features of life of the santhal community such as their present-orientedness (i.e. ignoring the future at the extreme), absence of 'free lunch' and dispersion in 'income distribution' have been explained in brief. The paper concludes that the existing school education systems have failed to attract majority of santhal children to school. It has also noted that only creating education facility for them cannot be expected to generate demand for education among the tribal children. It is suggested that education may be popular if due care has been given for their social tastes, preferences, aspiration and expectation.

Indian tea industry plays a significant part in terms of employment generation (for being labour intensive), production (accounting for over 27 percent of total world tea production), and foreign exchange earnings (on average Rs. 1,874 *core* per annum). The paper by Tamash Ranjan Majumdar studies the socio-economic background of tea producers especially the small gardens in North Bengal. It specially analyses the possible reasons for the expansion of land under tea. It aims at testing some relevant hypotheses on the basis of information on the socio-economic characteristics of the planters. The study revels that there has been a phenomenal expansions of small tea plantations across the region. It is noted that small tea plantations are largely represented by the small and marginal farmers. It indicates a negative consequence underlying the proliferation of small tea planters.

Development of human resources is an essential ingredient for enhancing the level of production in an economy. This requires improvement in the overall quality of life. An increase in the growth of economy in a sustainable manner automatically improves the quality of life of the people which again gives rise to the conditions of human resource development. Thus proper health facility, nutrition, skill and adequate education help contributing steady progress in productive activities. Govinda Choudhury and Biplab Chakraborty's paper examines the condition of female literacy in the North Bengal perspective with special emphasis on studying the gender inequality in literacy and education. The paper gives a snapshot of gender gap and literacy in various states of India taking census data from 1901 to 2001. The rank of states according to the female literacy rate has been shown comparing data between 1991 and 2001. The state wise sex ratio (1951-2001) has also been represented. Demographic change and literacy in North Bengal has been presented beautifully showing the trend in population growth. Also the gender gap and female literacy in North Bengal has been well documented.

North Bengal region of West Bengal state is famous for three Ts i.e. 'tea', 'timber', and 'tourism'. The paper of Anil Bhuimali and Nilanjan Biswas elaborately discusses the conditions of tourism and its impact on the economy of North Bengal. The nature and the scope of alternative tourism have been explained. The paper suggests that alternative tourism have been developed in two ways. One is for Himalayan and its adjoin districts. This covers Daljeeling, Jalpaiguri and Cooch Behar. The other potential areas may be sonthern districts of Malda, Uttar and Dakshin Dinajpur. The paper has cited two case studies relating to rural tourism. Social, economic and environmental problems associated with the development of tourism industry in North Bengal have been clearly identified.

Correlating fiscal imbalance is an important task before any government. It is commonly aggred that fiscal and monetary policies have a prominent and far-reaching role in economic development. Government expenditure and government revenue are two main instruments of fiscal policy. The paper of Chandan Kumar Mikhopadhyay and Biswajit Maitra explains causal relationship between government expenditure and government revenue in India. In this study the time series annual data of 1950-2005 for the government expenditure and government revenue in India have been used to examine the causal relationship between the variables concerned. The study enquires into the nature of the stochastic processes of the macroeconomic time series concerned. ADF test results for real government expenditure and real government revenue in India appear to be co-integrated and thus there exists a stable long run relationship between them.

Structural change in the developing countries does not follow Clarkian framework of economic development. This also does not follow the path of Kuznets framework. Different countries have, in fact, followed different paths towards economic development. Economic development of a country can be thought of in terms of short-term as well as long-term perspectives. Of this two the long-term perspective is more important because the question of sustainability is involved in the context of long-term perspective. According to the change in the structure of an economy the development path of it can be ascertained which again depends mostly on the inter-sectoral linkages. Kanak Kanti Bagchi and Subhabrata Chakraborty's paper analyses such an important issue relating to structural change of Sikkim and other seven north-eastern states of India. The pattern of structural change in the eight north-east states from 1980 to 2000 has well been documented representing the fact that the structural change in the north-east region is characterized by a process of jobless and joyless growth. Some research issues for the North-East region have been raised at the end.

Of the seven member country of SAARC India leads to sub regional growth, with its GDP growth outlook for 2003 and 2004 remaining at 6 percent and 6.3 percent respectively. It has now surpassed 9 percent. The highest GDP growth in 2007 reflects the expected uprising in the Indian business cyde in the world economy. The paper of Anil Bhuimali and Sidhartha Sankar Laha examines the Indo-Bangladesh trade patterns. The paper mainly deals with the issues of bilateral trading relations between India and Bangladesh. The paper begins with the discussion of Indo-SAARC trade relations showing India's growth rate of exports, imports and trade volume with the SAARC countries. Share of Indo-Bangladesh trade in SAARC perspective has been presented with the help of **IMF** data. India's intra-industry trade indices with Bangladesh, SAARC countries, and with the world as a whole have also been calculated and explained.

Most important task before the economy of Bangladesh during the 1990s had been the restructuring of public sector industries including the jute industries. **In** their paper Anil Bhuimali, Md. Gholam Kibria and Sidhartha Sankar Laha have dealt with the detailed analysis of two private jute mills in term of production, growth of output, exports, growth of exports and manpower position. Secondary as well as primary data have been employed to study the socio-economic background of trade union members of the private jute mills. An opinion survey has been conducted with the workers, employers, trade union leaders and the management.

It is of utmost importance of the central bank of any country to maintain price stability. It is in this context empirical analysis of money price relationship has received greater importance in recent years. Chandan Kumar Mukhopadhyay and Shyam Charan Barma's paper examines money and price relationship in the economy of Pakistan. This study deals with the state of short-run and long-run relationship between money supply and price and the direction of causality between money supply and price level.

Nepal is famous for its Wildlife. The biggest natural museum, Nepal is one of the richest countries of the world in terms of biodiversity. Nepal is eminently rich in its wild life and natural habitats. The paper of Anil Bhuimali and Kamanand Dev discusses different aspects of wildlife tourism in Nepal. It analyses the problems this particular sector confronts and points out future prospects of wildlife tourism in developing the economy of Nepal.

Before mid-1980s Nepal had adopted almost controlled economy with decisive government even in fixing day-to-day commodity price through public enterprises. To overcome huge balance of payment crisis Nepal had started liberalization by devaluating her currency significantly especially since 1989. The paper of Chandan Kumar mukhopadhyay, Arjun Kumar Baral and Sankar Prasad Achrya examines the twin deficit hypothesis to verify its presence or non-presence in the context of Nepal.

Chandan Kumar Mukhopadhyay and Kanchan Datta, in their paper also examine the long-run relationship between budget deficit and trade deficit in the context of the economy of Maldives. The paper investigates the relationship between the budget deficit and trade deficit for Maldives. The sample data of budget deficit and trade deficit used in this investigation hold for the period 1979 to 2003 for the annual observation.

Bhutan is an independent kingdom in South Asia whose capital is Thimphu. The people of Bhutan are mainly of Tibetan origin. The Bhutia are the major ethnic group who represents almost half of the Bhutan population. They refer themselves as the Drukpas or dragon people. Bhutan's head of state is a hereditary king but presently the power of the state is shared by the king, a council of ministers and a national assembly. Only 10 percent of land is under cultivation and the people are engaged in fanning. The country is not rich in manufacturing activity. Traditional handicraft is the main manufacturing item of the state. Bhutan was opened to tourism in 1974. Since then tourism becomes a major source of forging exchange earnings. The paper by Anil Bhumali and Anil Kumar Biswas deals with the impact of tourism sector on the economy of Bhutan. The study is mainly based on the secondary data available to the

Royal Government of Bhutan as well as some other national and international agencies. The paper starts with the description of global perspectives of tourism potentialities, analyses the pattern of tourism in Bhutan and major tourism attractions and tourism development plans of Bhutan. Impact of tourism on the economy of Bhutan has widely been examined examining the question of sustainability. Statistical tables have been used to understand the trend of important variables. Relationship between the variables has been discussed analytically without any causal test of non-availability of reliable data.

Anil Bhuimali and
Chandan Kumar Mukhopadhyay
. *Department of Economics,*
University of North Bengal, July 16, 2007

Chandan Kumar Mukhopadhyay

1

SANTHALS IN DUARS AND INVESTMENT IN EDUCATION

INTRODUCTION

Santhals constitute a major tribal community in the Duars region of West Bengal. They live along the Bengal-Assam border and their closest tribal neighbours are Bodos. However, Santhals lag far behind Bodos in the matter of educational progress. Inspite of intensive 'literacy drive' undertaken in the Duars region, a vast majority of Santhal children remain outside schools. [1] Again 'drop out' rate is exceedingly high among school-goers. All these seem to indicate that there exists an aversion among these tribal people for formal education at schools.

The present study is an attempt for enquiring into the nature of and reasons for such aversion for education. The study also seeks to develop a model of education and explain why these tribal people feel reluctant about investing in education. This will allow us for advocating some measures for making formal education popular among these tribal people.

INVESTMENT IN EDUCATION: MOTIVATION

People want to attend school when they believe that they will be better off by doing so. For some, benefits may be short-term. They like the life-style of a student. Students attending for these reasons regard education as consumption good. In this case, students go to school primarily for satisfaction it provides during the period of attendance.

Others, however, attend schools because of the long-term benefits it provides. These benefits are partly in the form of higher earnings, partly in the form of gaining access to more interesting, challenging or pleasant jobs and partly in the form of prestige or enhanced enjoyment of non-market activities. Attendance for the long-term benefits is the sole motivation for investment in education.

BENEFITS FROM INVESTMENT

Calculating the benefits of an investment over time requires the progressive discounting of benefits lying farther into the future. Benefits that are received in future are worth less to us now than an equal amount of benefits to be received to-day for two reasons.

First, if people plan to consume their benefits, they will prefer to consume earlier than later. This is because one is relatively sure of being able to enjoy such consumption now. But the uncertainties of life make future enjoyment less attractive.

Second, if people plan to invest the monetary benefits rather than use them for consumption, they can earn interest on the investment and enlarged their fund in future. Thus, no matter how people intend to use their benefits they will discount future receipts to some extent.

The present value of a stream of yearly benefits (B) over time (T) can be calculated as follows:

$$\text{Present Value} = \frac{B_1}{(1+r)} + \frac{B_2}{(1+r)^2} + \frac{B_3}{(1+r)^3} + \frac{B_T}{(1+r)^T} \qquad (i)$$

where the discount rate is r. As long as r is positive, benefits into the future will be progressively discounted.

COST INVOLVED

The costs of going to school are normally incurred over an extended period of 10/12 years. These costs include

(i) The direct cost of tuition , fees and books
(ii) The forgone earnings because during the investment period it is usually impossible to work, at least full time
(iii) Psychic costs of studying and being examined

CRITERION

Thus investment in education is worthwhile if the present value of the benefits were at least as large as the costs. In mathematical terms, this criterion can be expressed as

$$\frac{B_1}{(1+r)}+\frac{B_2}{(1+r)^2}+\frac{B_3}{(1+r)^3}+\frac{B_T}{(1+r)^T}\geq C \qquad (ii)$$

where C equals the total cost of education and B_i equals the annual differences in earning between school-educated and non-education persons over the period i =1, 2,......, T

There are two ways one can determine whether the criterion in equation (2) is met. Using the 'Present Value Method' one can specify a value for the discount rate(r) and determine if the present value of benefits is grater than or equal to costs.

Alternatively, one can adopt the 'Internal Rate of Return Method' which considers how large the discount rate could be and still render school education profitable. Clearly, if benefits are so large that even a very high discount rate would render school education profitable, then the investment is worthwhile.

In practice, one calculates this internal rate of return by setting the present value of benefits equals to cost and solving for r. The internal rate is then compared to the rate of return on other investments. If the internal rate of return exceeds the alternative rate of return, the investment project is considered profitable.

SOME IMPORTANT PREDICTIONS

No doubt very few persons make the precise calculations suggested in equation (2) in deciding whether to attend school.

Nevertheless, the equation (2) presents three predictions concerning the demand for school education.

(i) Present-oriented people are less likely to go to school than forward-looking people (other things being equal).
(ii) School-attendance will rise if costs of education declines (other thing being the same)
(iii) School-attendance will rise if the gap between earnings of school- educated persons and illiterate persons widens (again, other things being equal).

SANTHAL TRIBES IN DUARS AND INVESTMENT IN EDUCATION

These predictions may be of significant help in explaining the observed aversion of the Santhal people in the Duars region for formal education. The livelihood pattern and the philosophy of life of these people form the basis of their appraisal of benefits from and costs of education. In their case the present value of benefits usually fall short of cost and they, therefore, shy away from investing in formal education. These indicate that fair understanding of the philosophy of life and livelihood of these people need due attention for the explanation of observed attitude of these people towards formal education.

SOME FEATURES OF TRIBAL (SANTHAL) LIFE

Some basic features of the tribal (Santhals in Duars) life are stated below:-

1. Present-orientedness

Psychologists use the term *present oriented* to refer to people who do not weigh future events or outcomes very heavily. While all people discount the future with respect to the present, those who discount it more than average or, at the extreme, ignore the future all together, could be considered *present-oriented*. In terms of the equations (1) and (2), a present-oriented person is one with a very high discount rate (r). If r is large, the present value of benefits associated with education will be lower than if the discount rate being used is smaller.

Thus a present-oriented person would impute smaller benefits to school education than one who is less present-oriented, and those who are present-oriented would be less likely to attend school.

Santhals in Duars are found to be highly present-oriented. The rates of discount, that these people use in determining present value of future benefits, are rarely available because the decision are not made formally as equation (2) implies. However, the model does suggest that people who have a high propensity to invest in education will also engage in other forward-looking behaviors. On the other hand, present-oriented people with high discount rate of investment will abstain from having forward looking activities. Santhals in Duars region are found to be generally devoid of forward looking behavior like having concern for health status, medical relief, saving for future etc.

Present-orientedness of these people has given forth aversion for uncertain future gains related to education. They prefer "known present availabilities to higher but uncertain and unknown gains in future". This motivation among these people is nothing but the practical application in life of the dictum "A bird in hand is better than two birds in the bush".

2. Absence of Free Lunch

There exists no 'Free Lunch' system in this tribal community. A capable one is required to earn one's living as much as possible. Parents rear up and feed children until they attain the age five or six. Since that age tribal children participate in economic and domestic activities and earn their meals as much as possible. Some times they participate directly in productive or food earning process. They may help their parents in cultivation or related work. They may take part in other person's cultivation, tending of domestic animals or cultivation related activities. They may indirectly earn their living by performing domestic chores or taking care of kid brothers and sisters and let their parents take part in their economic activities. Thus they indirectly contribute to the earnings of their parents and thus earn their meals. They may not earn their complete subsistence but such earning is a part of subsistence. As they grow up, their earnings rise and at the age 15-16 years they take part in economic activities independently and earn their subsistence.

3. Minimal Dispersion in Income Distribution:

In this tribal community the spectacular and notable event is the absence of dispersion in income distribution. People in the community, barring a few, receive income very close to the average earning. The dispersion of income is very small.

People in this community are satisfied with low average income which is very close to the subsistence level. The small excess above the subsistence level is used for capital formation which is employed in their traditional productive activities. They are satisfied with this income distributions and it has become an integral feature of their social life. This feature has imbibed an established psychological set up among these people. This setup is marked by the absence of any significant urge among these people for having an income level which is glaringly higher than those of other members in society. Consequently, the society appears unwilling to approve any such action which can break this income distribution.

OVERVIEW OF THE FEATURES

Thus it is observed that among there tribal people their exist

(i) present-orientedness
(ii) stress on earning one's own living
(iii) satiety with subsistence level and lack of the desire for getting out of the income distribution pattern

These mean that these tribal people may indulge in any action only within the perimeter of these principles. Any activities, which are in clash with these principles, may not be of their choice. As a matter of fact, investment in education in many ways stands contrary to their accepted principles in life. So they shy away from investing in education. We seek to explain these points in the following section.

II

INVESTMENT IN EDUCATION: GRAPHICAL PRESENTATION:

The following figure presents the income streams with and without education. It also presents the costs of education. Thus the graph may be used for explaining the decision process for investment in education.

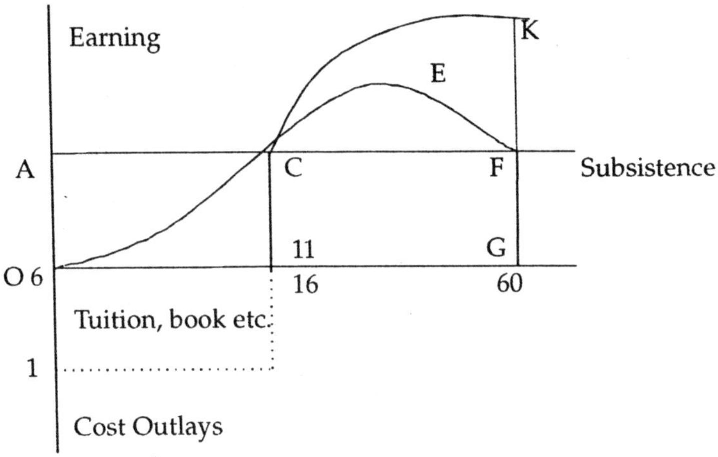

Here the curve OCF represents the income stream for any tribal child without having any formal education. The child starts earning livelihood at the age 6 and he/she earns less than subsistence until he/she become 16 years old. At the age 16 he/she earns his/her subsistence. Since that age his/her earning rises but it declines as he/she grows older. Consequently, for any illiterate tribal person.

Total earning (lifetime) = Area OCEFG
Earning Above subsistence = Area CEF
Social and Family support for livelihood = Area OAC
Net productive contribution
to the family and society = Area CEF-Area OAC....(3)

EDUCATION: EARNING AND COSTS

We assume that the child goes to the school at the age 6 and completes the school education at the age 16. Cost incurred in his/her education are as follows:

(a) Monetary Costs

For having formal education some monetary costs are incurred for tuition, books etc. These costs are represented by the area OHIJ. These costs are borne by the Government at present and so these are kept out of our analysis.

(b) Opportunity Costs

Education involves some opportunity costs and these are the earnings foregone during the period of school attendance (between 6 and 16 years). Here the foregone income = Area OCH

(c) Total Cost

Therefore,

the total cost = Monetary Cost + Opportunity Cost
= Area OHIJ + Area OCH
= Area OCHIJ

INVESTMENT IN EDUCATION: EARNINGS

We assume here that the educated person gets a job or is productively employed just after the completion of study at schools. In that case his/her income stream is represented by the curve CK which lies above the curve CEF over the entire productive period. Under this situation

Earning above the subsistence = Area CKF
Net productive contribution = Area CKF – Area OCHIJ

Social and family support for subsistence during the period of study = Area OACH .... (*iii*)

His/her net contribution to the family and society
= Area CKF – Area OCHIJ - Area OACH
= Area CEF + Area CKE – Area OCHIJ – Area OACH
= Area CEF + Area CKE – Area COH – Area OAC – Area OCH

= Area CEF + Area CKE - 2 Area OCH – Area OAC................ *(iv)*

Now education is profitable if and only if his/her net contribution to the family and society with education (as given by equation (iv), exceeds that without education (as given by equation (iii) i.e if

Area CEF + Area CKE – 2 Area OCH – Area OAC $\geq$ Area CEF – Area OAC

Or, Area CKE - 2 Area OCH ≥ 0

Or, Area CKE ≥ 2 Area OCH

Or, additional earning ≥ 2 (forgone income because of education over the period of study)

CONDITION OF EQUILIBRIUM

Every decision making process contains some conditions for attaining equilibrium and such condition needs to be stated for the completion of analysis. Accordingly, in case of investment in education equilibrium is reached when

Additional earning= 2 (forgone income) *(vi)*
following school education

IMPLICATION OF THE CONDITION

The tribal people are present-oriented and they, therefore, discount the future earning at a higher rate. They bear some pain when they forgo current earnings during the period of study at school. They may forgo current earning if they are assured of appropriate compensation in future in the form of additional earnings. The additional earning, which is twice as much as the forgone income, is considered by them to be an appropriate compensation.

FARTHER IMPLICATIOS

These people, after receiving school education, cannot engage themselves in traditional ways of earning livelihood. An educated tribal person cannot be expected nor do they themselves can afford to go to forests and search for their food. Therefore, they forgo the traditional income stream as depicted by the curve CEF. However, they can forgo the traditional income stream provided they are assured of appropriate compensation.

The compensation here refers to the additional income which an educated person gets over his/her traditional earnings. The additional income represents the difference between area under the curve CF and curve CK. Under this situation

Forgone income (Over the period 16-60 years) = Area HCEFG

Earning during the same period = Area HCKFG

Here Area HCKFG > Area HCEFG

[Since an educated person attains a higher income stream as represented by the curve CK]

Therefore,

Additional income following school education = Area HCKFG – Area HCEFG

= Area HCEFG + Area CKF – Area HCEFG

= Area CKF ..... *(vii)*

The equilibrium condition as given in (vi) shows that the educated person may forgo the traditional income and reach equilibrium when

Area CKF = 2 Area HCEFG

Or, Area CKF + Area HCEF = 2 Area HCEFG + Area HCEFG

Or, Area HCKFG = 3 Area HCEFG

Or, Area HCKFG/HG = 3 Area HCEFG/HG

(where HG = the productive years)

Average annual income earned following school education = 3 (Average annual income earned without having education) *(viii)*

EXPLANATION

These present- oriented tribal people have deep attachment for the traditional way of earning livelihood. As a matter of fact, they have remained self- contained for ages with the earnings from traditional activities. Moreover, they have been deeply accustomed to an income distribution pattern where dispersion of income is minimal with mean income standing close to the subsistence level.

These account for the existence of aversion among these people for departing away from the traditional way of living and earning their livelihood. Consequently, school education, which offers them an alternative scope for earning livelihood, has no appeal for these people.

The tribal children may go to schools for formal education and prepare themselves for alternative way of living provided they are assured of significant payoff. The relation (8) specifies the amount of the pay-off. *The pay-off required by these people is that the average annual income after the completion of school education must be three times as large as the average annual income earned through traditional means.* The tribal people are not sure of getting the required pay-off in future. As a result, they feel reluctant about investing in education.

IMPLICATIONS

Spread of education among the Santhal people of the Duars region of West Bengal appears to be hindered by the following facts:-

(i) There exist some elements of apprehension among these tribal people that the entire process of education has been so designed as to make them give up their culture and traditional way of living and earning livelihood.

(ii) These people are highly present-oriented and, therefore, worried about the earning foregone during the period of education.

(iii) They dislike the uncertainty about receiving the pay-off required for giving up their traditional way of living and earning livelihood.

(iv) They feel comfortable with the existing egalitarian distribution of income in their society with average income standing close to the level of subsistence. Their loyalty and concern for the society is so strong that they usually refrain from getting themselves involved with any kind of activities which does not benefit the entire society. Education is acceptable to them if gains from education could benefits all individuals in the society alike. In the present system, on the contrary, getting education is an exercise for personal gains. Consequently, formal education has not become popular among these people.

POLICY IMPLICATIONS

In order to make education more popular among these people, the present system of education needs to be modified in the light of the above noted concerns of the tribal people . A pointer to this direction is as follows:

(i) The courses and curriculam of school education must be well devised so that the tribal people consider them as a means for raising their productivity in traditional activities.

(ii) School going children must be provided with subsistence so that they don't have to worry about the foregone income any more.

(iii) The government must make appropriate arrangements for providing school educated tribal people with required pay-off in the event of their leaving the traditional way of earning livelihood

(iv) Tribal society be encouraged to send children in sizeable numbers to schools so that no one feels that taking education in an exercise for reaping individual benefits only.

(v) There must be some elements in teaching methods, courses and curriculum which arouse respect for the culture and livelihood of these tribal people.

CONCLUSION

The prevelant primary and secondary education systems lack in these necessary traits and have, therefore, failed to attract sizeable number of Santhal children to schools. Consequently, efforts undertaken so far for imparting education among the tribal children has lagged behind the 'critical minimum' level.

As a matter of fact, mere creation of education facilities cannot be expected to generate demand for the same. Education could be made popular among these tribal people if social tastes, preferences, aspiration and expectation of the concerned people were given due care and importance in our education system.

First Submission 20.03.2005

Submission on Revision 22.11.2006

Note

1. A recent survey conducted by the Department of Economics, North Bengal University, shows that only about 2% of Santhal children of school going age attend school in Santhal dominated areas like Santhalpur, Turturi, Yashodanga, Hatipota, Lokenathpur areas of the Duars region.
   In contrast, about 78% of Bodo children attend schools in the Bodo dominated areas like Mahakalguri, Kamakshyaguri, Khoardanga, Parokata, Nimti and Santali areas of the Duars region.

REFERENCE

Becker, Gary- *Hurman Capital*, New York, National Bureau of Economic Research, 1975

Berg, Ivar. *Education and Job: The Great Training Robbery*, New York: Praeger Publishers, 1970

Blaug, Mark. "Human Capital Theory: A Slightly Jaundiced Survey" *Journal of Economic Literature 14* (September 1976) : 827-55

Ehrenberg R.G and Robert S. Smith. *Modern Labour Economics*, Glenview,Illinois, Scott Foresman and Company, 1992

Freeman, Richerd B- "Over investment in College Training?" *Journal of Human Resources* 10, 3(September 1975): 287-311

Freeman, Richerd B- *The Overhead American*. New York: Academic Press, 1976

Griliches, Zvi, William M.Mason- "Education, Income and Ability", *Journal of Political Economy* 80,3 (May/June 1972)

Hause J.C, "Earnings Profile: Ability and Schooling", *Journal of Political Economy*, 80,3 (May/June 1972)

Hishleifer,J, " On the Theory of Optimal Investment Decision", *Journal of Political Economy* 66 (Aug 1968): 329-52

Mincer, Jacob, " On-the-Job Training: Costs, Returns and Some Implications", *Journal of Political Economy* (Supplement 1962), pp 50-79

Mincer, Jacob, *Schoolings, Experience and Earnings*, New York: National Bureau of Economic Research, 1974

Mincer, Jacob "The Distribution of Labour Income: A Survey with Special Reference to the Human Capital Approach", *Journal of Economic Literature* (March 1970), pp1-26

Mincer, Jacob and Salwman Polachek, " Family Investments in Human Capital: Earning of Women", *Journal of Political Economy* 82 (March/April 1974): S76-S108

Schultz, Theodore. *The Economic Value of Education*. New York: Columbia University Press, 1963

Spence, Michael, "Job Market Signalling", *Quarterly Journal of Economics* 87 (August 1993): 355-74.

Tamash R. Majumdar

2

A STUDY ON SOCIO-ECONOMIC BACKGROUND OF SMALL TEA GROWERS IN NORTH BENGAL

INTRODUCTION

The tea industry is one of the most important industries in India. The annual tea production has been around 800 million kg. for the last two years. The consumption is currently around 600 million Kg. India is the largest producer of tea in the world accounting for over 27 percent of global tea production. For almost five decades, tea continued to be the major item in India's export of principal commodities. India exports an average 180 million Kg. of the tea every year. The total net foreign exchange earned by the Indian tea industry per annum is around Rs. 1,847 crores. The four major tea producing states are Assam, West Bengal, Kerala and Tamilnadu. The total number of tea estates in the country is 1,634 (Tea Board : 2002) while permanent labours in the industry number around more than 1.1 million. Besides permanent labour, there is a significant number of casual labourers employed on the work-force in Indian tea estates.

West Bengal is the second largest tea growing state in India after Assam. It has around 343 tea gardens. There are three main tea-producing regions in West Bengal namely the Darjeeling Hills, the Terai or foothills area of Darjeeling district and the Doors in Jalpaiguri District. The Dooars is the largest of these tea regions in terms of labour employment, area under tea and production of tea. West Bengal produces nearly a fourth of the country's tea. The majority of the old tea plantations in the region are large production units of more than 400 hectares and are managed or owned by large tea corporate companies. Tea is the most important export earner of the state.

As tea is labour-intensive crop, tea plantation industry provides gainful employment to a large section of the population directly as well as indirectly. In the Darjeeling, Terai and Doors regions, the industry gives direct employment to around 3 lakhs of people and several lakhs of people are dependent on the industry in various ways. They include family members of the tea garden workers, petty traders of local settlements surrounding tea gardens and small suppliers and contractors. A noticeable feature of labour employment in tea gardens is that nearly half the tea labourers are female.

SUB-DIVISION OF THE TEA SECTOR

The General perception has been that tea production is a large scale enterprise – a single vertically integrated production – processing – marketing system. That perception has been thoroughly changed in all tea producing countries in the world including India. A substantial number of small tea growers (STGs) and medium size gardens now co-exist with large tea estate.

The estate orientation of the tea industry stems from two premises both of which are now being questioned. The first is that since tea production requires the proximity of processing facilities, it is best grown on large estates. This view has been eroded by estate factories increasingly going in for green leaf purchase, the setting up over the years of the privately managed bought-leaf factories (BLFs), and the emergence of government – sponsored cooperative factories. In the region of North Bengal, for instance, the BLFs are making huge profit from the leaf purchased from small holders. The second feature is historical; since labour was cheap and freely available, companies found it easy to open up large tea plantations. However, a combination of trade union influence and government instituted wages and welfare benefits through different labour legalisations, such as PLA, has put an end to the low labour costs that used to characterize the tea economy. It is worth emphasizing in this connection that the old estate system of tea production is highly labour intensive and the bulk of the costs of producing tea go in the form of labour wages (in some cases as much as 60%). Some stakeholders in the tea sectors have the opinion that the big companies are increasingly reluctant to operate in the old estate system of production due to rising labour costs and falling auction prices being witnessed in the last decade.

Basically, there are three sub-sectors in tea in North Bengal today, which are as follows: -

(1) **Estate Gardens :** Tea estates are privately owned large tea corporate companies of more than 400 hectares and they produce, process and market their own tea individually. They represent a single vertically integrated production – processing – marketing system run by large tea corporate companies.

(2) **Medium Size Gardens :** This category comprises newly established gardens above 10.12 hectares without having factory. Growers of this category are normally educated and they have a middle class background. They came to tea either from profession or from business. A large number of these growers were particularly connected with tea trading in different capacity.

(3) **Smallholder Gardens :** This category comprises plantations holding upto 10.12 hectares (or 25 acres) under tea without any processing facility (Tea Board). This sub-sector has contributed 55 million kg. (26%) in total production of tea in West Bengal in 2005. Prior to 1996, there was a very small number of small holder gardens in this region. However, during 1996 to 2001 they were increased on a large scale.

At present, the tea small holder sector, involving around 20,000 households, is of considerable importance to the economy of North Bengal. It is a major direct and indirect employment source for the people at large of this region.

A RECENT PHENOMENON: EXPANSIONS OF LAND UNDER TEA

One significant phenomenon of tea industry in North Bengal, which draws attention of many concerned people and creates debate, is the extension of tea plantation areas across several districts in this region. Many experts and agencies involved in tea-industry tried to provide possible explanations from two different viewpoints, one, declining productivity and the other, increase in demand. According to the first group, the ageing problem of tea bushes, which gradually reduces the productivity of century old tea garden, becomes so critical and acute that some measures are urgently needed to enhance productivity. The average age of tea-bushes of traditional tea estates is above 40 years, which causes diminishing return. In order to maintain total production at the same level as before, many gardens started to undertake replacement and replanting programme of tea bushes since early eighties.

According to the second group, it is the projection of possible enhancement of demand that initiated the expansion programme of tea gardens. They argue that the inclusion of tea in the list of products eligible for export to the then USSR under a liberal trade agreement in early eighties created huge additional demand for Indian tea. As a consequence of this, the expansion programme of plantation area of tea was started during this period.

The price behaviour of tea during this period, however, corroborates both the viewpoints. In either of these cases – shortage of supply or increase in demand- price would have increased. In fact, we observe that tea prices started to increase substantially since early eighties and continued till 1991.

THREE – PHASES OF EXTENSION OF LAND UNDER TEA

An analysis of expansion of tea plantation areas since early 1980s reveals that it has undergone there distinct phases during the period 1980-2001. The first phase covered a period from early1980s to late 1980s, the second phase covered a period from late 1980s to mid 1990s and the third phase covered the rest of the period.

The first phase has witnessed the expansion of tea plantation area by mostly traditional tea estates. Since early 1980s the large scale gardens began to undertake extension programme of plantation area in order to increase yield. There are both demand and supply side factors that have initiated the expansion of land area under tea. The extension programme has been undertaken either by utilizing the unused estate land or through acquiring new land, either owned or occupied by peasants of the surrounding villages. Technically, the extension of an established garden is known as a "project garden". It is to be noted in this connection that the process of land acquisition is accompanied by job creation for the affected people, besides the payment of monetary compensation for transfer of ownership. The land losens have got job in the tea plantation either as a permanent labour or as a casual labour depending upon the amount of land being transferred. The norm that was followed in providing employment was one permanent job and one casual job against a transfer of one acre of land, and one temporary job only against a transfer of less than one acre of land. However, the status of labourers in the project gardens (the extensions of main garden) is far low compared to their counterparts in the main gardens. Moreover, there are plenty of evidences of deprivation of workers in these gardens in terms of the disparity between the benefits that they were promised to be given and that they are actually deriving now. The range of fringe benefits is very narrow in such gardens in comparison to the provisions under the Plantation Labour Act.

The second phase is characterized by land conversion predominantly by local urban entrepreneurs with garden size more than 25 acres. It may be noted that tea has traditionally been cultivated in this region in large plantations employing migrant people. There has not been any direct involvement of local people in tea plantations. Consequently, there was lack of knowledge and experience regarding tea plantation among them. The general perception prevailing among the local people has been that tea plantations is a large scale enterprise requiring huge initial investment. This view of large scale orientation of tea plantation has began to change from the late 1980s following the extension programme of plantation area undertaken by large estates. A good number of local urban people who were connected with tea trading in different capacity had the opportunity to observe the whole process of expansion by the established garden. The high rate of return in this sector during this period with relatively less amount of investment attracted many of these people to initiate tea plantation. This segment of growers, being categorized as medium size plantations, initially identified a vast tract of uncultivable fallow land in different parts of Jalpaiguri, Uttar Dinajpur and Darjeeling districts. Two categories of fallow land have been brought under the cultivation : fallow land owned by villagers and vested fallow land occupied by villagers, which has subsequently been converted into leasehold land for a period of 30 years. Through persuasion along with money, they occupied the land from the local people and started tea plantation. In the initial period of this phase, these lands being uncultivable fallow land they did not face any hindrances to get "no objection certificate" (NOC) from the concerned authority. Gradually, as fallow land became scarce, this segment of growers has attempted to expand tea cultivation in cultivable land. In many instances, they tried to acquire cultivable land through fraudulent means establishing rapport with local political force. This gave birth social tension in villages. One factor that also contributed much to this growing social tension is less number of employment than the number promised at the time of land transfer. Besides, most of the jobs created against land transfer are casual in nature. Only a few number of permanent jobs were created. Again, there are evidences of violations of some other conditions of land transfer on the part of the new growers during this phase. The workers are paid out miserably low wages and practically no non-wage benefits. In many instances, the workers have received a daily wage to the tune of Rs. 18 - 20 only despite the substantially large size of the garden. This has also created lot of discontent among the local people.

This situation forced the government to impose ban on conversion of agricultural land into tea plantation with effect from 30th June, 2001 as the cut-off date for the tea nursery and tea plantation in new areas. It has been declared that any attempt to expand tea cultivation or tea nursery in new areas beyond the cut-off date will be viewed very seriously and appropriate legal action will be taken against the offender.

The third phase of land transfer to tea has begun in 1996-97 and is continuing till then. This third phase in characterized by small holder tea growers, or simply, small tea growers (STGs). A vast majority of growers under this category have a peasantry background. Prior to tea, they were small holders subsistence farmers producing paddy, jute or other type of traditional crop for earning their livelihoods. There are mainly two causes for migration of peasants from traditional crops to tea. In the first place, with the emergence of the "project gardens" as well as the "medium size gardens", the local people with a peasantry background have come to gather knowledge and experience about tea cultivation, because of their direct involvement in plantation work in these two categories of gardens. Gradually, these local people have come to learn that tea cultivation does not require much investment and tea can be grown on small plots of land. Subsequently, they started making plantation on their own land which were virtually left fallow for several years due to non-remunerative crop-production.

It is to be noted in this connection that the traditional crop cultivation was not a remunerative land use option to a significant number of peasants in different areas of this region. The areas of land under their possession were either unsuitable or poorly suitable for traditional farming activity. The use of land for the cultivation of traditional crops could have became remunerative for this group of peasants had a large amount of investment been made by them on land. However, in the absence of any alternative profession other than the traditional farming activity, they could not be able to make such investment. Besides, the economically non-viable size of holding coupled with the lack of irrigation facilities, the rising input prices and stagnant agricultural crop prices, the reduced access to institutional credit and other agricultural extension services (the supply side assistance) have prevented them from continuing traditional farming activity. In some cases, the landowners, who are traditionally pineapple growers, have also switched over to tea cultivation. Faced with multitude of problems such as the absence of well organized and well functioning market, non-realization of remunerative prices for the produce, the lack of preservation facility, the absence of good processing industries in the close proximity of plantations so on and so forth, the farmers in the pineapple sector have shifted to tea cultivation. It is probably the assurance of economic security in the tea plantation in the form of year round work and income, a fairly low risk of disease and disastrous crop failure, and a relatively little amount of investment requirement, which have motivated this segment of the peasantry class to switch over to tea.

Secondly, a significant number of small tea growers may be appropriately categorized as 'forced growers' as they were forced to move from traditional crop cultivation to tea. It is already noted that middle growers segment initially started tea plantation in uncultivable fallow land. Gradually, as fallow land became scarce, this segment of growers has attempted to expand tea cultivation in cultivable land. This has caused land degradation problem to the land surrounding the plantation area. As tea plantation requires draining off excess water from the land, digging up high drain is absolutely necessary for tea plantation. But, it causes draining off water from adjacent land too. Thus, land adjacent to tea garden being unable to hold required level of water becomes unproductive for traditional crop. Many peasants were forced to convert their land to tea because of non-remunerative rate of yield and productivity. However, this phenomenon is absent in the case of growers of the second category. They have initiated tea plantation in a planned manner.

With the emergence of the STGs, the tea sector has begun to experience a shift from estate-orientation to small-holder orientation in this region. Now the tea economy has been gradually becoming small holder oriented. As a matter of fact, the small holder tea is now a global phenomenon which have made its appearance in almost all tea producing countries of the world.

It is useful to make a comparison between medium size and smallholder gardens. In general, the owner of a medium size garden is sufficiently well off and for whom tea is only a part of the business activity. Thus, they seem to be "absentee growers". However, for most of the small growers, tea is the only source of livelihood. They do not have any other occupation. In few cases, only a few livestock and food and other cash crops are supplementing tea income.

OBJECTIVE OF THE STUDY

The basic objective of the study is to make a careful examination of the socio-economic background of the small tea growers in the region of North Bengal as little information is available on this aspect. The study also aims at testing certain relevant hypothesis on the basis of the primary information on the socio-economic characteristics of this segment of the growers. It would be relevant to note in this connection that these hypotheses primarily concern the general perceptions among the people about the land transfer phenomenon vis a vis the STGs. They are :

(i) Tea plantation is a large scale commercial activity requiring huge initial capital investment vis a vis big plots of land. It is not suitable for small holder schemes.

(ii) The small tea plantations (STPs) have emerged predominantly out of crop replacing land, replacing the cultivation of traditional crops and depriving the peasants from their means of subsistence.

(iii) The extension of tea plantation following the emergence of STGs has brought about the problems of land alienation, assetlessness and joblessness of the small holder cultivators in this region.

(iv) The STGs are basically unemployed educated urban people who are encroaching upon the sphere of economic activities of the peasant folk in this region.

SOURCES OF DATA

The present study is conducted on the basis of an empirical analysis of primary data on small tea growers in the region of

North Bengal. The data have been collected through field survey conducted in selected areas in two districts of this region during the period mid-December 2005 - mid-February 2006. A standard questionnaire has been set for data collection which seeks to elicit information on various social, demographic and economic characteristics of small tea growers. It also seeks to collect data on changes in land use pattern over the past couple of years. It seems important to mention that the present study is a part of the total research project which has been undertaken under the SAP-DRS of the department of Economics North Bengal University.

Thus, the present paper is based only on partial field-work that has been done among the small tea growers in two districts only. The complete field-work covering all the tea growing districts of this region is yet to be completed.

THE STUDY AREA

The small tea plantations (STPs) have taken root in four districts, Darjeeling, Uttar Dinajpur, Jalpaiguri and Coochbehar, in North Bengal region. The present presentation is based only on the partial survey among STPs conducted in five villages in four blocks in two districts. The blocks are Chopra in Uttar Dinajpur, Rajganj, Jalpaiguri Sadar and Mainaguri in Jalpaiguri district. The total number of respondents is 81. The sample is intended to capture as much diversity as possible in terms of the holding size of the respondents which ranges from 0.66 to 20 acres. The area wise distribution of respondents is given in the following table.

Table 1
Area-wise Distribution of Respondents

Sl. No.	*Area*	*No. Of Respondents*
1.	Chopra	23
2.	Fatapukur	8
3.	Jahari Talma	13
4.	Helapakri	12
5.	Panbari	25
Total		81

Source: Field survey

THE PERIOD OF EMERGENCE OF STPS

It is well-known that the STP is a mid-1990 phenomenon. The analysis of survey data substantiates this general perception about the STPs very clearly. The year-wise distribution of surveyed STPs is given in Table 2 and shown graphically in figure 1.

Table 2
Year-wise Distribution of STPs

Year	*Percentage of STPs*
1994	1.23
1995	3.70
1996	6.17
1997	7.14
1998	13.58
1999	33.33
2000	16.05
2001	18.52
Total	100.00

Source: Field survey

Figure 1
Distribution of STPs

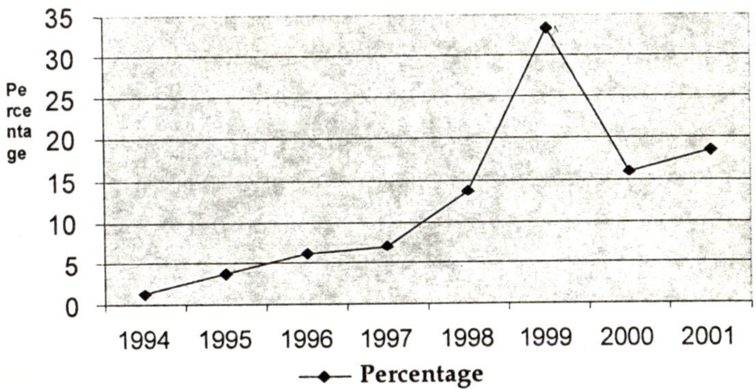

It is evident from the above table that a relatively small percentage of respondents have taken up tea cultivation prior to 1997. However, during 1998-2001, a maximum number of respondents have started tea plantation. It can also be seen that one-third of total STPs has come into existence in the year 1999.

THE SOCIO-DEMOGRAPHIC CHARACTERISTICS OF STGS

To know the identity as well as the social background of the STGs, it is necessary to study some socio-demographic characteristics of the STGs. These include educational status, the place of residence, ethnicity and age distribution. These characteristics are given in the following tables.

Table 3
Educational Background of the Respondent

Educational Status	*Percentage*
Illiterate	4.93
Primary School Level	25.92
Junior School Level	22.22
High School Level	21.00
Higher Secondary Level	13.35
Graduate Level	11.11
Post Graduate Level	2.47
Total	100

Source: Field survey

Table 4
Rural-Urban Distribution of the Respondents

Type	*Percentage*
Rural	86
Urban	14
Total	100

Source: Field survey

Table 5
Ethnic Background of the Respondent

Ethnic Group	*Percentage*
Bengali (Non Rajbanshi)	53
Bengali (Rajbanshi)	47
Total	100

Source: Field survey

Table 6
Age Distribution of the Respondent

Age-Group	Percentage
17-27	10
28-35	19
36-50	51
> 50	20
Total	100

Source: Field survey

The analysis of data on profile of education indicates that more than 25% of the respondents are educated only upto the primary level, 22% upto the secondary level and 21% upto the high school level only. The percentage of respondents educated upto the high school level comprises 69%. There are only 26% of the respondents who are having academic qualification above the secondary level. The respondents having academic qualification above the higher secondary level constitute only 14% of the total. Finally, nearly 5% of the respondents are illiterate. The analysis, therefore, indicates a relatively low educational profile of the respondents.

An examination of the table relating to rural-urban distribution of respondents shows that respondents having rural background comprise 86% while those having urban background make up only 14% of the total number. It is, therefore, seen that permanent village dwellers, who are predominantly peasants, have made their presence felt strongly among the STGs during the third phase.

An analysis of the ethnic background of the respondents shows that the respondents belong to two main ethnic groups of this region : (i) Rajbanshis and (ii) the Bengalis. The former group comprises 47% while the latter 53% of the respondents. The table indicates that Rajbanshi, a major constituent of ethnic minorities in this region, are key stake holders in the small tea sector. This is a noticeable feature of this sector in North Bengal. It may be noted in this connection that this ethnic minority group is the earliest settler of this region that numerically dominates much of rural North Bengal.

The observations revealed from the study of tables 3 & 4 amply contradicts the generally perceived notion that the STGs are basically unemployed educated rural people who are encroaching upon the sphere of economic activities of the peasant folk in this region. The presence of a markedly high proportion of rural Rajbanshi people in the small tea sector, as revealed from table 5, contradicts further this commonly - held view about the STGs.

The information on the age structure is of significance in the present context for drawing inferences on age pattern of self-employment generated by STPs. It is evident from the table that 29% of the respondents are falling under the age group 17-35 years, 51% belong to the age group 36-50 years, and only 20% are of above 50 years old. We see, therefore, that 80% of the respondents are falling within the younger and middle ages. This is one of the welcoming features in small tea sector. It has opened up a wide vistas of self-employment opportunities for the working age population of this region. It has already been seen from the rural-urban distribution of respondents that there is an overwhelming majority of rural people among the STGs. Taken this fact into account, it can be easily inferred that STPs have created self-employment opportunities for the rural working age population on a significant scale.

It can also be seen from the age- distribution table that a significant component of STGs is the younger people who fall in the age-group 17-35 years. This seems to indicate that small scale tea provides ample avenue for self-employment of unemployed rural youth, besides engaging the middle age rural people with this enterprise. In recent times, the unemployed youth in the rural areas of North Bengal is the most vulnerable group, which can be indulged by the extremist group easily, as the employment opportunities are very limited in this region. The engagement of these people, who are the potential trouble makers in the society, on a significant scale is one of the most remarkable success of this sector. An important point to note here is that small farm conventional agriculture failed to attract young people, who had a minimum level of secondary education, as producers. This is mainly because of the poor incentives and lack of support services for small farmers involved in agriculture. These young people are, however, keen to engage themselves in tea cultivation due to the fancy attached to it. The penetration of rural young people in STPs has surely helped mitigating social tension engulfing a vast rural area of this region.

OCCUPATIONAL PROFILE

It has already been observed that a significantly high percentage of STGs are village people having low educational profile. This observation is further substantiated by an analysis of occupational characteristics of the sample. Information are presented on both occupation prior to tea and additional occupation, if any, in the following table.

Table 7
Occupational Distribution

Category	*Percentage*
Prior to Tea	
Traditional Crop Cultivation (TCC)	60.50
Pineapple Plantation	3.70
Small Business (SB)	13.58
SB in addition to TCC	2.47
Service	8.64
Tea Garden Workers	2.47
Others	6.17
Nothing Significant	2.47
Total	100
Additional Occupation	
Traditional Crop cultivation	37.00
Pineapple Plantation	1.24
Small Business	14.82
SB in addition to TCC	2.47
Service	8.64
Tea Garden Worker	4.94
Others	1.24
Solely depends on Tea Plantation	29.63
Total	100

Source: Field survey

The table shows that nearly 65% of the respondents were engaged in the cultivation of paddy, jute and pineapple prior to tea. Only 14% of them were involved in small business. The other occupations do not appear to be much significant in the field study. The table clearly indicates that the expansion of land area under tea plantation during the third phase is largely due to peasants of this region, besides persons engaged in small business. This is in sharp contrast to the general notion among the public that the process of land transfer is accompanied by displacement of peasant community from the cultivable land in this region. The process of land transfer during this phase is, in fact, characterized by migration of peasants from traditional crops to tea.

The distribution pattern of additional occupation (i.e. occupation in addition to tea) reveals that the maximum percentage (40%) of the respondents are still associated with traditional crop cultivation. This is followed by small business which comprises 15% of the respondents. What emerges from the field study is the existence of mixed agriculture involving a significant number of STGs. Some parts of land are being used for tea while the remaining parts being put under paddy, jute and pineapple. There is, thus, the evidence of crop diversification being undertaken by the STGs. One possible reason for this phenomenon might be the diversification of risks and uncertainty associated with traditional crop cultivation and the maintenance of a steady flow of farm income over the year. It may be noted in this connection that the risk of serious disease prevalence or disastrous crop failure is fairly low in case of tea plantation.

One noticeable feature of the occupational characteristics is that almost one fourth of the respondents do not have any occupation other than tea plantation. They are solely dependent on tea. In other words, tea remains the only source of family income for them. This is probably indicative of the fact that a substantial number of STGs are small holder farmers who are not left with any land for the cultivation of traditional crops after they have taken up tea cultivation.

PATTERN OF INVESTMENT

An important aspect of the present study is to investigate into the source of finance for developing STPs. The hypothesis relevant in this context is the general perception that the establishment of tea plantations requires huge capital investment and hence tea can not be grown as a small holder crop. Whether this hypothesis is true or not is to be examined by the field study. Information on the arrangement of finance for developing STPs are detailed in the following table.

Table 8
Source of Finance

Source	Percentage
Solely Self-Finance	68
Private Loan in addition to Self-Finance	20
Bank Loan in addition to Self-Finance	11
Both Private & Bank Loan in addition to Self-Finance	1
Total	100

Source: Field survey

It is evident from the above table that initial capital investment for tea plantation was covered by growers themselves through mobilizing their own resources and / or through taking loans from mostly relatives or in some cases from village money lenders. Thus, the small tea plantations have been build up out of self-finance predominantly. This phenomenon contradicts the general perception that tea plantation is a large-scale enterprise which requires huge initial investment. The view of large-scale orientation of tea plantation has been amply eroded by this new phenomenon. As a matter of fact, a low initial capital investment for the establishment of tea plantations is a key identifying factor which allows STPs to proliferate in this region.

The table also indicates that there is a lack of financial support to the STPs from various funding institutions, such as commercial banks or Tea Board. This has put them under problem with regard to the use of both labour and non-labour inputs in adequate quantities. An important cause for the absence of bank or Tea Board funding is the non-possession of N.O.C. of tea cultivation with them. As most of the STGs have come from peasantry, they are not quite familiar with the procedure of getting N.O.C. There was clearly lack of awareness among the growers with regard to this aspect in the initial period. Without N.O.C. they could not apply for registration and without registration they could not apply for any sort of support from official agencies like banks, tea board etc. Later on while the state government banned conversion of agricultural land into tea plantation with effect from 30th June 2001, small growers felt the necessity of registration of their garden. As the grower has to prove that he has completed plantation before the cut-off date, this legal barrier has prevented may growers, many of whom are illiterate or semi-literate peasants, from obtaining clearance (N.O.C.) from Land and Land Revenue Department. In fact, they are facing huge problem in getting N.O.C. The problem is particularly more acute in case of "forced growers" who are basically marginal farmers. If N.O.C. is not granted to them they would be the sufferer. The role of Land and Land Revenue Department in giving N.O.C. is far from appreciating till date.

As we have mentioned already, without having a N.O.C. a grower could not get himself registered with the Tea Board and hence could not take financial benefit in the form of subsidy (Rs. 26,000/- per hectare) offered by the Board. It is only a few number of growers who are registered with the Tea Board and have received plantation subsidy. Moreover, most of the growers do not have access to bank finance mainly due to non-possession of N.O.C. Our study finds that, with a few exceptions, the banks are also reluctant to provide loans to them, neither for working capital nor for long term fixed capital. It is obvious that the absence of financial backup from banks and Tea Board have prevented them from making adequate investment on plantation and thereby making a good amount of profit.

LAND USE ANALYSIS

A study of land and use pattern is necessary in order to understand the various dimensions of the land-use transformation phenomenon which draws attention of many concerned people and creates debate. First of all, the size distribution of land holding is presented in the following table.

Table 9
Respondents under different holding sizes

Holding Size (in acre)	*Percentage*
Upto 2	46.84
2-4	27.85
4-6	8.86
6-10	10.13
Above 10 & below 25	6.33
Total	100.00

Source: Field survey

It is evident from the table that 47 percent of the respondents are under 2 acres, 75 percent under 4 acres, and 94 percent under 10 acres. There are only 6 percent respondents with holding size between 10 and 25 acres. The study, therefore, reveals the small holder dominated character of new tea plantations during the period 1995-2001. This seems to indicate the concentration of villagers with a peasantry background in small tea plantations (STPs). Though the optimum size holding is yet to be determined analytically, the preliminary study seems to indicate that smaller plantations are economically viable.

An exercise is now necessary in order to examine the pattern of land use change. The hypothesis central in the present context is the general perception among the people that STPs have emerged predominantly out of crop-replacing land. An area-wise pattern of land-use change is depicted in the following table.

Table 10
The Pattern of Land-Use Change (Percentage)

Area	*Virgin Land (Acre)*	*Crop-Replacing Land (Acre)*	*Total Land (Acre.)*
Chopra	5.975734	17.78595	23.76169
	(25.14861)	(74.85139)	(100)
Fatapukur	10.17864	8.696956	18.87559
	(53.92486)	(46.07514)	(100)
Jahuri Talma	2.112983	8.16453	10.27751
	(20.55928)	(79.44072)	(100)
Helapakri	12.75861	5.670173	18.42878
	(69.23197)	(30.76803)	(100)
Panbari	19.89605	8.760374	28.65643
	(69.42963)	(30.57037)	(100)
Total	50.922202	49.07798	100

Source: Field survey

The table shows that two categories of land have come under new tea plantations : (a) virgin land; (b) crop replacing land. The former category includes grazing grounds, bamboo clumps, hemp field etc. the latter category, on the other hand, makes up replacement of paddy, mesta jute, pineapple, vegetable cultivation etc. It can be seen from the table that the overall distribution of land over these two categories is by and large even. It supports the general perception that crop lands are being replaced by plantation. At the same time, the table also indicates a high virgin land ratio out of total land. This seems to indicate that the emergence of STPs has led to expansion of agricultural land through gainful employment of fallow land into a remunerative crop cultivation like tea. However, there are two areas, Chopra and Jahari Talma, where there is a large dominance of crop-replacing land over the virgin land.

One explanation for this phenomenon may be that before marginal farmers decide to go for tea plantation in these region, the virgins, non-cultivable land areas were possibly being fully transferred to plantation by middle growers. A relatively high small-holding concentration in new plantations in both regions seems to justify this pattern of land use change. Another explanation may be that there is a high concentration of "forced growers" in these regions who involuntarily decide to switch over from traditional crops to tea. This is because of the fact that their land have become unproductive for traditional crops due to the expansion of tea plantation in areas adjacent to their plots of land. This negative externality factor, which is being mostly generated by middle growers gardens of earlier phase, may have been responsible for this. The study has also found that agricultural land in these areas are essentially mono-cropping land without irrigation facilities in most of the cases. The traditional agricultural operation seems to be economically non viable in these regions due to these factors. On the other hand, in terms of net benefit, the rate of yield of tea is attractive than the rate of yield of traditional crop. This possibly one of the factors that justifies the conversion of a higher proportion of crop land to tea plantation from an economic point of view. A case in point in this regard is the Jahari Talma village in Jalpaiguri Sadar block. It has been observed during the field survey that farmers who have access to Teesta canal irrigation water have not converted their crop land to tea plantation. However, those without having access to irrigation water have decided to switch over from traditional crops to tea. Finally, in

Chopra, the conversion pineapple land into tea has been found to be occurred. This seems to explain partly why crop land under tea is more than virgin land in this area.

A study of the pattern of land possession is now made on the basis of the following table.

Table 11
The Pattern of Land Possession (Percentage)

Area	*Own Land (Acre)*	*Acquired Land (Acre)*	*Total (Acre)*
Chopra	13.95779	9.803893	23.76169
	(58.74075)	(41.25925)	(100)
Fatapukur	12.63466	6.240938	18.87559
	(66.93647)	(33.06353)	(100)
Jahari Talma	7.348557	2.931655	10.27756
	(71.47505)	(28.52495)	(100)
Helapakri	5.909433	12.51935	18.42878
	(32.06632)	(67.93368)	(100)
Panbari	17.59858	11.05785	28.65643
	(61.41233)	(38.58767)	(100)
Total	57.44632	42.55368	100

Source: Field survey

The table shows that in all the areas, except Helapakri, the possession of own-land is more than acquired land. This is clearly indicative of the fact that peasants themselves have decided to change traditional crop production to tea plantation. It is also indicative of a high penetration of villagers into STPs. This clearly refutes the view that STGs are mostly non-villagers who have given rise to the problems of land alienation and joblessness of the small holders cultivators in this region. On the other hand, STPs provide evidences of better land utilization, job creation and income stabilization of the small and marginal farmers of this region. However, in Helapakri, the acquired land possession is more than the own-land possession. This probably points to the fact that the non-villagers penetration in this area is more than in other places.

Finally, a comparison of the distributions of owned and acquired land over the categories of virgin and crop-replacing land has been made on the basis of the following table :

Table 12
Distribution of Owned and Acquired Land (Percentage)

Area	Owned			Acquired		
	Virgin	*Crop-Rep*	*Total*	*Virgin*	*Crop-Rep*	*Total*
Chopra	21	79	100	32	68	100
Fatapukur	54	46	100	54	46	100
JahariTalma	14	86	100	36	64	100
Helapakri	34	66	100	86	14	100
Panbabi	70	30	100	68	32	100
Total	44	56	100	61	39	100

Source: Field survey

The table reveals that 44 percent of owned land is virgin and 56 percent crop-replacing; the corresponding figures for the acquired category are 61 percent and 39 percent respectively. It is, therefore, seen that there is a dominance of crop-replacing land over virgin land in case of owned land. However, the opposite situation emerges in case of acquired land where virgin land dominates over the crop-replacing land. This result is quite similar to what we can expect normally. Since the investment for tea plantation in crop-replacing land is much more higher than that in virgin land, there is a predominance of the latter type of land in the case of acquired land. On the other hand, since no such differences usually exist in the case of owned land, it is quite possible that a high proportion of crop-replacing land has underdone land use changes. Again, as virgin land is better suited for tea plantation, it has converted to tea initially. But due to non-availability of virgin land later on, the crop-replacing land has been converted to tea. This might also explain the predominance of crop-replacing over virgin land in the case of owned land.

SOME CONCLUDING OBSERVATIONS

One significant phenomenon of tea industry in North Bengal in the recent years is the emergence of small tea plantations (STPs) across several districts in this region. The sector has emerged beyond the traditional tea growing area and has seen growth in terms of numbers, acreage and production. This paper is primarily aimed to give attention to questions : who are the small tea growers and what is their socio-economic background? These questions assume importance in view of the fact that there are many misperceptions among the people about the socio-economic position of the small tea growers in this region. One common perception is that non-villagers have penetrated mostly in small tea plantations and this has led to the encroachment of the sphere of economic activities of the villagers with a peasantry background. The analysis of data based on field survey, however, does not substantiate this view. The study distinctly reveals the small and marginal farmers concentration in STPs. Another important aspect of the study is the analysis of the three-phase expansion of land area under tea in recent times. A careful examination of various phases of expansions shows that a multitude of factors have contributed to the proliferation of STGs in this region. A key identifying factor which allows STPs to proliferate is low capital investment, besides the adaptation of the concept that tea can be grown as a small holder crop. The study also indicates a negative consequence underlying this proliferation phenomenon. It is the forced growers concentration in STPs who decide to go for tea cultivation involuntarily. Finally, the growth of STPs is accompanied by land use change on a significance scale. The study has addressed this issue in details. The observations of the study again do not fully support the general view about changes in land use pattern.

REFERENCES

Bimal Baruah : Land and Labour Productivities of Tea : A Case Study of Sonitpur District, Assam, Hill Geographer, Vol. XV (1999) No. 1 and 2.

B. Sivaram : Productivity Improvement and Labour Relations in the Tea Industry in South Asia, International Labour Organization.

John Bafffes : Tanzania's Tea Sector, Constraints and Challenges, the World Bank.

S. E. Kabir, Crisis in the Tea Plantation of North Bengal.

Surendra Singh and T. C. Daimari : Determinants of Labour Productivity in Tea Cultivation in the Upper Brahmaputra Valley, Trans. Inst. Indian Geographers, Vol. 25, Nos. 1 and 2, 2003.

Swapan Baruah and Madan Taparia : Small Tea Growers of Assam : Status and Strategies. The Assam Review and Tea News, Vol. 93 No. 10 December, 2004.

Yujiro Hayami : Development Economics - From the Poverty to the Wealth of Nations, second edition, Oxford University Press.

Govinda Chaudhury & Biplab Chakraborty

3 FEMALE LITERACY: A NORTH BENGAL PERSPECTIVE

INTRODUCTION

The central objective of any development planning is optimal utilisation of human resources through improvement in the overall quality of life. A high level of economic growth over time is considered to be necessary as well as a significant condition of human development. If people are healthy, educated and adequately skilled, they can participate fully and contribute more to economic development process. Inadequate provision of health, education and working skill therefore deprives the society as people are not adequately equipped to contribute to the fullest extent possible. An equitable distribution of human capital (basic literacy and nutrition/ health) is a precondition for increased productivity and ability to their income. What constitutes "Equity" has been a source of continuous debate in economic literature. Sen (1980) considers literacy and nutrition as attributes to be equalized, while other's advocates the opportunities people face as the attributes to be equalized (Arneson 1989, Cohen 1989, and Roemer1993). For others it is amount of resources which need to be equalized (Dworkin 1981). Inequality in attributes are evident from gender discrimination, inter and intra regional disparity in development, and as well as in deprivation of the marginalized communities. An attempt in this context has been made in this paper to study gender inequality in literacy & education in North Bengal.

Sen in his essay "Many Faces of Gender Inequality" suggests seven types of gender inequalities that exists in a developing society namely; mortality inequality, natality inequality, basic facility inequality, special opportunity inequality, professional inequality, ownership inequality and, household inequality.[1] For some neo-classical economists the income effect of growth does not necessarily have gender-biasness nor does it strengthen gender inequality. This is because, as per capita income increases there is more resource to share with women at the household level, more job opportunities for women, and increased government spending on female education and health. An alternative hypothesis is growth does not ensure improvement of women's relative position. Rather the improvement of parity depends on the policies, strategy of development, and affirmative action of the government. There is thus, no need for growth to occur at the first place for reallocation of jobs and expenditure to women (Seguino, 2002).

The growth gender inequality polemic seems intriguing as the causal relationship between the two appears to be rather complex. As long as growth leads to a reduction in gender inequality in Quality of Life (QL), we may adhere to such policy to improve the status and well-being of women in the society. Measuring quality of life is fraught with conceptual difficulties from its inception. A group of preferred indicators which are most frequently used includes life expectancy, child survival rates, income per capita, and adult literacy rates, individually or in some composite index. The UN composite index for QL is based on life expectancy, literacy rates, and per capita income which is better known as Human Development Index (HDI).

Gender sensitive QL measures of relative well-being of women is based on some indicators like gender-gap in health, nutrition, literacy, and less frequently access to resources. One such adjusted index that reflects these categories is the Gender Development Index (GDI), created in 1995 (UNDP 1995). This composite index is based on measures of life expectancy, literacy rates, and per capita income. Another alternative gender sensitive measure as suggested by Seguino (2002) includes the following indicators;

(1) Health indicators: the ratio of females to males in the population (FMR), male to female mortality rates, and the fertility rate;
(2) Education indicators: the ratio of female to male educational attainment for those over 15 and the ratio of female to male gross secondary school enrollment rates; and
(3) Indicators of women's relative access to material resources: the ratio of female to male wages, and women's share of employment.

Of all the indicators mentioned above gender gap in educational achievement is considered to be most sensitive. The existence of gender gap in literacy rate and education is not unique to India only, but is also found in other countries in varying degree. Existence of gender gap in literacy not only means inequality or denial of human rights, but also do have economic, demographic, health, and social ramifications. (Spratt, 2000) Studies[2] undertaken at different points of time shows that literacy is positively correlated to employment, survival of infants and children and inversely with fertility rate (Drèze, 2001). Recent growth literature considers human capital along with the physical capital as an important factor for economic growth. Literacy and education is a primary component of human capital, as it not only increases human productivity but also have positive externalities that benefit society. Study shows that it is female literacy at all levels of education which has the potential to increase the pace of growth more than their male counterpart (Self, 2004).

From recent different empirical studies it has clearly emerged that a close relationship between education and demography exist.[3] A wide range of theoretical analyses from different disciplines points in the same direction (see Dasgupta, 1993). Female literacy contributes to reduction of fertility and desire for a large family size. Literate women tend to have more autonomy in reproductive decisions (Murthi, Guio and Drèze, 1995). Moreover, literate women tend to be less dependent on their children for old age security (Dyson and Moore 1983; Cain 1984. *c.f.* Murthi, Guio and Drèze, 1995) and have high aspiration for their child that tends to reduce the family size. Further, the opportunity cost of educated women is high and this discourages childbearing and childrearing (Becker 1960 and Olsen 1994).

However, some recent studies have raised doubts about the nature of relation between literacy and other variables mentioned above (Jeffery and Basu, 1996b). As, absence of any substantial degree of positive relation between women's education and autonomy led to doubts on the modus through which the former was supposed to reduce fertility (Jeffery and Jeffery 1996; Vlassoff 1996; and Visaria 1996, *cf.* Drèze, 2001). Further as some studies show, observed differences in fertility across groups over time are attributed to other factors, including reductions in infant mortality (Kolenda 1998), family planning programmes and the rising cost of children (Vlassoff 1996), and different risk environments (Jeffery and Jeffery 1997).[4]

On the other hand, studies show that poverty and income level are strong determinants of 'who goes to school and for how long,' (Bajpai, 2004) But, states like Kerala and Himachal Pradesh have been able to achieve much better educational and health standards compared to rich states like Punjab and Haryana. This is also evident from table 1 below for some neighbouring countries of India. For example, Sri Lanka and Myanmar do much better in education and health than would be predicted based on their level of resources. The adult literacy rate of India for both male and female is much below than that of China, Sri Lanka, and Myanmar. In sharp contrast to other countries gender gap in literacy rate in India is higher and the adult female literacy rate is not yet 50 percent. This explains why the per-capita income level of women in India is much lower than their sisiters in other countries.

Table 1
HDI rank of India and neighbouring countries.

Name of the country	*HDI rank*		*GDI*		*Estimated earned income (PPP US$) 2004*		*Adult literacy Rate (% age 15 and above) 2004*		*Life Expectancy at birth 2004*	
	Rank	Index	Rank	Index	Female	Male	Female	Male	Female	Male
China	81	0.760	64	0.765	1561	7159	86.5	95.1	73.7	70.2
Sri Lanka	93	0.755	68	0.749	2561	6158	89.1	92.3	77.0	71.7
India	126	0.611	96	0.591	1471	4723	47.8	73.4	65.3	62.1
Myanmar	130	0.581	-	-	-	-	86.4	93.9	63.5	57.8
Pakistan	134	0.539	105	0.513	997	3403	36.0	63.0	63.6	63.2
Bhutan	135	0.538	-	-	-	-	-	-	64.6	62.2
Bangladesh	137	0.530	102	0.524	1170	2540	-	-	64.2	62.5
Nepal	138	0.527	106	0.513	995	1993	34.9	62.7	62.4	61.6

Source: *Human Development Report 2006*, UNDP, OUP.

The trend in HDI & GDI value given in table 2 and 3 shows that it is only a couple of years back that China's HDI has exceeded that of Sri Lanka. This has been possible due to the universal and compulsory elementary education programme taken up in China during the eighties. Also, during the same period China's GDI has bettered that of Sri Lanka. Whereas, the Indian HDI figure in 2004 is not better than what Sri Lanka has achieved in 1975 or for that matter what China had achieved by 1990. The gender development index does not fair as well and the gap in achievement of female attributes is rather dismal. Trends in HDI or for that matter of any index do not reveal much unless we take a closer scrutiny of the various components of such index. At the aggregate the index shows a gap exists and that it would require greater effort on our part to bridge this gap. On the other hand, GDI reveals the gender inequality that exists in a society which requires immediate attention. 'Growth with equity and social justice' has been the primary objective of development planning for many developing countries including India. Experience shows that growth does not necessarily ensure equity and social justice. 'How best to remove this inequality in general and gender inequality in particular?,' has been constantly debated by scholars and researchers. It is important therefore, to locate attribute(s) of GDI which requires our highest attention to achieve desired results within least possible time and given our limited resource base. Our discussion has shown the role literacy, health and income can play to reduce gender gap in the society. Of which literacy is considered to be the most sensitive attribute with a high forward & backward linkage effect.

Table 2
HDI & GDI of some select countries.

Country	*Human development index (HDI)*			*HDI Rank*			*Gender development index (GDI)*			*GDI Rank*		
	2000	*2003*	*2004*	*2000*	*2003*	*2004*	*2000*	*2003*	*2004*	*2000*	*2003*	*2004*
Norway	0.942	0.963	0.965	1	1	1	0.941	0.960	0.962	3	1	1
Australia	0.939	0.955	0.957	5	3	3	0.956	0.954	0.956	1	2	3
Sri Lanka	0.741	0.751	0.755	89	93	93	0.737	0.747	0.789	70	66	68
China	0.726	0.755	0.768	96	85	81	0.072	0.075	0.765	77	64	64
Indonesia	0.684	0.070	0.711	110	110	108	0.068	0.069	0.704	91	87	81
India	0.577	0.602	0.611	124	127	126	0.560	0.586	0.591	105	98	96
Pakistan	0.499	0.527	0.539	138	135	134	0.468	0.508	0.513	120	107	105
Bangladesh	0.478	0.520	0.530	145	139	137	0.468	0.514	0.524	121	105	102
Nepal	0.490	0.526	0.527	142	136	138	0.470	0.511	0.513	119	106	106
Mozam-bique	0.322	0.379	0.390	170	168	168	0.307	0.365	0.387	144	133	128
Niger	0.277	0.281	0.311	172	177	177	0.263	0.271	0.292	146	140	136

Source: HDR 2002, 2005 & 2006.

Table 3
Trend in HDI index of some select countries.

HDI Rank	*Country*	*1975*	*1980*	*1985*	*1990*	*1995*	*2000*	*2004*
1	Norway	0.868	0.888	0.898	0.912	0.936	0.956	0.965
3	Australia	0.848	0.866	0.878	0.893	0.933	0.947	0.957
81	China	0.527	0.560	0.596	0.628	0.685	0.730	0.768
93	Sri Lanka	0.612	0.653	0.684	0.706	0.729	0.747	0.755
126	India	0.413	0.439	0.477	0.515	0.548	0.577	0.611
134	Pakistan	0.365	0.388	0.420	0.463	0.493	0.511	0.539
137	Bangladesh	0.347	0.366	0.391	0.422	0.454	0.510	0.530
138	Nepal	0.299	0.366	0.378	0.425	0.467	0.500	0.527
168	Mozambique	..	0.302	0.290	0.316	0.330	0.364	0.390
177	Niger	0.234	0.250	0.240	0.246	0.254	0.268	0.311

Source: Human Development Report 2006, UNDP, OUP

A close examination of literacy figures reveal that there exists a substantial number of children deprived of access to education, primarily because their families have not gained from the development process of the past. These children belong to families which are poor, marginalized, cut-off from the mainstream, and families subjected to all forms of discriminations. They have kept away from school not by their choice but forced by circumstances and inequality of opportunities. Literacy & education is both cause and effect of unequal and lopsided development, it is therefore, very difficult to break this vicious circle of illiteracy, poverty, and marginalisation.[5] The problem becomes more acute with existence of gender discrimination in the society. Marginalization and deprivation of women has been a result of combination of social, cultural, and economic factors. Full potential of women's capabilities could not be realised due to the partition attitude of the patriarchal society, exploitation of the girl child, low female literacy level, etc.

Gender equity can be achieved through enhanced participation of women both at the household and community level (Ranadive, 2003). Greater participation of women can be ensured with increase in female literacy and education. Thus, passionately pursuing universal targets without giving adequate consideration to gender issues will not be sufficient to come out of the trap of low level of development. India's ranks 126th out of 177 countries as compared to Sri Lanka's 93 and China's 81 and the GDI rank of 96, 68 and 64 respectively is a testimony to this argument.

GENDER GAP AND LITERACY IN VARIOUS STATES

Literacy is considered to be an important means to break this vicious circle. Literacy rate in general and female literacy rate in particular, is an important determinant of development of population and its QL.[6] The largest disparity in educational attainment in the country is by sex and rural-urban location. The crude literacy rate has increased three fold during the first half of the century, but a little over three fold during the second half. The trend in decadal change in literacy rate shows that the male literacy rate exceeded the female literacy rate during 1991-2001. This has been possible due to a change in policy approach by the government in the nineties and it is a welcome change. The thrust of the educational policy in the nineties has been attainment of higher literacy rate with a decrease in gender literacy gap. The literacy figures for 1991 and 2001 shows that all states show a decrease in gender gap in the nineties except Kerala and Rajasthan. The increase in gender gap in literacy rate for Kerala is not of much concern as literacy rate for both male and female is almost universal for the state. The near universal literacy in Kerala is the outcome of conscious policy actions that were able to overcome barriers to access along physical, economic and social dimensions. Physical barriers to schools were overcome by establishing schools within walking distance from homes. Economic access was provided by making schools progressively free until high school. The census 2001 for the first time shows that the rate of increase in female literacy exceeds that of the male counterpart. Also, the decadal change in literacy rate for 2001-1991 is the highest in the census history of the country.

Though, the all India literacy rate shows that there has been a quantum increase in literacy rate for both males and females over the years[7], yet, between rural and urban areas the differences continue to be unacceptably large, especially for females. Only 46% of females in rural areas were literate as opposed to nearly 73% in urban areas in 2001, a gap of around 27 percentage points. For males, the gap was lower at around 15% percentage points with 71.18% of males in rural areas and 86.42% in urban areas being literate in 2001 (Census, 2001).

Fig. 1
Crude literacy rates by sex, India, 1901-2001

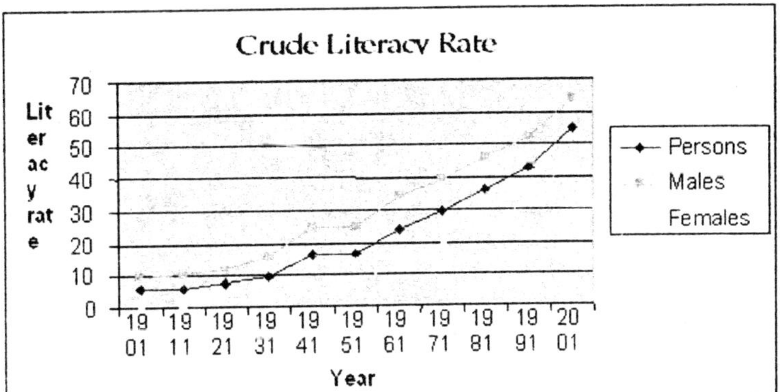

Source: Census, Govt. of India.

According to the literacy rate of Census 2001 the states can be grouped together into following three categories as in table 4a or according to female literacy rate given in table 4b. States which have attained ± 10% of the national average has been grouped together in middle level for both the tables. Literacy rate above the middle level is considered high or else below it as low. Except for Maharastra none of the states in the 'high literacy level' category are highly industrialised. Delhi, Chandigar and Pondichary are metropolitan urban areas and so naturally tend to have high literacy rate. But, it is states like Kerala, Mizoram, Himanchal Pradesh, and also Andaman & Nicobar, and Daman & Diu which has achieved a high level of literacy for both rural and urban population. The states in the high literacy level also show a corresponding high level of female literacy. It is states like Uttaranchal, Haryana, Chatisgarh, Orissa, Rajasthan, Dadar & Nagar Haveli, Uttar Pradesh, Jammu & Kashmir, Jharkhand, and Bihar those which comparatively shows a high level of gender literacy gap compared to the national average figures of 2001. The drop-out rate for girls compared to boys is greater in all states (except Karnataka) and in the five states, namely Uttar Pradesh, Bihar, Rajasthan, Madhya Pradesh and West Bengal, the drop-out rates for girls is more than 50% of the total enrolment of girls at the primary level. Thus, there is considerable 'waste' in the school system, and this in effect reduces the efficiency of resources allocated to education.

Table 4a

Classification of States & Union Territories according to Literacy rate.

Literacy level	*Literacy rate (2001)*	*States/Union Territories*
High	Above 75%	Kerala, Mizoram, Lakshdeep, Goa, Delhi, Chandigar, Pondichary, Andaman & Nicobar, Daman & Diu, Maharastra, Himanchal Pradesh
Middle	75% to 55%	Tripura, Tamil Nadu, Uttaranchal, Gujrat, Punjab, Sikkim, West Bengal, Manipur, Haryana, Nagaland, Karnataka, Chatisgarh, Assam, Madhya Pradesh, Orissa, Meghalaya, Andhra Pradesh, Rajasthan, Dadar & Nagar Haveli, Uttar Pradesh
Low	Below 55%	Arunachal Pradesh, Jammu & Kashmir, Jharkhand, Bihar

Table 4b
Classification of States & Union Territories according to Female Literacy rate.

Female literacy level	*Female literacy rate (2001)*	*States*
High	Above 65%	Kerala, Mizoram, Lakshdeep, Goa, Delhi, Chandigar, Pondichary, Andaman & Nicobar, Daman & Diu, Maharastra, Himanchal Pradesh
Middle	65% to 45%	Tripura, Tamil Nadu, Uttaranchal, Gujrat, Punjab, Sikkim, West Bengal, Manipur, Haryana, Nagaland, Karnataka, Chatisgarh, Assam, Madhya Pradesh, Orissa, Meghalaya, Andhra Pradesh,
Low	Below 45%	Rajasthan, Dadar & Nagar Haveli, Uttar Pradesh, Arunachal Pradesh, Jammu & Kashmir, Jharkhand, Bihar

Table 6
Rank of states according to female literacy rate.

States	Female literacy rank 2001	1991	States	Female literacy rank 2001	1991
Kerala	1	1	Sikkim	16	17
Mizoram	2	2	Meghalaya	17	20
Lakshdeep	3	3	West Bengal	18	19
Chandigar	4	4	Manipur	19	18
Goa	5	5	Gujrat	20	16
Andaman & Nicobar	6	8	Karnataka	21	21
Delhi	7	6	Haryana	22	23
Pondichary	8	7	Assam	23	22
Daman & Diu	9	9	Andhra Pradesh	24	25
Himanchal Pradesh	10	12	Orissa	25	24
Maharastra	11	11	Rajasthan	26	28
Tripura	12	15	Arunachal Pradesh	27	26
Tamil Nadu	13	13	Dadar & Nagar Haveli	28	27
Punjab	14	14	Uttar Pradesh	29	29
Nagaland	15	10	Bihar	30	30

Sex-ratio is considered to a better alternative than other vital statistical estimates calculated from life tables because of underreported number of deaths and births (Bardhan and Klasen, 1999). Moreover, life expectancy measure does not show age-specific differences in mortality due to gender discrimination. The ratio of females to males in the population, on the other hand, reflects society's valuation of women as well as women's ability to protect herself and the girl child during the first few years after birth. We may therefore; safely say that higher sex-ratio can be interpreted as a higher quality of life, or greater welfare for females, even when it is difficult to trace the exact nature of the relationship (Seguino, 2002).

Table 6
State-wise Sex-Ratio (1951-2001)

State	*Sex Ratio*					
	1951	*1961*	*1971*	*1981*	*1991*	*2001*
States with high level of female literacy						
Himachal Pradesh	912	938	958	973	976	970
Kerala	1028	1022	1016	1032	1036	1058
Maharashtra	941	936	930	937	934	922
Mizoram	1041	1009	946	919	921	938
States with middle level of female literacy						
Andhra Pradesh	986	981	977	975	972	978
Assam	868	869	896	910	923	932
Chhattisgarh	1024	1008	998	996	985	990
Goa	1128	1066	981	975	967	960
Gujarat	952	940	934	942	934	921
Haryana	871	868	867	870	865	861
Karnataka	966	959	957	963	960	964
Madhya Pradesh	945	932	920	921	912	920
Manipur	1036	1015	980	971	958	978
Meghalaya	949	937	942	954	955	975
Nagaland	999	933	871	863	886	909
Orissa	1022	1001	988	981	971	972
Punjab	844	854	865	879	882	874
Sikkim	907	904	863	835	878	875
Tamil Nadu	1007	992	978	977	974	986
Tripura	904	932	943	946	945	950
Uttaranchal	940	947	940	936	936	964
W. Bengal	865	878	891	911	917	934
States with low level of female literacy						
Arunachal Pradesh	...	894	861	862	859	901
Bihar	1000	1005	957	948	907	921
Rajasthan	921	908	911	919	910	922
Uttar Pradesh	908	907	876	882	876	898
Jammu & Kashmir	873	878	878	892	896	900
Jharkhand	961	960	945	940	922	941
INDIA	946	941	930	934	927	933

Source: Census, Govt. of India.

The sex-ratio trend given in table 6 shows that India is yet to achieve the sex-ratio of 1951 once again. Kerala is the only state which not only has a favourable sex-ratio for all the census years but, has also improved it. Bihar on the other hand has transformed itself into a state with unfavourable sex-ratio from being one with a highly favourable sex-ratio in 1951. J&K, Sikkim, Haryana, Punjab, Nagaland, Arunachal Pradesh, Uttar Pradesh and West Bengal are states which require special attention as far sex-ratio is concerned. Sikkim, Himanchal Pradesh, Punjab and Haryana are not only state to have shown a decrease in sex-ratio in 1991-01 decade. The sex-ratio of West Bengal has never exceeded the national average and it has only for the first time just equaled the national sex-ratio in 2001 census. The states with poor female literacy rate are also those that show a lower sex-ratio. Also, the sex-ratio in enrolment at the primary level is much lower than the sex-ratio of the population in 6-11 years age group. The ratio gets further lowered at the upper primary, secondary level. Mere enrolment is not enough; it is the number of effective years of schooling that helps women to increase their earning opportunities Education is an important means for empowerment.

Studies suggest that, both at the micro level (household) as well as at the macro level (countrywide), there is a positive relationship between income (and wealth) and educational attainment. Women work participation rate is considered as an important indicator of socio economic progress. High gender gap in employment rates is a universal phenomenon in the developing economies. Female work participation rates depend upon the nature of development, economic & social equity, and female literacy rate etc. Women workers as a percentage of the total female work force is high for the unorganised sector in both urban and rural areas. Primarily, in the unorganised sector women join the work force to supplement low family income, rather than for her own well being. The gender based disparities are a matter of concern, as women labour constitutes half of the labour force. Their marginalization and deprivation can adversely affect development of a nation. Long term data reveals that the female work participation rate has always lagged behind their male counter part for both rural and urban sector.

FEMALE LITERACY IN WEST BENGAL

In West Bengal the overall literacy rate was only 24.42% in 1951. The female literacy rate was even lower and the gender gap in literacy rate stood at 21.4% for the same year. In 1990s the decadal growth in literacy rate of West Bengal has been the highest so far. Yet, we find that it has slipped to 18th position in 2001 in the overall literacy ranking of states from its earlier 17th position in 1991. However, a 14 percentage point increase in the female literacy rate during 1991-2001 has placed the state in 18th rank up by one since the earlier census. This has narrowed the gender gap in literacy rate of the state. Development is related with literacy and education but it is more so with the quality rather than with the quantity of education. One important measure of the quality of education is the effective years of schooling. This include the number of years of schooling, promotion to higher standards, attendance rate etc. It is alarming to note that West Bengal has an overall second highest drop-out rate in the country below Sikkim (Jayanthi C, 2003).

Table 7
Literacy rate of West Bengal according to sex.
Literacy rate in West Bengal

Year	*Person*	*Male*	*Female*	*Gender Gap*
1951	24.42	34.14	12.74	21.40
1961	34.46	46.57	20.27	26.30
1971	38.86	49.56	26.56	23.00
1981	48.64	59.93	36.07	23.86
1991	57.70	67.81	46.56	21.25
2001	69.22	77.58	60.22	17.36

Source: Census, Govt. of India

From table 8 we find that Kolkata is the only district with high level of literacy rate but it has entirely an urban population. There are in all twelve districts that fall under the category of middle literacy rate level in West Bengal. Only seven districts in the middle level has a literacy rate higher than the state average, of which four districts are in immediate neighbourhood of Kolkata and Darjeeling in north being traditionally a high literate district. Out of the five districts in the middle level with literacy level below the state average, there are as many as three districts from North Bengal region of the state. These three districts not only have a low overall literacy level but their female literacy is much below the state average. Malda and North Dinajpur the two North Bengal districts have the lowest literacy rate for both male and female in the state. The female literacy rate of these two districts is as low as that of the BIMARU states. A study of the North Bengal literacy situation in general and that of the female literacy in particular is thus required.

Table 8
Literacy rate in different Districts of West Bengal.

Districts	2001 Person	2001 Male	2001 Female	1991 Person	1991 Male	1991 Female
Districts with high level of literacy						
Kolkata	81.01	84.07	77.95	77.61	81.94	72.09
Districts with middle level of literacy						
N. 24-Parganas	78.49	84.35	72.13	66.81	74.72	57.99
Haora	77.64	83.68	70.93	67.62	76.11	57.83
Hooghly	75.59	83.05	67.72	66.78	75.77	56.90
Mednipur	75.17	85.25	64.63	69.32	81.27	56.63
Darjeeling	72.87	81.28	63.92	57.95	67.07	47.84
Bardhaman	71.00	79.30	61.93	61.88	71.12	51.46
S. 24-Parganas	70.16	79.89	59.73	55.10	68.45	40.57
Districts with literacy rate below the state average						
Coochbehar	67.21	76.83	57.04	45.78	57.35	33.31
Nadia	66.55	72.67	60.06	52.53	62.05	44.42
South Dinajpur	64.46	73.30	55.12	46.40	56.75	35.33
Bakura	63.84	77.21	49.80	52.04	66.75	36.55
Jalpaiguri	63.62	73.64	52.90	45.09	56.00	33.20
Districts with very low level of literacy						
Birbhum	62.16	71.57	52.21	48.56	59.26	37.17
Purulia	56.14	78.18	37.15	43.29	62.17	23.24
Murshidabad	55.05	61.40	48.33	38.28	46.42	29.57
Maldah	50.71	59.24	41.67	35.62	45.61	24.92
North Dinajpur	48.63	59.27	37.16	38.58	45.24	22.85
West Bengal	s69.22	77.58	60.22	57.70	67.81	46.56

Note: High literacy level: > 79%, middle level: ± 10% point of the state average (2001 figures), low level: < 49%.

Source: Census 2001 (P), 1991.

LITERACY AND GENDER GAP IN NORTH BENGAL

Demographic change & literacy in North Bengal

North Bengal comprises of six northern districts of West Bengal, *viz.*, Koch Bihar, Jalpaiguri, Darjeeling, Uttar Dinajpur, Dakhin Dinajpur and Malda which accounts for 21,855 sq.km. i.e., 24.64% of the total land area of West Bengal. This region is bounded by Assam & Bangladesh in the east, Sikkim & Bhutan in the north, Bihar & Nepal in the west and river Ganga in the south. A large number of people have migrated to this region in various times and the region witnessed a large influx of migrated population during the post partition period. According to Census 2001, the total population of North Bengal is 1,47,22,015 of which male and female population is 75,71,926 & 71,50,089 respectively. The population of North Bengal is 18.35% of the state, and male and female proportion is 18.25% and 18.46% respectively. The comparative figures of population and area for the districts of North Bengal are given in table 9 below.

Table 9
Area and population of the districts of North Bengal as a proportion of the State.

Districts	*Percentage of total State Population*	*Percentage of total land area of the State*
Darjeeling	2.00	3.55
Jalpaiguri	4.24	7.02
Koch Bihar	3.09	3.82
Malda	4.10	4.21
D Dinajpur	1.87	2.50
U Dinajpur	3..04	3.54
North Bengal	18.34	24.64

Note: Figures in the table is calculated from Census, 2001.

This region has been one the sparsely populated region in the country. Table 10 shows that the growth of population has increased immediately after independence. Thought the average density of population for North Bengal is less compared to the state. Yet, the density of population is much higher than the national average. This transition from a sparsely populated region to an increasingly populated region within a span of few decades is largely due to the post partition migration. Demographic pattern of the region has witnessed a radical change during the last few decades. The rapid growth of population is not dispersed evenly over the region. This is because of the difficult terrain, agro-climatic differences, large tea plantations, vast tract of forest lands and difference in the urbanisation pattern of the region.

Fig. 2
Trend in Population Growth in districts of North

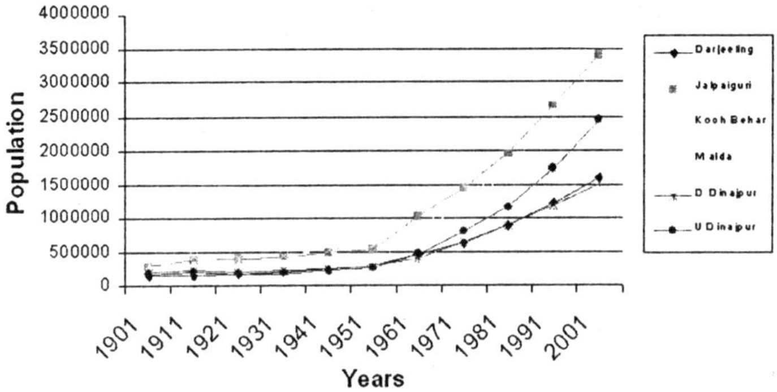

The rate of growth in population of this region has been almost four and a half times during the last fifty as compared to the growth rate in the first half of the twentieth century. Whereas, the growth rate for the state as a whole has increased less than three times for the corresponding period (see fig. 2 and table 10). Uttar Dinajpur, Koch Bihar and Jalpaiguri the bordering districts have shown the highest increase in population growth. Such high growth in population has put enormous pressure on the regional physical and social infrastructure. The total fertility rate estimated from the census 2001 by Guilmoto and Rajan (2002) for U. Dinajpur (4.3), Malda (4), D. Dinajpur (3.3), and Koch Behar (3) is three or more and that of Jalpaiguri is almost three.[8] A value of three or more for TFR is a matter of concern as this implies an increase in population. The vast open tract of land in this region which has been settled by the growing population is required to be provided with adequate infrastructure. New areas settled had to be provided with basic amenities of life. Also, absence of contiguous settlement in different parts of this region increases the cost per capita of providing such social goods. Thus, providing adequate social goods to the settlements in the hills, forests, and remote villages pose a challenge to the planners.

Table 10

Rate of growth of population in different districts of North Bengal

Districts	*1901-1951*	*1951-2001*	*1991-2001*
Darjeeling	1.27	3.43	2.72
Jalpaiguri	1.20	3.78	2.45
Koch Behar	0.36	3.94	1.54
Malda	1.03	3.43	2.89
D Dinajpur	0.69	3.29	2.53
U Dinajpur	0.69	4.61	3.44
NB	0.89	3.74	2.58
WB	1.05	2.95	1.98

Note: Rates estimated from Census data. Figures are per annum

North Bengal has a rich diversity in its demographic composition. It has been traditionally the home of different ethnic groups and its diversity has expanded with vast population who have migrated to this region over the centuries. A large tribal population has been brought from central India to be engaged as workers in the tea gardens. The vast open tract of agricultural land is home of the marginalised communities of the region. This region has a substantially large proportion of SC/ST communities. SC/ST population as a percentage of the total district population is given in table 11 below. Over 50% of the population in Koch Behar district belong to the SC community and also, 53% of the rural population in the district is SC. Jalpaiguri has a higher percentage of SC population in urban areas compared to other districts of the region. Darjeeling has the lowest percentage of SC population among all districts of the region and it even lower for urban areas in the district. The highest number of both SC and ST people is in Jalpaiguri. The ST community in Jalpaiguri and

Darjeeling are found in the tea growing areas of the districts. Figures in table 11 shows that both SC and ST communities are less urbanised. High percentage of marginalised communities to the total population in this region speaks about the relative backwardness of North Bengal.

Table 11
Distribution of SC/ST population in North Bengal.
% of SC/ST Population to Total District Population

Name	*SC Population*			*ST Population*		
	Total	*Rural*	*Urban*	*Total*	*Rural*	*Urban*
Darjiling	16.09	19.05	9.89	12.69	16.43	4.86
Jalpaiguri	36.71	40.24	20.46	18.87	22.39	2.65
Koch Bihar	50.11	53.14	19.91	0.57	0.58	0.49
Uttar Dinajpur	27.71	29.04	17.98	5.11	5.69	0.94
Dakshin Dinajpur	28.78	30.44	17.86	16.12	18.09	3.08
Maldah	16.84	17.02	14.60	6.90	7.37	0.97
West Bengal	23.00	26.90	13.10	5.50	7.20	1.20

Source: Primary Census Abstract, 2001.

The West Bengal HDR 2004 shows that except for Darjeeling, various attributes determining the quality of life are very low for the districts of North Bengal As noted in the HDR, 2004 (WB); the pattern of development in West Bengal appears to fall in concentric circles as distance from Kolkata increases. This is true for literacy also. Of the six districts of North Bengal all except Darjeeling has a literacy rate less than the state. Malda and Uttar Dinajpur are two districts with the lowest male and female literacy in the state. The poor state of literacy and education in this region has been more due to its relative isolation from other parts of the country in the past, poor transport and communication and lack of adequate infrastructure. Added to these are the ethnic diversity and various linguistic groups of the region that makes it even more difficult to provide adequate facilities for spread of literacy among children in their own vernacular. Rapid increase in population during the second half of the last century has increased the demand for education.

Table 12
Ranking of North Bengal districts according to literacy rate.

Districts	*Ranks (2001)*	*Ranks (1991)*	*Change in rank*	*Districts*	*Ranks (2001)*	*Ranks (1991)*	*Change in rank*
Darjeeling	6	7	+	Jalpaiguri	13	14	+
Coochbehar	9	13	+	Maldah	17	17	...
South Dinajpur	11	12	+	North Dinajpur	18	18	...

Note: Ranking has been done on the basis of total literacy rate.

Table 12 shows the relative position of different districts of North Bengal according to literacy rate for 1991 and 2001. Four districts of North Bengal show an improvement in relative position in the overall ranking of the districts by literacy rate. The position of Maldah and North Dinajpur has not only remained unchanged at the bottom but also slipped in the female literacy ranking along with other two districts of the region. Darjeeling and South Dinajpur are the only two districts to have improved relative position for both female and overall literacy rate.

GENDER GAP AND FEMALE LITERACY IN NORTH BENGAL

Female demographic profile and gender gap in North Bengal

The overall growth rate of female population in North Bengal has been higher than the state average rate of growth. The decadal rate of female population growth has exceeded that of the male counter part in this region. From table 13 it is evident that the increase in female population has been more during the second half of the last century compared to the first half. The highest growth in female population during 1951-2001 was in South Dinajpur, followed by Koch Behar. Maldah though has a higher growth of female population than the state average yet, it shows a declining trend in the sex-ratio (see fig. 3). The female population growth rate has however declined in 1991-2001, but it is still higher compared to the state rate of growth in female population for the same period. There has been a substantial fall in the growth rate of female population in Koch Behar district followed by Uttar Dinajpur during the period 1991-2001. The percentage of SC population is highest in Koch Behar and the lowest being in Darjeeling according to the 2001 census. The percentage of SC to total urban population is highest for Jalpaiguri and is followed by Koch Behar district. Koch Behar on the other hand has the highest percentage of SC population in rural areas. Darjeeling and Jalpaiguri with large tea plantations have the highest percentage of ST population. For the SC and ST population rate of urbanisation is very low. Also, the growth rate of ST population has been decreasing for all districts of North Bengal and more so as a percentage of the urban population.

Table 13
Growth rate of Female Population in North Bengal

Districts	*Growth rate of Female Population*		
	(1901-2001)	*(1951-2001)*	*(1991-2001)*
Darjeeling	2.39	3.53	2.89
Jalpaiguri	2.54	3.93	2.53
Koch Behar	2.17	4.05	1.62
Malda	2.19	3.41	2.94
D Dinajpur	2.00	3.37	2.56
U Dinajpur	2.64	4.67	3.54
North Bengal	2.32	3.81	2.66
West Bengal	1.99	3.04	2.08

Note: Estimated from Census figures.

The sex-ratio in different districts of the region during the last century trends towards a value of 950. Malda's sex-ratio has declined continuously over the last century. At the beginning of the last century sex-ratio for all other districts of North Bengal was well over 900. The sex-ratio took a dip in the 1951 census, but has gradually increased over the years and the overall ratio was found to be around 950 in 2001 census.

Community wise the sex-ratio is given in table 14 for different districts of North Bengal. Darjeeling with highest urbanisation rate has an overall sex-ratio of 899, but the sex-ratio for urban ST population is 1016. The sex-ratio for rural ST community in Maldah shows a very health figure as well as its district average. But, the sex-ratio for the district is much lower for urban population. This raises a question, whether the high sex-ratio is due to out migration of the male population form the rural areas in desperate search of income. The rate of urbanisation of the ST population is highest in Darjeeling and its corresponding sex-ratio is favourably at 1016. Urban sex-ratio for Jalpaiguri, Uttar and Daskin Dinajpur is lower than the rural sex-ratio for the same year. For the SC population Darjeeling and both Dinajpur have a lower urban sex-ratio compared to the corresponding rural ratio. In all the districts sex-ratio is higher for the ST population compared to the SC population. The sex-ratio for ST community is even better than

Fig. 3

Sex-ratio trend in North Bengal

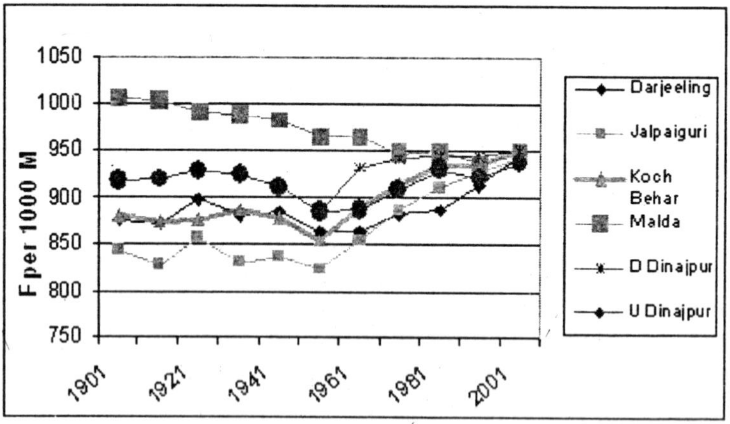

the combined sex-ratio for all population in the districts. However, the urban sex-ratio for SC population is better than that of the ST population for all districts except Darjeeling. Sex-ratio for urban population does not show a healthier ratio for all districts and for all communities in the region.

Table14

Sex-ratio by rural-urban and SC/ST population of North Bengal

Districts	*Sex Ratio 2001*								
	Total Population			*SC*			*ST*		
	Person	*Rural*	*Urban*	*Person*	*Rural*	*Urban*	*Person*	*Rural*	*Urban*
Darjiling	937	956	899	949	950	941	996	993	1016
Jalpaiguri	942	944	933	942	942	944	979	980	927
Koch Bihar	949	947	964	952	951	988	919	916	947
U Dinajpur	938	945	893	940	944	897	978	982	817
D Dinajpur	951	950	958	948	949	942	979	980	943
Maldah	948	948	947	946	946	958	1000	1001	924

Source: Primary Census Abstract, 2001

Sex-ratio as mentioned earlier is useful to understand how a society values women in general, but it is not a comprehensive measure to understand the degree of sex discrimination that exists in a society. GDI helps us to understand the degree of such discriminations that exists in a society. The GDI ranks of the districts of North Bengal are not encouraging. The gender gap that exists is quite evident from table 15 below.

Table 15

Gender Development Index

	Life expectancy rate		*School enrolment rate*		*No. of workers to population (%)*			
Districts	*Male*	*Female*	*Male*	*Female*	*Male*	*Female*	*GDI Index*	*GDI Rank*
Darjeeling	67	71	71.50	68.80	25.10	10.18	0.57	2
Jalpaiguri	61	63	60.60	43.20	27.06	11.30	0.45	12
Kooch Behar	53	57	65.70	51.90	28.26	10.73	0.45	12
U Dinajpur	61	63	57.20	42.00	26.87	11.47	0.46	10
D Dinajpur				28.61	12.14			
Maldah	54	55	45.90	37.20	27.05	13.70	0.39	17

Source: West Bengal HDR, 2004. Development and Planning Department, Govt. of West Bengal.

Female literacy rate of the different districts of North Bengal is low. The average female literacy rate for the region is much less than the state average. From table 16 we find that the Malda and North Dinajpur are at the bottom of the table and there has been no substantial change in the relative position of the districts during the decade 1991-2001. Factors which are favourable for higher female literacy rate like rate of urbanisation, women employment in the formal sector etc., have changed marginally during the decade in this region.

Table 16

Ranking of North Bengal districts according to female literacy rate

Districts	*Ranks (2001)*	*Ranks (1991)*	*Change in rank*	*Districts*	*Ranks (2001)*	*Ranks (1991)*	*Change in rank*
Darjeeling	6	7	+	Jalpaiguri	12	11	"
Coochbehar	10	8	"	Maldah	16	15	"
South Dinajpur	11	12	+	North Dinajpur	17	16	"

Note: Ranks estimated from Census, 2001and 1991

The rate of urbanisation is very low in North Bengal with only 14.14% of the total population living in urban areas. This is much below the all India figure of 27.8%, and the only exception is Darjeeling district with a 32.44% of the population being urbanised. A high urbanisation rate has been always considered to contribute positively towards higher literacy rate particularly female literacy rate. The rural-urban literacy rate by sex as shown in table 14 show that the literacy rate is high for both male and female in urban than in rural areas. Also, it is found that there exists a gender gap in the literacy rate in urban as well as in rural areas. The gap is larger for rural areas than urban areas for all the districts. The worst rural literacy figures are from Uttar Dinajpur. Male and female literacy rates of the district are the lowest in North Bengal, while the gender gap in rural literacy rate being the highest among all the districts. Though Maldah has marginally better literacy figures than Uttar Dinajpur yet, its GDI index shows much lower value for other attributes of the index. The enrolment figures both for male and female are lowest in Maldah as shown in table 17 and is therefore a matter of concern. Moreover, the overall enrolment figures in all the districts of North Bengal are low and therefore, require special attention to improve them.

Table 17
Rural-Urban Literacy Rates by sex in North Bengal for 2001.

Districts	*Rural*				*Urban*			
	Person	*Male*	*Female*	*Gender gap*	*Person*	*Male*	*Female*	*Gender gap*
Darjeeling	66.92	77.21	56.14	21.07	84.63	89.14	79.68	9.46
Jalpaiguri	59.73	70.75	47.97	22.78	80.73	86.27	74.74	11.53
Kooch Behar	65.21	75.32	54.49	20.83	85.93	91.11	80.55	10.56
U Dinajpur	43.68	55.12	31.43	23.69	80.74	85.49	75.38	10.11
D Dinajpur	61.27	70.83	51.16	19.67	83.92	88.47	79.17	9.30
Maldah	48.21	57.03	38.85	18.18	79.47	84.65	73.99	10.66

Source: Census of India, 2001 (P)

Access to school in North Bengal

The objective of the national policy has been to provide a primary school within 1 km. of all habitations and upper primary schools within 3 km. of all habitations. Table 18 & 19 shows that out of 23,311 habitations in the region 2944 habitations are not served by primary school and 7473 habitations does not have upper primary within 3 km. of the settlement. The worst sufferer being Maldah, 643 habitations are not served by primary school within 1 km. of the settlements. The figure for Darjeeling is high but that is more due to the difficult terrain and isolated settlement in the hills of the district. The figure for upper primary schools within 3 km. of the habitations is not healthy for Maldah, and as well as for Uttar Dinajpur. It is female literacy that suffers if the distance of school from habitations increases. This may explain why Darjeeling even with a GDI rank 2 has such a high gap in gender literacy rate.

Table 18
Schooling facilities available

District	Number of Habitations having Schooling Facility at Primary Stage: Within them	Primary Stage: Within 1 km but not within them	Primary Stage: Beyond 1 km	Upper Primary Stage: Within them	Upper Primary Stage: Within 3 km but not within them	Upper Primary Stage: Beyond 3 km
Coochbehar	1640	2501	421	299	3309	937
D Dinajpur	1114	2351	325	134	2770	886
Darjeeling	889	767	552	135	1044	1029
Jalpaiguri	1500	1369	501	213	1705	1452
Maldah	1771	2825	643	281	3509	1449
U Dinajpur	1345	2292	502	158	2281	1700
NB	8259	12108	2944	1220	14618	7473
WB	40883	65874	8928	7310	84592	23783

Source: 7th All India Education Survey.

Table19
District wise distribution of school in villages of North Bengal

District Name	*Total Number of Villages*	*Total Number of Habitations*	*Villages without Primary Schooling Facility*	*No. of Unserved Habitations by primary school*	*No. of Unserved Habitation by Upper Primary*	*Total Primacy Schools*	*Primary Schools with No Teacher*	*Primary Schools with ONE Teacher*
Coochbehar	1202	4565	72	2925	4266	1801	5	34
D Dinajpur	1637	3790	26	2675	3656	1195	4	34
Darjeeling	708	2208	60	1319	2073	1167	5	72
Jalpaiguri	756	3370	62	1870	3157	1969	16	109
Maldah	1799	5239	64	3468	4958	1885	9	42
U Dinajpur	1504	4139	67	2794	3981	1427	18	262
NB	7606	23311	351	15051	22091	9444	57	553
WB	40787	115685	1769	74802	108375	49851	266	3824

Source: 7th All India Education Survey.

Table 17 shows that out of 9444 primary schools 57 schools have no teacher and another 553 schools have only one teacher. North Bengal has 18.5% of the state population and the corresponding number of primary schools is 18.9% of the state. Whereas, out of 8928 habitations without primary school within 1 km. in the state almost 33% are in North Bengal. Of the 266 primary schools with no teacher in the state, 57 (21.4%) are in this region. Another 533 (14%) of primary schools in the region reported schools with one teacher. Uttar Dinajpur, Maldah, and Jalpaiguri are the worst sufferers as far primary schools with one or no teachers are concerned. To pull up these districts from the low rural literacy rate steps need to be taken to provide better schooling facilities in these districts. The All India Educational Survey also shows that a substantial number of the primary and upper primary schools lack toilets in general and separate toilets in particular. This discourages girls from attending school as it does provide sufficient privacy for the girl child.

Schooling infrastructure in North Bengal

A closer examination of table 20 shows that it is the rural schooling infrastructure that is comparatively in bad shape than urban schools. Out of 776 primary schools without building in the state 246 (31.7%) are in North Bengal, of which, 238 are in rural areas. Maldah has the highest number of primary schools without building in the rural areas followed by Uttar Dinajpur. Primary schools with *kachha* building account for 27.3% (876 in nos.) of the total such schools in West Bengal, of which 834 are in rural areas of the region. Almost 12% of the primary schools in North Bengal are either *kachha* or without building. Poor infrastructure will naturally affect the schooling of a child especially when North Bengal has extreme climatic condition with longer rainy season. The student-teacher ratio is also not satisfactory as 56.5% of the schools in the region have a ratio over 50 which do not help to impart quality education to students. Coochbehar, Jalpaiguri, Maldah, and Uttar Dinajpur have 52.9%, 65.9%, 59.4%, and 78.2% respectively of their primary schools with a pupil-teacher ratio over 50. Only 5% of the schools in this region has a pupil-teacher less than or equal to 20. The highest number of such schools is in the Darjeeling districts. The higher number of such schools in Darjeeling is more due to the spatial distribution of the habitations and also because of less population of such remote and isolated habitations.

Table 20
Distribution of schooling infrastructure in North Bengal

District NameTotal Number of VillagesPrimary Schools without Building (Tent or Open Space)Primary Schools with Pupil-Teacher Ratio >= 50Primary Schools with Pupil-Teacher Ratio <= 20Primary Schools with Kachha Building

		Total	Rura	Urban			Total	Rural	Urban
Coochbehar	1202	23	22	1	954	17	111	110	1
D Dinajpur	1637	23	19	4	441	51	137	133	4
Darjeeling	708	7	6	1	406	189	352	330	12
Jalpaiguri	756	8	7	1	1299	81	83	71	12
Maldah	1799	141	141	0	1119	96	165	163	2
U Dinajpur	1504	44	43	1	1116	34	28	27	1
NB	7606	246	238	8	5335	468	876	834	32
WB	40787	776	713	63	21952	2842	3208	3076	132

Source: 7th All India Education Survey

Gender gap in SC/ST literacy

Literacy of the SC/ST community is an important indicator of development, especially as a measure of social inequality (SRE, Vol.I, 2006). In terms of literacy the worst affected group is the backward class in general and the backward class women in particular. Gender gap in literacy is especially high among the backward class communities. The literacy rate of the SC/ST community in West Bengal was not high compared to other states in the country. *Adivasi* women of West Bengal were found to lag behind *adivasi* women of other states in respect of literacy (Ramachandran et al, 2003). Districts with substantial SC/ST population thus show a low literacy level in general and female literacy level in particular. There has been an increase in literacy rate for all districts of North Bengal, for both male and female and as well as for rural and urban population during the period 1991-2001. The following patterns of the literacy rate have been observed to have emerged from the data of 1091 and 2001. Firstly, the urban literacy rate greater than the rural literacy rate in general and also holds true for SC/ST population. Darjeeling has the highest rate of literacy for both male and female ST population, particularly for the urban ST population. This is because of the greater urbanisation of the ST community in Darjeeling. Rural Koch Behar has a better ST literacy rate than Darjeeling. The predominantly ST labourers in the tea estate have a low level of literacy.

Notes

1. Interested readers may refer to A.K. Sen's essay in Frontline, Oct. 27 - Nov. 09, 2001
2. See Bulatao and Lee (1983), Subbarao and Raney (1995), and Schultz (1997), Jain and Nag (1985,1986), Sharma and Retherford (1990), Satia and Jejeebhoy (1991), Basu (1992), UN (1993), International National Institute for Population Sciences (1995), GOI (1997), Gandotra et al. (1998), Parasuraman et al. (1999), and Arokiasamy (2000a). – c.f. (Murthi, Guio and Drèze, 1995)
3. Note: In neo-classical economic model if children are "normal goods", then the demand for children increases with rise in mother's shadow wage (opportunity cost of a factor) through education while the substitution effect lowers the demand. If on the other hand we consider that parents derive utility not only from the number of children but also from their quality, then increase in shadow wage (income effect) decreases the demand for children and the substitution effect increases it.
4. c.f. Drèze, 2001
5. Taken from Yash Aggarwal's, "Disparities in Educational Development," – Discussion Draft (posted in web.)
6. HDR 2004, Govt of West Bengal.
7. All India literacy rate in Census, 1991 & 2001 was 52.2% and 65.38% respectively.
8. Figures in the parenthesis denote TFR for the district.

REFERENCES

Arneson, R. (1989), "Equity and Equality of Opportunity for Welfare." *Philosophical Study* 56: 77-93.

Arokiasamy, P. (2000a.), "Gender preference, contraceptive use and fertility in India," mimeo, International Institute for Population Sciences, Mumbai.

Bajpai, N. and S. Goyal (2004), *Primary Education in India: Quality and Coverage Issues.* CGSD Working Paper No. 10.

Baker,G and H.G. Lewis (1965), ' On the Interaction Between the Quantity and Quality of Children', *Journal of Political Economy,* pp s279-s228

Bardhan, K. and S. Klasen. (1999), 'UNDP's Gender-Related Indices: A Critical Review', *World Development* 27 (6): 985-1010.

Basu, Alaka.M. (1992), *Culture, the Status of Women and Demographic Behaviour.* Oxford: Clarendon Press.

Becker, G. (1960), "An economic analysis of fertility," in *Demographic and Economic Change in Developed Countries.* Princeton: Princeton University Press.

Bulatao, R.A. and R.D. Lee, (1983), "An overview of fertility determinants in developing Countries," in R.A. Bulatao and R.D. Lee (eds.), *Determinants of Fertility in Developing Countries,* New York: Academic Press.

Cohen, G. A. (1989), "On the Currency of Egalitarian Justice." *Ethics* 99: 906-944.

Dasgupta, Partha (1993), *An Inquiry into Well_being and Destitution.* Oxford: Clarendon Press.

Drèze, J. and M. Murthi (2001), "Fertility, Education, and Development: Evidence from India," *Population and Development Review,* Vol. 27, No. 1. (Mar., 2001), pp.33-63.

Drèze, J. and A. Sen. (1995), *India: Economic Development, and Social Opportunity,* Oxford University Press, Oxford.

Dworkin, R. (1981), "What is Equity: Part 2. Equality of Resources." *Philoophy. & Public Affairs;* 81,10. pp.283-3 45.

Dyson, Tim and Mick Moore. (1983), "On kinship structure, female autonomy, and demographic behaviour in India," *Population and Development Review* 9, No. 1: 35-60.

Gandotra, M.M. *et al.* (1998), "Fertility in India," NFHS Subject Reports Number 9, International Institute for Population Sciences, Mumbai.

International Institute for Population Sciences. (1995), *National Family Health Survey: India 1992-93.* Bombay: IIPS

Jain, A.K. and M. Nag. (1985), *"Female primary education and fertility reduction in India,"* Working paper No. 114, Centre for Policy Studies, Population Council, New York.

—— 1986. "The importance of female primary education for fertility reduction in India," *Economic and Political Weekly,* 6 September.

Jayachandrana, U. (2002), *"Socio-Economic Determination of School Attendance in India,"* Centre for Development Economics, Working Paper No.103.

Jayanthi C., (March 2003), "Role of Education and Social Change", *Yojana*, Vol 47, No 3, pp 15-17

Jeffery, P. and R. Jeffery. 1996, "What's the benefit of being educated: Women's autonomy and fertility outcomes in Bijnor," in Jeffery and Basu 1996a.

Jeffery, P. and R. Jeffery. (1997), *Population, Gender and Politics: Demographic Change in Rural North India.* Cambridge: CUP.

Jefery, R. and A.M. Basu (eds.) (1996a), *Girl's Schooling, Women's Autonomy and Fertility Change in South Asia.* New Delhi: Sage.

Kambhapati, U.S and S. Pal (2001), "Role of Parental Literacy in Explaining Gender Difference: Evidence from Child Schooling in India', *European Journal of Development Research*, Vol.13 No.2, pp97-119

Kingdon, G. G. (2002), 'The Gender Gap in Educational Attainment in India: How Much can be Explained?," *The Journal of Development Studies*, Vol.39, No.2, Dec. pp25-53

Mukherjee, N and J. Roy (2006), "Gender discrimination in Literacy and Employment Pattern in Relation to Economic Development of North Bengal," *Economic Affairs*, Vol.51, No.1, March, pp.55-64.

Murthi, M., A. C. Guio and J. Drèze (1995), "Mortality, Fertility, and Gender Bias in India: A District-Level Analysis," *Population and Development Review*, Vol. 21, No.4., pp. 745-782.

Olsen, R.J. (1994), "Fertility and the size of the U.S. labour force," *Journal of Ecdonomic Literature* 32: 60-100.

Pal, S. (2004), "How much of the Gender Difference in Child School Enrolment can be Explained? Evidence from Rural India," *Bulletin of Economic Research* 56:2, 0307-3378

Parasuraman, S. *et al.* (1999), *Role of Women's Education in Shapping Fertility in India: Evidences from National Family Health Survey.* Mumbai: Himalaya.

Rajan, S.I and A. Jaikumar (1992), "Impact of Noon-Meal Programme on Primary Education- An Exploratory Study of Tamil Nadu," *Economic and Political Weekly*, Oct.24-31

Ramchandran,V.K, M. Swaminathan and V. Rawal (2003), '*Barriers to Expansion of Mass Literacy and Primary School in West Bengal: A Study Based on Primary Data from Selected Villages'*, Centre for Development Studies, Working Paper No.345, April.

Ranadive, J. Deshmikh- (2003), "Placing Gender Equity in the Family Centre Stage: Use of 'Kala Jatha' Theatre, *Economic and Political Weekly*. Vol. 38. No. 17.

Roemer, J. E. (1993), "A Pragmatic Theory of Responsibility for the Egalitarian Planner." *Philosophy and Public Affairs* 22: 146-66.

Roy, S.K. : *Tribes Education and Gender Question: Tribes of North Bengal*, Centre for Women's Studies, North Bengal University.

Saith, R. and B. Harriss-White. (1999), 'The Gender Sensitivity of Well-Being Indicators', *Development and Change* 30: 465-97.

Satia, J.K. and S.J. Jejeebhoy (eds.) (1991). *The Demographic Challenge: A Study of Four Large Indian States*. Delhi: OUP.

Schultz, T.P. (1997), "Demand for children in low income countries," in Rosenzweig and Stark 1997.

Self, S. and R. Grabowski (2004), "Does education at all levels cause growth? India, a case study," *Economics of Education Review*, 23, pp. 47-55.

Sen, A.K. (1980), "Equality of What?" In S. McMurrin, ed., *Tanner Lectures on Human Values*, vol I. Cambridge, U.K.: Cambridge University Press.

Sen, A.K and Sengupta, S. (1983), "Malnutrition of Rural Children and Sex Bias," *Economic and Political Weekly*, 19 (Annual Number), pp. 855-64

Sharma, O.P. and R.D. Retherford. (1990), "Effect of female literacy in India," *Occasional Paper 1 of 1990*, Office of the Registrar General, New Delhi.

Spratt, J.E. (2000), "Women and Literacy in Morocco," *Annals of the American Academy of Political and Social Science*, Vol. 520, World Literacy in the Year 2000. (March, 1992), pp. 121-132.

Subbarao, K and L. Raney. (1995), "Social gains from female education: A cross-national study," *Economic Development and Cultural Change* 44: 105-128.

United Nations, (1993), *Women's Education and Fertility Behaviour: A Case Study of Rural Maharastra*. New York.

Visaria, L. (1996), "Regional variations in female autonomy and fertility and contraception in India," in Jeffery and Basu 1996a.

Vlassoff, C. (1996), "Against the odds: The changing impact of schooling on female autonomy and fertility in an Indian village," in Jeffery and Basu 1996a.

Anil Bhuimali & Nilanjan Biswas

4

NORTH BENGAL– A POTENTIAL HOT-SPOT FOR ALTERNATIVE TOURISM

INTRODUCTION

Travel and Tourism is a composite phenomenon, which embraces the incidence of mobile population of tourists who are the strangers to the places they visit. It is essentially the outcome of general curiosity of human being to know and learn more. It is a long journey to the history to trace the beginning of travel and tour. In the begining, it was largely unconscious and simple affair. People traveled for sake of leisure and entertainment. Now, leisure is a term that is used to encompass a whole series of experiences that people can undertake in their free time. [Horner and Sweerbroke, 2005, 22]. Believing this fact, it can be inferred that traveling in old days were merely a private affair.

GROWTH AND DEVELOPMENT OF TOURISM INDUSTRY

Situation has been changed dramatically especially since the last two decades or so following he mass movement of people across the globe. It is worthwhile to mention in this connection that tourism industry is expected to be the largest industry of the world in terms of earnings now-a-days. From the data published by the World Tourism Organisation, tourism industry creates opportunity for 10.6 percent of globe workforce, contributes 10.2 percent to world's Gross Domestic Product (GDP). Not only that, it is estimated that cross-country movements of tourists will increase to 1.5 billion by the year

2020. This reveals the proximity of the size and expansion of world tourism . From the tourist arrivals from 1950 to 1998, it will clearly indicate the enormous potential of the tourism industry at the international level. Table1 depicts the annual flow of international Tourist Arrivals from 1950 to 1998.

Table 1
International Tourist Arrivals 1950-1998

Year	*Total Thousands*	*% Change over previous year*	*Index 1950=100*
1950	25,282		100
1960	69,296	174.09	274
1961	75,281	8.64	298
1962	81,329	8.03	321
1963	89,999	10.66	356
1964	104,506	16.12	413
1965	112,729	7.87	445
1966	119,797	6.27	474
1967	129,529	8.12	512
1968	130,899	1.06	517
1969	143,140	9.35	566
1970	159,690	11.56	631
1971	172,239	7.86	681
1972	181,851	5.58	719
1973	190,622	4.82	753
1974	197,117	3.41	779
1975	214,357	8.75	847
1976	220,719	2.97	945
1977	239,122	8.75	847
1978	257,366	7.63	1017
1979	273,999	6.46	1083
1980	284,841	3.96	1127
1981	288,848	1.41	1143
1982	286,780	-0.72	1134
1983	284,433	-0.82	1125
1984	311,167	9.10	1231
1985	325,725	4.68	1288
1986	332,924	2.21	1317
1987	358,659	7.73	1419
1988	390,000	8.74	1543
1989	450,000	3.85	1602
1990	415,000	2.47	1642
1996	595,000	-	-
1997	612,835	-	-
1998	625,236	-	-

Source: WTO Year Book, 1999

Considering this huge potentiality of tourism business, an integrated approach is of utmost importance. Integrated approach signifies the public-private participation. Therefore, tourism is now under the domain of governmental affair. It automatically calls for the precise and exact definition of tourist for the purpose of official measurement. It was, however, the League of Nations which did a pioneering work in defining the term for measurement. The committee of Statistical Experts of the League of Nations in the year 1937 established the definition of term 'tourist' and synonymously "foreign tourist" as, "any person visiting a country other than that in which he usually resides, for a period of at least 24 hours and a maximum of one year" (OECD 1974:7).

The following persons were to be considered tourists with in this definition:

(i) persons traveling for pleasure, for domestic reasons, for health etc.

(ii) persons traveling to meetings, or in a representative capacity of any kind (Scientific, administrative diplomatic religious, athletic, etc).

(iii) persons traveling for business purposes.

From the holistic point of view Jafari (1977:8) defines tourism as – "the study of man away from his usual habitat, of the industry which responds to his needs and of the impacts that both he and industry have on the hosts socio-cultural economic and physical environments". It emphasizes on the impact of the tourists on the host environment.

It is however, matter of motivation which engages people to travel. There is a degree of variation in selecting the holiday but mostly internal and external stimuli influences the behaviour of a person. This factors include ——

(a) income, (b) mobility, (c) age, (d) education, (e) sex, (f) travel cost.

In short, we can make it in a functional form

$T = f(Y, M, A, E, S, T_c)$

Where T stands for tourism and Y stands for income, M stands for mobility, A stands for age, S stands for sex, E stands for education, Tc stands for travel cost: Also we have

$f\ y¢ > o$, $fm¢ > o$, $fa¢ > o$, $ft¢_c < o$ where (¢) refers to propensity.

Income is positively related with travel. Higher the level of income, more the people travel and vice versa. Mobility refers to the transport and communication system. Advancement of transport facilities induces more people to travel. Age is also important factor determining the demand for travel. People with younger age more likely to engage in traveling because of physical strength and also due to more adventurous nature of mind. Education and such other factors like health, religion, business influences the demand for tourism. However, transport cost is inversely related with demand for tourism. In order to maintain the steady demand for tourism, we must consider affore mentioned factors. Any policy regarding the tourism development must encompass those factors.

IMPACT OF TOURISM

Impact of tourism business on the host country is manifolds. It encompasses not only economic benefits but also social and cultural benefits. Among the all effects, economic benefits are most significant and widespread. The impact of tourism business from the economic point of view can be judged from two angles — one from cost and benefit analysis and other is economic significance. Impact study mainly focuses the multiplier effect. Uncertainty arising out from the international market for manufacturing and with declining terms of trade for primary commodity prices forced the developing countries to shift alternative sources for foreign earnings. Here comes the importance of tour and travel industry at the international level. Tourism is considered as an alternative source of foreign exchange. Besides, there is also cultural and social impacts. For example, when a foreigner visits the host country, he interacts with local cultures and vice versa. It creates some intrinsic benefits also. Apart from this metaphysical and intrinsic benefits , if we consider purely material benefits, investment on tourism is more than sufficient to cover the cost of investment.

All this facts leads to the conclusion that tourism is a great economic force. Therefore we must foster this vast potential of tourism industry by creating suitable environment and inducing more and more public-private integrated effort to wake up this sleeping jiant and prosper.

ECONOMIC PERSPECTIVE OF TOURISM FOR DEVELOPING COUNTRY WITH REFERENCE TO INDIA:

From the economic point of view, the two most important benefits of tourism industry are the foreign exchange earnings and multiplier effect created through tourism and related business. These two effects are specially crucial for developing countries which are generally lacking foreign exchange and high level of income. It is, thus, genuinely found that most of the developing countries, now-a-days thrive for international tourism. Also it is observed that out of 40 world's most favoured nations ,18 are developing nations. Most of them are enriched with scenic beauty and with vast cultural, ethnic diversities.

However, the major shift towards tourism in the post- world –war period by the developing countries is attributed to the economic consequences. Due to the long run declining trend in international terms of trade for primary commodities coupled with increasing uncertainty in global manufacturing due to oil price shocks forced most of the develoing countries to look for alternative source of foreign business or trade. As a consequence, tourism emerged as the third largest industry of the world after oil and automobiles.

One of the most favourable argument for promoting international travel and tourism is its capacity to earn much desired foreign exchanges which solves the problem of Balance of Payment (BOP) for developing nations. Table 2 will provide a glimpse of foreign exchange earnings of tourism industry for handful of countries.

According to Sinclear (1991), Dicke (1993) and Huband (1997) tourism has gained the prime status in earning foreign currency for Kenya, Gambia and Egypt. For India it is true also. Not only that foreign currency also provides critical support for industrial development.

Second most important economic significance of travel and tourism is the multiplier effect that occurs on the host country due to the forward and backward linkage of tourism activity. He effect is generated in two ways-direct and indirect. Direct effect means the direct payment of tourists in forms payments to the hotel, restaurant, goods and services brought by them etc. Which further paid to the providers of those goods and services, they, in turn, pay to producers of goods. In this way it transits through the entire economy. For developing countries this is particularly beneficial because It simulates overall demand.

Table:2

International Tourism Receipts by Regions (Billion US $)

	1990	*1991*	*1992*	*1993*	*1994*	*1995*	*1996*	*1997*
WORLD								
Receipts (US $ Billion)%	266.2	272.7	310.8	317.8	347.8	393.3	433.9	443.8
annual change	21.3	2.4	14.0	2.3	9.4	13.1	10.3	2.3
AFRICA								
Receipts (US $Billion)%	5.3	5.0	6.0	6.1	6.5	7.0	8.3	8.7
annual change	18.3	-6.1	20.2	1.8	6.2	7.2	18.6	4.8
AMERICAS								
Receipts (US $ Billion)%	70.2	77.7	85.5	91.2	95.1	100.2	112.9	120.3
annual change	16.5	10.7	10.1	6.6	4.3	5.4	12.7	6.6
EAST AS/PACI								
Receipts (US $ billion)%	38.8	40.2	47.3	52.4	62.2	72.7	81.4	83.2
annual change	13.8	3.5	17.6	10.9	18.7	16.9	12.0	2.2
EUROPE								
Receips (US $ Billion)%	144.6	143.1	163.7	160.5	175.4	202.5	219.7	218.9
annual change	27.8	1.0	14.4	- 2.0	9.3	15.5	8.5	- 0.4
MIDDLE EAS								
Receipts (US $ Billion)%	- 5.1	4.3	5.4	4.8	5.4	7.2	7.7	8.61
annual change	-5.3	16.8	26.2	10.5	12.5	32.2	6.9	1.7
SOUTH ASIA								
Receipts (US $ Billion)%	2.1	2.4	2.8	2.8	3.2	3.6	3.9	4.1
annual change	2.8	15.7	17.7	-1.6	13.8	14.6	8.3	5.2

Source: World Tourism Organisation, Year Book (2000)

Development of infrastructure is another vital benefit of tourism. Developing countries generally lag in infrastructure. Road, airways, water supply – all are important constituents for tourism industry may be generally shared by other sectors of the economy.

Tourism contributes significantly in creating jobs for both formal and informal sectors. This can be measured by separate multiplier, namely – Employment Multiplier. In brief, the underdeveloped regions of any country can greatly benefit from tourism development. For instance, Khajuraho in India, which is now, globally renown tourism spot, was least known, remote village just 40 years ago. Today, thousands of tourists visit there by air, rail, and roadways frequently.

SUCCESSFUL TOURISM DEVELOPMENT

(Depends upon)

Table 2

ECONOMICS	ENVIRONMENT	ENRICHMENT	EXCHANGE
1. Satisfaction in tourism Activities provided	1. Enhancing Attractiveness of the area	1. Consideration for the environment.	1. Increasing Trade Opportunities
2. Absorbing revenues Generated within the area.	2. Using without Using up	2. Building up academic institution	2. Developing Healthy attitude.
3. Avoiding spoliation And unnecessary Depletion.	3. Consideration.	3. Promoting International mutuality	3. Soft Tourism.
	4. Restoration.	4. Tourist experience	4. Coordinating Needs.

RETHINKING TOURISM – IDEA OF SUSTAINABILITY:

Assessing the impact of tourism and travel on host country through income generation multiplier, employment multiplier effects, foreign exchange earning – it seems that it is the best way to promote development and also remedy for many economic ills such as backwardness, unemployment, poverty etc. unfortunately, this is not the case in reality. Indiscriminate and unplanned growth of tourism infrastructure has created enormous destruction of environment. As a consequence in some places resultant economic benefits of tourism is outweighted by the negative externalities of tourism with higher level of air pollution, destruction of forestry etc. this calls for rethinking the progress of tourism industry. The policy option therefore can be either to stop tourism or to make it environment friendly. This is exactly the idea of sustainability.

Unprecedented growth of tourism industry may lead to enormous increase in the level of income for host countries. It may open avenues for creating new employment opportunities but we can not ignore negative impacts of it. Following points may be a reckoner for those who are ardent supporters of travel and tourism industry:

(i) Globally about 7% of total carbon emissions are attributed to air travel from tourism.

(ii) In USA, tourism consumes 870 billion litres of water per year, produces 317 million tones CO_2 equivalent, and generates 11 million tones of suspended solids in sewage.

(iii) Increases ocean levels and disturbed weather patterns due to climate change may affect all major destinations in the world.

(iv) Least developed countries contributes only 8% of tourism flows and over 85% of tourism revenues are lost in leakages by the time they reach destinations in Africa (collected from WTO report 2004).

It is clear from the above that tourism must encompass economic, social, environmental, wildlife and cultural set-up of host nation. This is the essence of sustainable tourism. Sustainability has become a fundamental issue in tourism development and growth.

Therefore, the concept of sustainable tourism is a challenge to prosper the tourism capacity and the quality without deteriorating the environment that foster them. Alternatively, we can term it 'environment led tourism'.

In this context we can make note of Hawie's (1990) concept of sustainable tourism. According to him, main features of the sustainable tourism can be grasped through following factors.

- The influence of tourism in regional economic and social development.
- The impacts on environment and culture of host population.
- The participation rate for the host community
- Inclusion of intangible assets such as heritage, landscape and spirit of the place and

- Formulating the strategic cover for the development in a given locality.

It will be relevant to mention Indian scenario in this domain. The new National Tourism Policy of India, 2003 perceives that our mission is to promote sustainable tourism as a means of economic growth and social integration and to promote the image of India abroad as a country with a glorious past, a vibrant present and a bright future. The policies to achieve these ends will be centered around three broad areas – welcome (Swagat), Information (Suchna). The objectives of tourism development are to nurture the understanding between people, to create employment opportunities and to bring about socio-economic benefits to the community in order to enrich and promote India's cultural heritage.

The World Tourism Organisation has defined sustainable tourism as tourism development that "meets the needs of present tourists and host regions while protecting and enhancing opportunities for the future leading to management of all resources in such a way that economic, social and aesthetic needs can be fulfilled while maintaining cultural integrity, essential ecological processes, biological diversity and support systems".

There are, however, number of definitions of newly adopted terminology "Eco-tourism". The notion of eco-tourism was initially developed in 1987 by Ceballos Lascurin who defines Eco-tourism as experience of "traveling to relatively undisturbed areas with specific objective of admiring and enjoying the scenery and its wild plants i.e. flora and fauna as well as many extinct cultural manifestation found in the areas" (Boo, 1990). Black developed a comprehensive definition of eco-tourism. He defines eco-tourism as being an "experience with a focus on the natural and cultural environment, ecological sustainable activity with a predominant education and community groups and projects to the conservation of surrounding environment". (Black, 1986).

Thus, we have to think of 'Alternative Tourism' which includes not only eco-tourism but many more, all that sustainable to the local community. For example, rural tourism, nature tourism, cultural and ethical tourism etc. basic idea is the management of environment as well as the active participation of local people. With this insight, let us now identify the prospects of the North Bengal as the destination for potential tourists and viability of alternative tourism.

THE GEOGRAPHICAL OVERVIEW OF NORTH BENGAL:

North Bengal lies in the northern part of West Bengal, comprising six districts – Malda, Dakshin Dinajpur, Uttar Dinajpur, Cooch Behar, Jalpaiguri and Darjeeling. It extends approximately 24°45′ N to 27°20′ latitudinally and from 87°45′ E to 89°50′ E longitudinally. The total area of the region is about 21859 sq.km.

Except the Northern Himalayan zone entire region belongs to plane. Geographical character is diverse since; Northern part belongs to lofty hilly area while to the immediate foothills there is weavy landscape, called Terai and Dooars. Again, on the southern part monotous plain exists.

Basically, entire region can be classified into three distinct zone or units. These are —

(a) The Northern Hilly Tract

This region consists of two districts namely –Darjeeling and Jalpaiguri. The region consists of long tortuous range running generally from north to south throughout the length. The Singalila range is the most interesting part of it. Its highest peak is Sandakphu (11,299 ft.). The only mountainous tract in the Jalpaiguri district is the part of the Bhutan range in the immediate neighbourhood of the frontier outpost of Buxa. Sinchula range here works as the boundary between India and Bhutan. It has an elevation varying from 4000 feet to little over 6000 feet.

(b) The Terai and Dooars

The foothills part of Himalayas known as Terai and Dooars. It is the Teesta River which demarcates the region into two parts – the western part known as the Terai while the eastern one known as Dooars. The region is typical alluvial fan (Geog-Review of India, Vol. 26) surface of the Himalayan foothills, general elevaion of which is over 280 feet. The entire area is built up by the washed out elements (debris) from Himalayan slopes.

(c) The Northern Plain

Third unit of North Bengal includes the southern part of Jalpaiguri district, Uttar and Dakshin Dinajpur, Koch Behar and Malda districts. Depending on the nature of soil, the region is divided into three parts – Barind, Talland and Diara.

Some par of Malda district and some part of Dakshin Dinajpur is known as Barind. Its characteristic feature is the relatively highland of red clay soil of the old alluvium.

Tal land characterized by low-lying plain which floods deeply by the streams (meanders). Cooch Behar and major par of Uttar and Dakshin Dinajpur district and some part of Malda belongs of this region.

Southern part of river Kalindri of Malda district is known as Diara. The region is formed by the currents of Ganges and featured with numerous lines of islands and accretions.

One of the important factor behind the possibility of growth of tourism is the tolerable climate. North Bengal has diversity of climate although it is moderate in nature.

Darjeeling mountain region is endowed with cool and humid climate. Rainfall is high though it varies in some part. Average annual temperature is 12.6^{0}c. during cold monthly temperature often falls below zero. Short-lived summer with temperature on the average lies between 18°C to 22^{0}C very soothing and attracts tourists from all over the world.

On the contrary, the plains of North Bengal broadly the districts of Jalpaiguri, Cooch Behar, Utter and Dakshin Dinajpur, Malda the summer is hot and humid with high level of moisture, obviously not suitable for tourist movement. The Barometer rises to almost 32^{0}C on the average and sometimes it clmibes to nearly 40^{0}C in some part of this area in summer season.

Finally, we must make note about the treasure of flora and fauna of the region. Depending on the climate, nature of soil, rainfall, natural vegetation of the area is intensely diverse and varied in character. This enriched bio-diversity with whispering forests and roaring rivers of the region lure a large number of interested people to flock here every year. The natural vetation can be summed up from following table 3 below:

Figure 6
Physiography and River system of North bengal

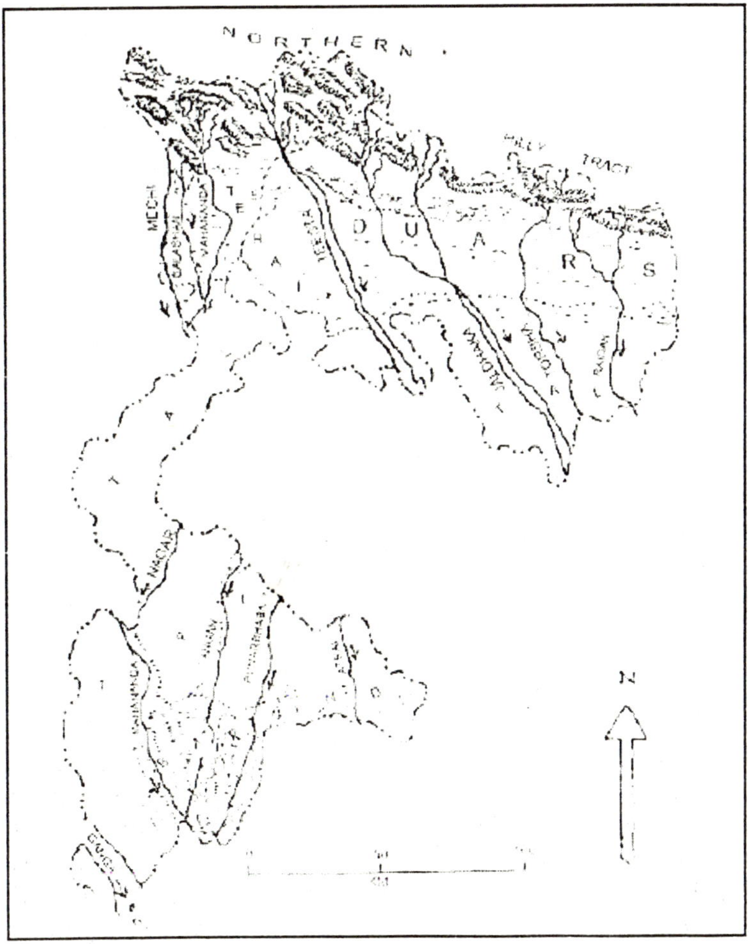

Table- 3

Area	*Floral Type*
1. DARJEELING	1. TROPICAL ZONE (Upto 6000 feet) Sal (Shorea Robasta) Palash, Sissoo, Khair Semal, Mehgony, Pine (Pinus Longifolia). 2. TEMPERATE ZONE (MORE THAN 6000 feet) Oaks, Chestnuts, Magnolias, Laurels, Maples, Birches.
2. JALPAIGURI	1. RIVERINE FOREST: Sal, Mehogoni etc. 2. PLAINS FOREST: Semal, Khair, Asathwate Amaki (Phyllanthus emblica) Arjuna. 3. SAVANNAH FOREST: Sacchuram, Arundo donax, etc.
3. COOCH BEHAR	1. The Betel – nut palms, Date palm, Coconut etc. 2. Bambooms and plantains. 3. Mango, Bat (Ficus Bengalensis), Peepal etc.
4. DINAJPUR (UTTAR, DAKSHIN)	1. Babla, Kadam, Mahua, Krishnachura etc.
5. MALDA	1. Moist deciduous riverine forest. 2. Dry deciduous Sal forest. 3. Dry deciduous hijal forest.

North Bengal is enriched with spectacular range of faunal variety. The forest cover of Jalpaiguri and Dooars is hospitable ground for numerous herbivores of the region such as elephant, Rhinosaur, Sambar, Chital, Barking Deer, Stispid Hara etc.

The one-horned rhinos and the Indian elephant are the prime attraction for the tourists. The migratory birds of Kulik bird sanctuary is also another attraction. These enriched wild-life resources and large varieties of Orchid treasure of Himalayan makes North Bengal genuinely a potential hub for eco-tourism.

EXISTING SCENARIO OF TOURISM IN NORTH BENGAL

From the view point of travel and tourism, most-sought spots center around Darjeeling and Jalpaiguri districts. Darjeeling retains an international acclaimation, lures travelers throughout the world. Jaldapara forest and nearby region is also famous for the wild-life treasures. Other districts such as Malda and both Uttar and Dakshin Dinajpur are less known owing to its low level of natural resources. But from the historical angle Malda has unique status being the capital of famous Hindu dynasties such as Sen, Pal. Dakshin and Uttar disricts also bear some historical importance specially the Maurya dynasty.

Hills of West Bengal encompasses an area of 3149 sq.km is the star attraction for tourists. Apart from Darjeeling hill station (2134m. above sea level) Kalimpong and Kurseong are two frequent visited hill stations. As a halting station, Siliguri occupies central position on the tourist map of travelers of North Bengal.

Let us now have a glimpse of tourist spots of 6 districts of North Bengal from the following table 4.

Table 4

Districts	*Tourist Spots*	*Location*
MALDA	(a) Nimasarai, historical place. (b) Gour famous for its historical resource. Capital city of sen, Pal's dynasty. Numerous forts, i.e. Dakhil Darwaja, Barasona Masque, Quadam Rasul Mosque, Lattam Mosque. (c) Ramkeli religious holy place for hindus. (d) Pandua famous for religious and mosques of sultani period i.e. Qutb Sahi Mosque, Bari Dargah etc.	(a) District tow, 4km North to the town. (b) 3 km south from the town towards Farakkah. (c) 11 miles north from town.
UTTAR DINAJPUR	(a) Chakulia- place with historical relics, mosques. (b) Kulik Bird Sanctuary: the most frequent and popular destination for nature-lovers as well as local commuters Host place for lot of migrating birds such as stock, Egret, Herons etc.	(a) Under Goalpokhar 2 No. Block. (b) 3.5 km North from Raiganj- the district headquarters of Uttar Dinajpur.

Contd.....

Districts	Tourist Spots	Location
DAKHIN DINAJPUR	(a) Bangarh excavation work discovered structural remains of mosques, temples of Maurya Gupta, Pala and Islamic periods.	(a) One km North to Gangarampur, the district town of Dakshin Dinajpur. (b) Situated in Tapan Block.
COOCH BEHAR	(a) Palace of Maharaja, Modan Mohan Temple, Sagar Dighi. (b) Baneswar – famous for shiva temple. (c) Rasik Bill Bird sanctuary natural wetland with covered area of 178 sq.km.	(a) Situated in center of the district town. (b) 10 km from the town. (c) Under Tufanganj sub-division of the district.
JALPAIGURI	(a) Jaladhapara wild-lie sanctuary is established in 1941 with covered area of 114 sq.km. Famous for Indian Rhinos (Rhinoceros unicorniz), Totapara – settlement of an indigenous tribal group. (b) Buxa Tiger Reserve: 761 sq. km area covered for Tigers, enriched with natural bio-diver-sity, Hotspot for nature-lovers, zoologists and as such. Rajabhatkhhawa – gateway of Buxa Tiger Reserve Forest, famous for or chidarium and Nature Interpcetation center. Jainti – frequent visited spot for not only nature lovers but also other tourists for Mahakal Gumpha. (c) Garumara Sanctuary– homeland or number of carnivorous and hervivorous, total area is around 8.62 sq. km.Malbazar – nearly town, small town with scenic beauty of tea gardens, forests and blue sky.	(a) 119 km away from siliguri. (b) Nearly 50 km journey from Cooch Behar town. (c) 60 km away from Jalpaiguri town. (d) Jalpesh is situated 70 km away from siliguri.

Contd....

Districts	*Tourist Spots*	*Location*
	(d) Jalpesh: famous for Jatileshwar temple. Also known or Rus fair.	
DARJEELING	(a) Darjeeling- Most amous, most saught tourist spot of West Bengal, World amous for scenic beauty. Numerous locations to watch – Mall (ridge), Tiger Hill (11 km away from Darjeeling), Batasia loop, Sinchal Lake, Monasterys and so on. (b) Kurseong – Place of white orchid, enriched with healthy climate and natural beauties. (c) Kalimpong's attractions three gomphas, sericulture center and brekking acilities. (d) Artificial lake of Mirik is point of interest for tourists surrounded by tea gardens, orange orchards, cardamom plantations lure tourists from far. Besides bokar Gompha is also frequently visited spot.	(a) District town 80 km away from Siliguri. (b) 51 km from Siliguri sub-division (c) Kalimpong is 72 km North to Siligurid) Mirik is 50 km away from both Darjeeling and Siliguri.

Source: Compiled from different Travel Guide Book.

SCOPE FOR "ALTERNATIVE TOURISM" IN NORTH BENGAL

Tourism has its impact on the local or host country. It must encompass the tolerance level of the host locality. The idea of carrying capacity comes into play here. In simple words, before creating tourist infrastructure we must consider the carrying capacity limits. It will mitigate the adverse environmental effects on the host locality. Not only environmental effects, tourism leaves impact on economic and social life of host population profoundly, therefore we must encompass the economic and social carrying capacity of the locality or destination.

Conventional tourism neglects the idea of sustainability. For example, indiscriminate use of natural resources of local environment and building up of infrastructure leaves an adverse effect on the host country. This gives the birth of idea of alternative tourism a tourism which not only optimizes tourist satisfaction but also manages environmental degradation.

Again, if destination is more commercialized, it looses its charm and authentic qualities which attracts the tourists. WTO (2000) suggests some capacity standards in terms of visitors per hectare:

- Forest park: upto 15
- High density picknicking: 300-600
- Sports/team games: 100-200
- Golf: 10-15
- Hiking: 40
- Ski-resorts: 100 skiers per hectare of railways.

North Bengal has vast store of natural, ethnic, cultural resources. There is huge potentiality of tourism. Some part of it, i.e. Darjeeling hills, Terai and Dooars, forest area of Jalpaiguri already known for is tourism potentiality. But we must concern ourselves about the environmental impacts of rampant development of travel and tourism of this region. Proper sewage systems, water supply, proper care of flora and fauna should be undertaken. In brief, we must broaden our outlook from mere conventional tourism to the alternative tourism. Following are the instruments of the alternative tourism on which North Bengal has the vast potentiality.

(i) Eco-tourism – tourism with environmental consideration.

(ii) Cultural Tourism – tourism activity related to human cultural heritage.

(iii) Adventure tourism – a form of tourism that involves physical efforts and risk taking activity.

(iv) Plantation Tourism – Tourism activity in tea-garden (Tea – Tourism)

(v) Rural Tourism – A visit to rural village without disturbing flora and fauna.

(vi) Religious Tourism – A visit to religious spots such as temples, Gomphas, Monasteries.

For developing proper alternative tourism an integrated approach is necessary. Detailed planning is also required. Table – 2 gives a brief idea.

Till recently tourism growth of North Bengal is mainly confined with Darjeeling hill areas and maritime areas. Rests of the areas of North Bengal are lagged behind. The scope and policies for developing the alternative tourism can be divided into two ways. One is for Himalayan and its adjacent districts covering Darjeeling, Jalpaiguri and Cooch Behar. Other is Southern districts including Malda, Uttar and Dakshin Dinajpur.

Darjeeling has excellent opportunity and prospect for nature tourism. It is already renown for its natural beauty and floral treasures. Darjeeling and its nearby hill areas can be made a hub for eco-tourism. Source projects are already being undertaken. For example in Mirik number of projects has been developed to attract tourists. The on going construction of Tourist Village in Chalsa of Dooars is living example of it. Eco-lodges should be set up in these regions. The Darjeeling Gorkha Hill Council has already constructed tents in Lolay Gaon for tourists. Tents are kind of alternative hospitality outlets found in natural areas like mountainous areas, forest areas mainly to cater the needs of adventure tourists. Tarkhola, which is 80 km. away from Siliguri, can be made for adventure tourism such as hand gliding, rafting. Rock climbing or trekking through the virgin forest of this region can be an attraction for the tourists.

Similar kind of alternative tourism can be developed in number of places such as Mongpong, Rongpo, Suntaleykhola, and Lava.

Malbazar, which falls under Jalpaiguri district, is another potential hot spot for alternative tourism. Enriched with scenic beauty, Malbazar would be an important center for eco-tourism. Nearby Lataguri, Chalsa, Garumara National Park can be developed for nature tourism. Bhutan Ghat, 35 km away from the Alipurduar is endowed with similar kind of natural beauty, with steel-blue water of Raidak and lashy green forest cover, Bhutan Ghat is genuinely potential place for nature tourism.

Not only nature tourism, Dooars region has potential for ethnic tourism. For example, Totapara, near to Jaldhapara, is the last remaining settlement of Totos, an indigenous tribal group is an important destination for interested people.

Figure 7
Potential Toursim Nuclei in North Bengal

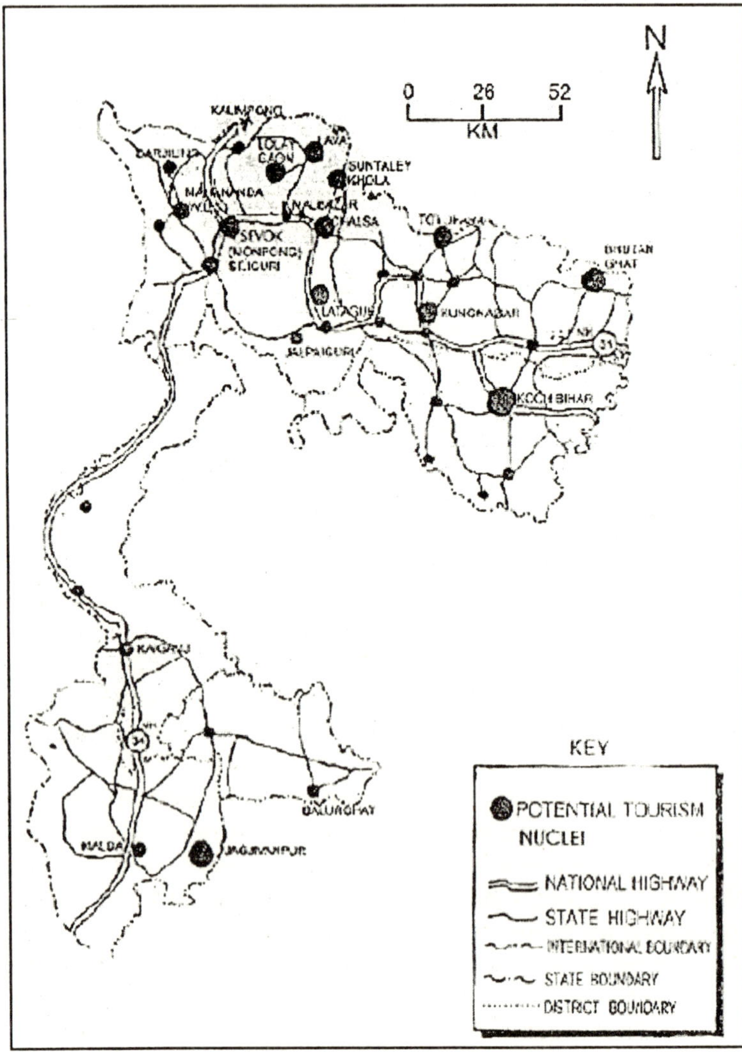

Apart from natural and cultural heritage Northern hill areas and Cooch Behar have some religious values. For instance, Gomphas and Monestry of Darjeeling and various famous temples of Cooch Behar. These religious places attract numbers of devotees throughout the year. A tourism industry can be developed centering these areas if proper initiative can be undertaken. 'Rus' of Cooch Behar is famous in entire West Bengal. People from various parts of North Bengal's flock to the 'Rus Fair' of Cooch Behar. Rus can be proposed for heritage tourism. It offers a vivid opportunity to exchange cultural values of the people of North Bengal.

The second area of development for alternative tourism includes three districts – Malda, Uttar and Dakshin Dinajpur. This region is less known owing to its fragile resources. However, Malda and both Dinajpur is treasured with historical relics. Specially Malda is enriched with historical wealth. Gour, Adina, Pandua all are with historical importance. There is excellent opportunity to develop package tourism in these regions. Barasona Mosque, Dakshin Darwaja and many more are the instances of historical relics. A package covering the visit of the historical places along with staying in 'eco-tents' can be attractive programme for tourists. These types of projects are yet to be developed. It is worthwhile to mention he name of Jagjivanpur in this connection. Located to the 41 km. east of Malda town is prized destination for historians, archaeologists and scholars due to its historical importance.

AN INTEGRATED APPROACH FOR COMMUNITY PARTICIPATION: TWO CASE STUDIES:

Village tourism or rural tourism is one component of sustainable tourism. Some village resorts with all modern facilities and standards can be built rural areas where tourists can experience apart from the marvel of he nature, the glimpse of village life also. They may enjoy culture of rural folk. Especially this may be point of attraction for foreign tourists. Another important benefit of rural tourism is he community participation. A large number of Himalayan villages have he potential to the development of rural tourism.

Initiatives are already being undertaken but not yet in large scale. Here we can depic two particular cases – one is village Tinchuley near Takdah and other is Chuikhim.

In Tinchuley first step was to make the villagers programmes. This was undertaken by World Wildlife Fund (WWF) in early 1990. Necessary training and financial support was provided for organic cultivation, small fisheries and biogas plant.

The next step was to built tourism infrastructure. At the initial stage paying guest system or family hospitality was introduced. Now, more than three guesthouses all ready established. One renowned NGO named 'Help Tourism' cooperated and facilitated the development programme.

In April 2005, joint approach was developed by Share Department of Urban and Rural Community Development, Tata Institute of Social Sciences. The project was titled as "Chuikhim Social Development- cum- Tourism Initiative". Necessary framework was devised with the help o village people, specially with women. Number of Self-Help Groups (SHG) were formed. They got the training for modern cooking and guide service, in order to provide adequate facilities to the tourists. The young generation learnt the techniques providing services to the tourists in treks, bird watching, rock climbing and rafting tours.

In this way Chuikhim and also the Tinchuley have successfully changed their way of life. Through the active participation on village tourism, they not only benefited economically, but also culturally, and socially.

PROBLEMS OF TOURISM IN NORTH BENGAL

The optimum growth of tourism sector depends on some conducive and allied factors . Absence of any of these factors sustained growth of tourism never be possible. It required proper management, integration and awareness. In North Bengal initiative to develop tourism industry has been started much later. Again central attention has been given to Darjeeling hill and adjacent Dooars areas, other part of North Bengal largely remained understated. The problem of tourism in this region ranges from financial, structural to attitudinal and cultural. However we can classify the problem into three broad categories——economic, social and cultural. This is represented in the following chart.

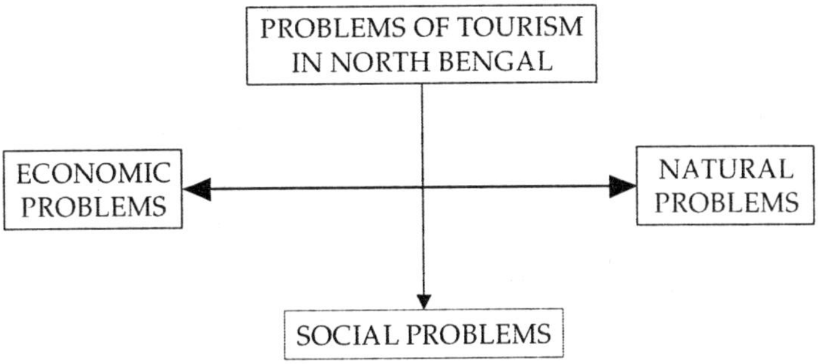

ECONOMIC PROBLEMS

Tourism industry is newly grown industry in North Bengal. Most of the initiatives have been undertaken by Government. Private players are largely absent. Recently, scenario has been changed. Some private companies are investing in tourism industry.But they are largely investing in conventional form o tourism infrastructure i.e. building up lodges, motels. resorts without considering viability. Sustainability is a vague concept for those investors. Again, if they are interested to set-up eco friendly resorts fund crunch is the major constraint. Most of these projects are high cost because of consideration regarding proper sewage system, water treatment plant, solid waste management systems. These involve high cost which in most cases makes the profitability at low level.

Infrastructure is another major problem of the region. Infrastructure includes transport and communications buildings, water supply, electricity etc. Most of the potential tourist spots are ill-communicated. Road transport is the main source for communication. The rich potential·tourist spots such as Buxa-Jayanti, Chalsa, Gour, Pandua, Fallut, Sadakpu are linked up only with road which is also not proper state, Bagdogra Airport is only air-port in the region. This creates severe barrier for foreign traffic.

Another important aspect is the lopsided policy from the authorities. Major projects are directed towards Darjeeling. Other districts are largely deprived. This creates problem for Darjeeling also. Building up to rampant tourism infrastructure in Darjeeling town without considering carrying capacity makes Darjeeling most vulnerable for living. For example, according to North Bengal perspective plan 2001-2010 report the average population of Darjeeling town is 1,266 per sq. km whereas at the sametime average density for West Bengal was 767 per sq.km.

SOCIAL PROBLEMS

Social problems arise out of the difference between the culture, life-style of the tourist population and host population. The interaction between tourists and local people is obvious. Some times it creates problem of adjustment. This becomes serious when tourists are often foreigners .They become alienated cultural tourism depends on the active participaion between local community and tourists or visitors. Unfortunately, if visitors are not treated properly it will collapse miserably.

Instances of cheating by local people is a point of worry ,specially in hill areas where behaviour of Taxi, Jeep drivers are point of concern. They often try to cheat foreign tourists by charging high prices. This meanace must be stopped. Proper co-ordination between people and authorities should be maintained.

ENVIRONMENTAL PROBLEMS

Environmental degradation is the most common problem associated with tourism development. It is always a burden or local environment. Most of the tourist spots are developed basing on natural beauty. Therefore, nature is most vulnerable and easy deplorable resource due to the growth of tourism. In North Bengal symptom of over- crowding and natural degradation is already visible in tourist spots, specially in Darjeeling and Dooars region. Concept of eco-tourism is yet to be popularized. Lack of proper publicity, information and awareness of local people make the scenario more serious.

CONCLUSION

Travel and tourism is regarded as the most varied and diverse industry. Basically, it is a service-oriented industry, depends on management ability of the provider. North Bengal with its rich bio-diversity and natural resources carries a huge potential for development of nature tourism. It is fair to say that major attraction for tourist in this region is the Darjeeling hill and Terai, Dooars. At the time of formulating integrated plan for tourism development, we must consider this point. North Bengal can be a hub of tourism centering Darjeeling and adjoining areas Other parts of North Bengal both Dinajpurs and Malda comparatively less resourceful. But they have their own historic values. Thus, nature and eco-tourism centers can be built around Darjeeling and Dooars, whereas center for cultural tourism can be built around Malda and Uttar, Dakshin Dinajpur.

Second point is that any tourism development policy must address the local community participation. Encompassing local community not only economically viable but also culturally viable. It is related to empowerment specially, for women, when we find that large part of Female workforce lying idle in this region. Development of tourism must establish a platform for the women of the North Bengal to work suitably and make themselves empowered.

Lastly, most important consideration is the measure of 'carrying capacity'. The common problem of nature based tourism is over exhustation of resource, beyond its carrying capacity. This symptom is already visible in source part of Darjeeling hills. We must therefore, formulate our tourism planning in accordance with carrying capacity with the North Bengal.

Marketing problem is another aspect to be highlighted. Leaving Darjeeling hill and Jaldapara most of the other spots are less known and published. Specially, tours of Dinajpur, Malda are seriously lagging in this respect. Tourism development requires proper marketing, both private and public initiative is necessary. Therefore, rejuvenation, revitalization and reconstruction of the poor tourism scenario of North Bengal calls for initiation of a separate Organisation, a Territorial and Financial Planning. The active efforts of these measures would give impetus to overall regional development of the area concerned.

REFERENCES

Bose, S.C. (1977), Geography of West Bengal, Calcutta Publishing House.

Bhatia A.K (2002), International Tourism Management, Sterling Publishers Private Limited. New Delhi.

Bryden J.M. (1999), Tourism and Development. The University Press, London.

Batta R.N. (2001), Tourism and Environment, Indus Publishing Company, New Delhi.

Chakraborty Saikati (2006), Scope, Emergence of Rural Tourism Development in Sikkim and Dooars.

Das Arunaua (2006), Community Base Village Tourism in Eastern Himalayas .

George and Nigam (2003), Tourism and Tourism.

Karmakar, M (2002), Growth and Prospects of Tourism in North Bengal (Thesis Paper).

Puneet, Aneja (2006), KuruKshetra; vol-54, no-7, May 2006.

Ranga Mukesh (2003), Tourism Potential in India, Abhijeet Publishers, New Delhi.

Singh, Ratandeep (1997), Dynamics of Modern Tourism.

Travel Guide (2004), Manorama Publishing House, Karnataka.

Chandan Kumar Mukhopadhyay
Biswajit Maitra

5

CAUSAL RELATIONSHIP BETWEEN GOVERNMENT REVENUE AND GOVERNMENT EXPENDITURE IN INDIA

– An Econometric Study for the Periods 1950-2005

INTRODUCTION

In modern days almost all economists and policy makers agree that, fiscal and monetary policies have a prominent and far-reaching role in economic development. In case of fiscal policy the two main instruments are government expenditure and government revenue. The efficacy of the policy depends on how the government regulates these instruments through budgetary management. For the effective policy formulation, the relationship between these two parameters needs to be examined.

In economic literature, four alternative explanations regarding the relationship between government revenue and government expenditure have been stated. These are:

1. Tax-and-Spend Hypothesis

This hypothesis suggests that the amount of tax revenue determines the size of government expenditure. More specifically, if the amount of tax collection rises, the government spends more. So, there is a unidirectional causal relationship between government tax revenue and government expenditure. Friedman (1978), Buchanan and Wagner (1977 and 1978) hold this view.

2. Spend-and-Tax Hypothesis

This view postulates that government expenditure determines tax revenue. Government takes the expenditure decision first, and then imposes tax on the people. So there exists a unidirectional causality running from government expenditure to government revenue. This hypothesis has been supported by Barro (1974 and 1978), Peacock and Wiseman (1961 and 1979).

3. Tax-and-Spends and Spend-and-Tax Hypothesis:

This hypothesis viewed that government expenditure and government revenue are interdependent. So, there exists a bi-directional causal link between the variables concerned. Specifically, government expenditure can cause government revenue and/or government revenue can cause government expenditure. This hypothesis is also known as *Fiscal Synchronization Hypothesis*. Musgrave (1969), Meltezer and Richard (1981) have supported this view.

4. No relationship between tax and spending of the government:

This view suggests that government expenditure and government revenue are independent. There is no relationship between them.

A brief survey of the literature to highlight such major studies is given below:

LITERATURE SURVEY

Manage and Marlaw(1986) enquired into the pattern of causality between receipts and expenditure of the U.S. government for the period 1929-1982. They found the evidence that in most of the cases (58%), bi-directional causality existed. In no such case where the causality from expenditure to receipts was observed.

Anderson, Wallace and Warnar (1986) conducted their study in the United States for the period 1929 – 1982. Their study reveled that higher spending led to higher taxes implying uni-directional causality from expenditure to revenue.

Von Furstunberg, Green and Jeong (1986) applied VAR Methodology incorporating quarterly federal data for the period 1954 – 1982 and supported the "Spend-and-Tax" hypothesis. This study corroborated the findings of Anderson, Wallace and Warner.

Chowdhury, A.R. (1988) re-examined the result of Manage and Marlaw (1987) study and confirmed bi-directional causality.

Blackley, P.R. (1986) applied Granger-Sim causality on U.S. federal data (1929 – 1982) and held that increasing revenue led to increasing expenditure.

Millaer, S.M. and F.S. Russck (1990) used Co-integration and error correction model and found the evidence of bi-directional causality between revenue and expenditure.

Joulfaial, D. and R. Mookerjee (1990) assessed the revenue-expenditure nexus involving Granger causality and reported unidirectional causality from revenue to expenditure.

Jones, J.D. and D. Joulfaian (1991) reported unidirectional causality running from expenditure to revenue in the short run and bi-directional causality in the long run. This confirmes 'Spend-and-Tax' hypothesis in the short run and 'Spend-and-Tax and Tax-and-Spend' hypotheses in the long run.

Naidu, C.R., Md. Mohsin and V. J. Naidu (1994 – 95) examined the causal relationship between revenue and expenditure for the period (1969 –1990) in Andra Pradesh, India and found bi-directional causality.

Dhanasekaran, K (2001) examined the relationship in the Indian context using annual time series data for the period 1960 – 1997. The study was based on the use of Co-integration, Gewek Decomposition Models and Granger causality test. The study showed the absence of co-integration, implying that there was no stable long run relationship between the variables. With revenue as dependant variables, the Gewek tests supported the existence of bi-directional causality, while with government expenditure as dependent variable, no evidence of causality was observed. On other hand, Granger causality supported the unidirectional causality flowing from expenditure to tax.

Darrat, A.F. (1998) examined if Turkish budgetary process followed Tax-and-Spend, or Spend-and- Tax hypotheses. The study did not find any evidence to support any of the above hypotheses.

Regmi, Uday Raj (2006) reported unidirectional causality running from government expenditure to tax revenue in Nepal for the period 1977 – 2004. This study used the methodology of co-integration, Vector Error Correction and Granger causality.

II

DATA AND METHODOLOGY

In this study time series annual data (1950 – 2005) for the government expenditure and revenue in India have been used. The data set has been collected from Reserved Bank of India Bulletins and different issues of International Financial Statistics. Wholesale price index (1995 = 100) has been used.

STUDY PROCEDURE

We seek to examine the causal relationship between the variables concerned through the following steps:

(i) The stationary of the data set is examined, since the regression on non-stationary time series gives spurious relationship resulting in erroneous conclusions.

(ii) The non-stationary time series may be used to find long run stable relationship provided the series are co-integrated. Therefore, co-integration between the variables has been studied.

(iii) We enquire into the direction and the nature of causality through VAR techniques and Granger causality.

STATIONARITY TEST

The study involves the use of time series data. These series are not deterministic variables. They share some typical pattern. The realization of such patterns are viewed as being generated by some stochastic processes. Specification of the underlying stochastic process is preceded by the identification of the nature of the stochastic process. More specifically, it is necessary to know whether the underlying stochastic process is invariant with time or whether it describes a random walk. If the process is non-stationary, it is difficult to represent the time series over past and future intervals of time by an algebraic model. By contrast, if the stochastic process is fixed in time i.e., if it is stationary, then one can model the process through an equation with fixed coefficients that can be estimated from the past data.

Charles. R. Nelson and C.I. Plosser (1982) hold that macro-economic time series usually behave like random walks. So these series are not 'trend reverting.' Consequently, these variables do not tend to revert back to a long run trend after a shock. In such case, standard regression with non-stationary data makes all regression coefficients misleading, and therefore, leads to spurious relationships with erroneous conclusions. It, therefore, becomes pertinent to enquire into the nature of the stochastic processes of the macroeconomic time series concerned, viz. government expenditure and government revenue in India.

ADF Unit Root Test: The Model

Figure 1 presents the time plots of Government expenditures and Revenues in India over the period 1950 – 2005. Stationarity of the variables are examined through ADF test.

Fig. 1
Real Govt. Expenditure and Real Govt. Revenue (Base = 1995)

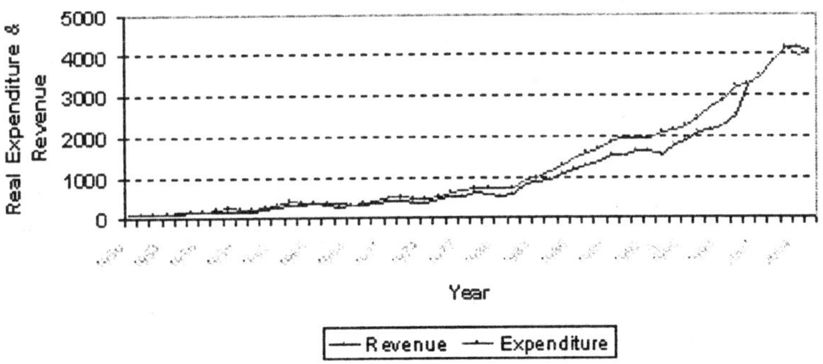

If government expenditure and government revenue follow random walk with drift around a stochastic trend, the ADF test equation will take the form:

$$\Delta E_t = \alpha + \beta t + \delta_i \sum_{i=1}^{n} \Delta E_{t-1} + \varepsilon_t \qquad (i)$$

$$\Delta R_t = \gamma + \omega t + \rho_i \sum_{i=1}^{n} \Delta R_{t-1} + \upsilon_t \qquad (ii)$$

Where, E_t is logarithm of real government expenditure,

R_t is logarithm of real government revenue,

$\varepsilon_t \sim$ iidN $(0, \sigma_\varepsilon^2)$,

$\Delta E_{t-1} = (E_{t-1} - E_{t-2})$,

$\Delta E_{t-2} = (E_{t-2} - E_{t-3})$,

$\upsilon_t \sim$ iidN $(0, \sigma_\upsilon^2)$

$\Delta R_{t-1} = (R_{t-1} - R_{t-2})$,

$\Delta R_{t-2} = (R_{t-2} - R_{t-3})$, etc.

The Results

The results of the estimations of the equation (i) and (ii) are shown in the table bellow:

Table-1
ADF Test Results For Real Govt. Expenditure And Real Govt. Revenue

Variables	*ADF test statistic*	*Critical Values* 1%	5%	10%
E_t	-3.326752	-4.1348	-3.4935	-3.1753
ΔE_t	-5.951951	-4.1383	-3.4952	-3.1762
R_t	-3.254852	-4.1348	-3.4935	-3.1753
ΔR_t	-5.879414	-4.1383	-3.4952	-3.1762

The Findings

From the Table 1, it appears that:

(i) The absolute value of the ADF test statistic is less than the absolute critical values for the variable E_t at 1% and 5% level of significance.

(ii) For the variable R_t the absolute value of ADF test statistic is lower than the critical values at 1%, 5% levels. Consequently, the hypothesis of unit root (non-stationarity) is accepted for both the variables (E_t and R_t).

(iii) In case of the first differenced series (ΔE_t and ΔR_t), the absolute value of ADF test statistic is greater than the corresponding absolute critical values at 10%, 5% and even at 1% levels. Consequently, first difference series are stationary. The Autocorrelation Functions (ACF) and Partial Autocorrelation Functions (PACF) diagrams (Fig. 2 - Fig. 9 given in the Appendix) also testify for stationarity. Therefore, the real government expenditure and real government revenue in India are non-stationary at levels and stationary upon first differencing.

CO-INTEGRATION

Random walk process attains stationarity by differencing. But differencing the data has a cost. The cost arises from the fact that differencing may result in a loss of information about the long run relationship between the variables concerned. Engle and Granger (1987) hold that there are situations where one can run a regression between two variables even though both are non-stationary. This will be possible if the linear combination of the non-stationary variables were stationary. In such case, the variables are said to be co-integrated. Engle-Granger techniques are being applied in this study on co-integration.

The Model for Co-integration

The following model is used for the study of co-integration between Government expenditure (E_t) and Government revenue (Rt)

$$E_t = \alpha + \beta R_t + u_t \qquad (iii)$$

$$R_t = \gamma + \delta E_t + v_t \qquad (iv)$$

The Results of Co-integration study

The estimated equations are:

$$E_t = -0.08533 + 1.004763 R_t \qquad (v)$$

S.E. (0.04) (0.3778)

t [-2.14] [72.93]

$R^2 = 0.99$

Adjusted $R^2 = 0.99$
Sum Squire of Residuals = 0.127
d.f. = 55

$$R_t = 0.113186 + 0.985256 E_t \quad (vi)$$

S.E. (0.03832) (0.021)
t [2.85399] [72.93]

$R^2 = 0.99$
Adjusted $R^2 = 0.99$
Sum Squire of Residuals = 0.125
d.f. = 55

Table 2
Adf Tests Results On Resuduals And

Variables	*ADF test statistics*	*Critical Values* 1%	5%	10%
u_t	-4.007557	-4.1383	-3.4952	-3.1762
v_t	-4.009218	-4.1383	-3.4952	-3.1762

The Findings

The ADF tests on the residual series indicate that both the residuals are stationary. The ACF and PACF plots also confirm the stationarity of the residuals (Fig. 10 - Fig. 13 given in the Appendix). Consequently, real government expenditure and real government revenue in India are appear to be co-integrated and therefore there exists a stable long run relationship between them.

III

Vector Error Correction (VEC)

The Vector Error Correction specification restricts the long run behavior of the endogenous variables to converge to their co-integrating relationships while allowing a wide range of short run dynamics. The co-integration term is known as the error correction term since the deviation from the long run equilibrium is corrected gradually through a series of partial short run adjustments. Therefore, VEC modeling gives important information about the short run relationship between the co-integrated variables.

The Model

Vector Error Correction (VEC) model between government expenditure and government revenue is as follows:

$$\Delta E_t = \gamma_1 + \rho_1 z_{t-1} + \alpha_1 \Delta E_{t-1} + \alpha_2 \Delta E_{t-2} + \alpha_3 \Delta R_{t-1} + \alpha_4 \Delta R_{t-2} + \varepsilon_t \quad (vii)$$

$$\Delta R_t = \gamma_2 + \rho_2 z_{t-2} + \beta_1 \Delta R_{t-1} + \beta_2 \Delta R_{t-2} + \beta_3 \Delta E_{t-1} \; \beta_4 \Delta E_{t-2} + \omega_t \quad (viii)$$

Where ε_t and ω_t are white noise error terms.

Estimation and Results

The results of the estimation of the equations (vii) and (viii) are being presented through the Table 3

Table - 3
THE RESULTS OF THE VEC ESTIMATIONS

Dependent Variable	*Explanatory Variables*	*Coefficients*	*'t' statistics*	*Standard errors*
ΔE_t	Constant	0.029	3.81	0.00775
	z_{t-1}	-0.3132**	-2.34	0.13385
	ΔE_{t-1}	0.2614	1.57	0.166
	ΔE_{t-2}	-0.1831	-1.11	0.16557
	ΔR_{t-2}	0.0347	0.22	0.15945
		-0.0809	-0.514	0.15738
ΔR_t	Constant	0.0309	3.73	0.00831
	z_{t-1}	0.1748	1.22	0.14355
	ΔR_{t-1}	0.057	0.34	0.171
	ΔR_{t-2}	-0.2058	-1.22	0.16878
	ΔE_{t-1}	0.1845	1.04	0.17811
	ΔE_{t-2}	-0.0687	-0.39	0.17756

** indicates that the co-efficient is significant at 5% level.

The Findings

It is observed from the Table 3 that,

(i) The coefficient of Z_{1t-1} in the co-integrating equation (vii) is significant at 5% level. This indicates that the system is in the state of short run dynamics.

(ii) The negative sign of the coefficient for Z_{1t-1} indicates that the change in the value of depends inversely on the past error.

(iii) The coefficient Z_{1t-1} is not significant in the co-integrating equation (viii). It indicates short run disequilibrium is the system.

GRANGER CAUSALITY TEST ON GOVT. EXPENDITURE AND GOVT. REVENUE:

The Model

The long run causal relationship between the variables can be study by applying Granger Causality Test. We have found two co-integrating equations between E_t and R_t. So there is a possibility of two-way causal relationship between the variables. This is studied through Granger causality test with the following equations:

$$E_t = \alpha + \beta E_{t-1} + \gamma_1 R_t + \gamma_2 R_{t-1} + \gamma_3 R_{t-2} + \gamma_4 R_{t-3} + u_t \quad (ix)$$

$$R_t = \delta + \omega R_{t-1} + \rho_1 E_t + \rho_2 E_{t-2} + \rho_3 E_{t-3} + \rho_4 E_{t-4} + \upsilon_t \quad (x)$$

Where and u_t are υ_t white noise error terms.

The Results

The results of estimation of the equations (ix) and (x) are given below:

$$E_t = -0.0763 + 0.585 E_{t-1} + 0.704 R_t$$

$$-0.273 R_{t-1} - 0.0257 R_{t-2} + 0.02869 R_{t-3} \quad (xi)$$

S.E.	(0.35)	(0.112)	(0.120)	(0.1850)	(0.179)	(0.115)
t	[-2.181]	[5.236]	[5.851]	[-1.479]	[-0.144]	[0.250]

$R^2 = 0.996,$

Adjusted $R^2 = 0.995$,
Sum Squire of Residuals $R^2 = 0.046$,
F = 2196.564,

$$R_t = 0.112 + 0.592R_{t-1} + 0.629E_t - 0.18E_{t-1} - 0.069E_{t-2} + 0.00352E_{t-3} \qquad (xii)$$

S.E.	(0.03)	(0.106)	(0.106)	(0.164)	(0.15)	(0.102)
t	[3.7]	[5.568]	[5.954]	[-1.099]	[-0.46]	[0.034]

$R^2 = 0.996$,
Adjusted $R^2 = 0.995$
Sum Squire of Residuals $R^2 = 0.04122$,
F = 2268.526,

The Findings

It is observed from the estimated equation (xi) that,

(i) The coefficient of R_t is positive and significant at 1% level. It implies that current government revenue affects current government expenditure significantly.

(ii) The coefficient of E_{t-1} is positive and significant at 1% level. Consequently, the immediate past expenditure significantly affect current government expenditure.

(iii) All other coefficients, i.e., γ_2, γ_3 and γ_4 are not statistically significant. Consequently, revenue obtained in the previous periods do not offer to exert any significant effect on current government expenditure.

It is further observed from equation (xii) that,

(i) The coefficient of R_{t-1} is positive and significant at 1% level. Consequently, government revenue of previous period significantly affect current government revenue.

(ii) ρ_2, the coefficient of E_t, is positive and significant at 1% level. This indicates that current government expenditure significantly affects current government revenue.

(iii) Other coefficients in this model such as ρ_2, ρ_3 and ρ_4 are not statistically significant. It, therefore, appears that expenditure of past periods fail to affect current government revenue.

IV

SUMMERY AND CONCLUSIONS

It is therefore, observed that:

(i) The real government expenditure and real government revenue in India for the period (1950-2005) display non-stationarity, i.e., random walk process.

(ii) Both the series become stationary upon first differencing. Therefore, these series follow I(1) process.

(iii) The ACF and PACF plots also confirm the stationarity of the variables.

(iv) The variables concerned are co-integrated and the study gives forth two co-integrating equations. This testifies for the existence of stable long run relationship between the variables.

(v) Error correction model confirms short run dynamics between government expenditure (dependent variable) and government revenue. Specifically, government expenditure is negatively related to the past error terms.

(vi) There exists bi-directional causal (Granger) relationship between real government expenditure and real government revenue. Specifically, the current government expenditure and current government revenue are found to affect and be affected by the other variable.

In short, these results seem to support the "Tax-and-Spend and Spend-and-Tax" hypothesis in case of India for the periods (1950 – 2005). These results have some policy implications to correct fiscal imbalances. Results suggests that spending cuts will ultimately lead to revenue reductions; and revenue increases will correspondingly lead to expenditure increases. Therefore, fiscal adjustment based on expenditure side and revenue side of the budget should be independent of each other.

APPENDIX

Figure 2 (ACF of Et)

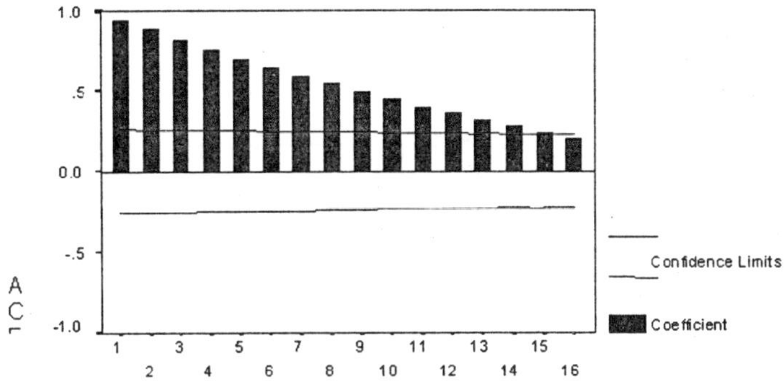

Figure 3 (PACF of Et)

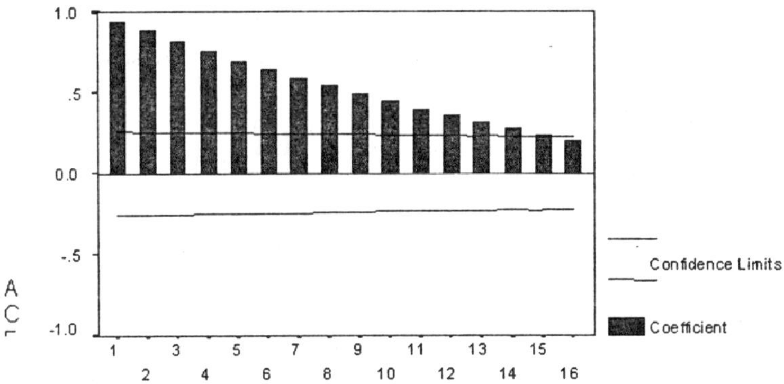

Figure 4 (ACF of Rt)

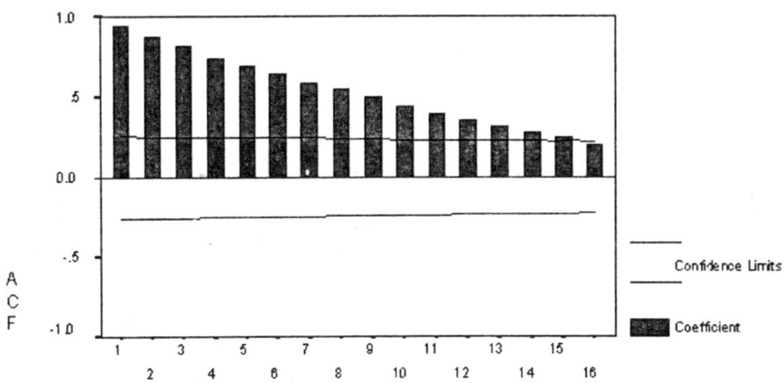

Figure 5 (PACF of Rt)

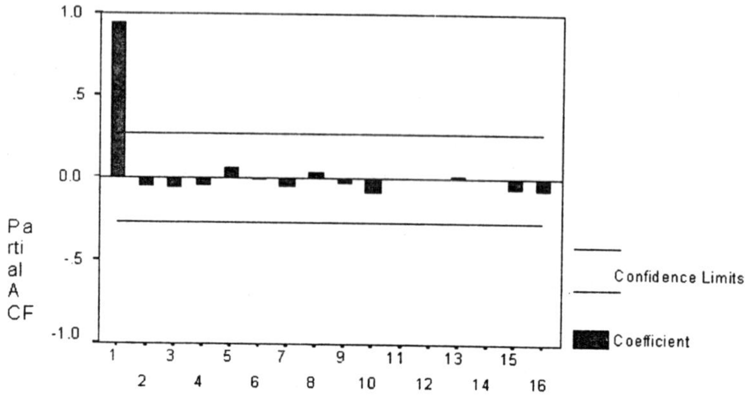

Figure 6 [ACF of D (Et)]

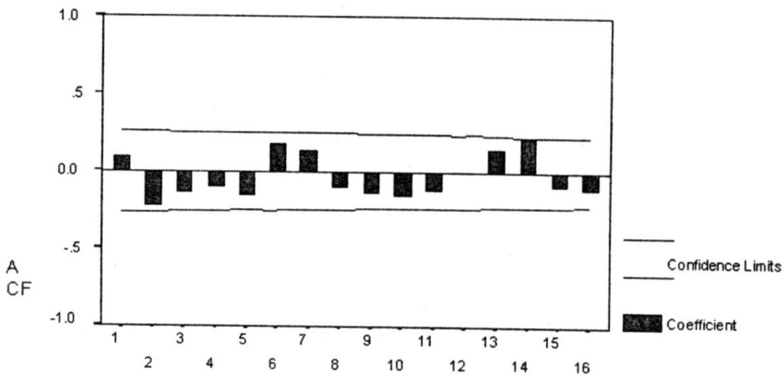

Figure 7 [PACF of D(Et)]

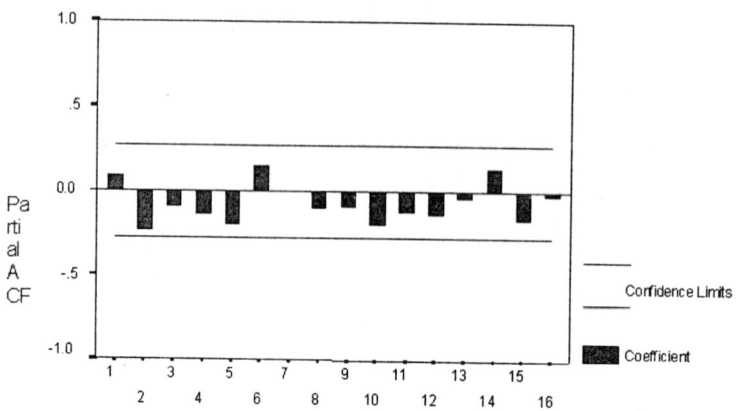

Figure 8 [ACF of D(Rt)]

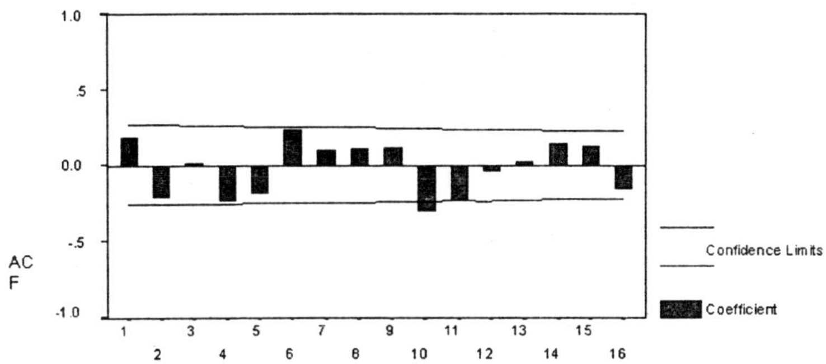

Figure 9 [PACF of D(Rt)]

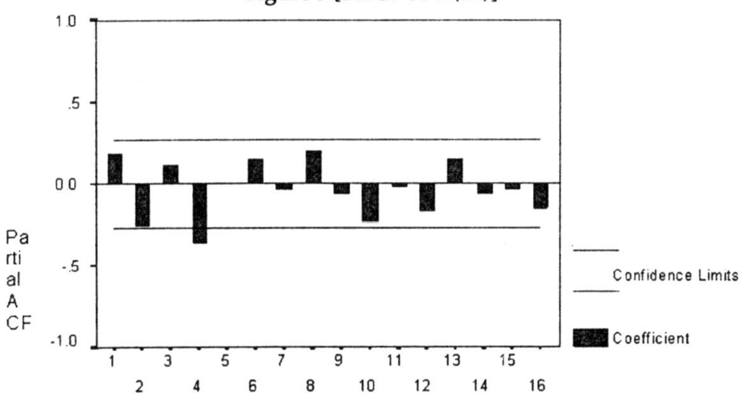

Figure 10
ACF of Resuduals in Equation (v)

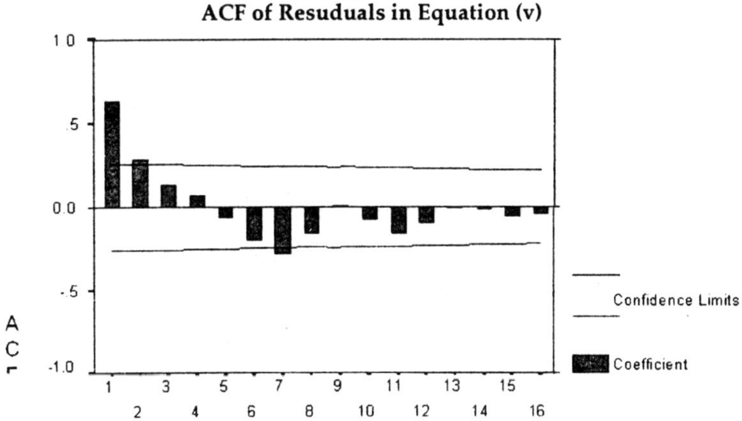

Figure 11
PACF of the Resuduals in Equaction (v)

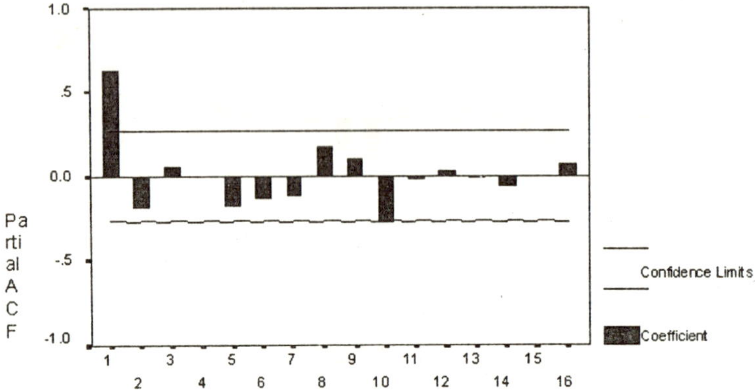

Figure 12 (ACF of the Resud)

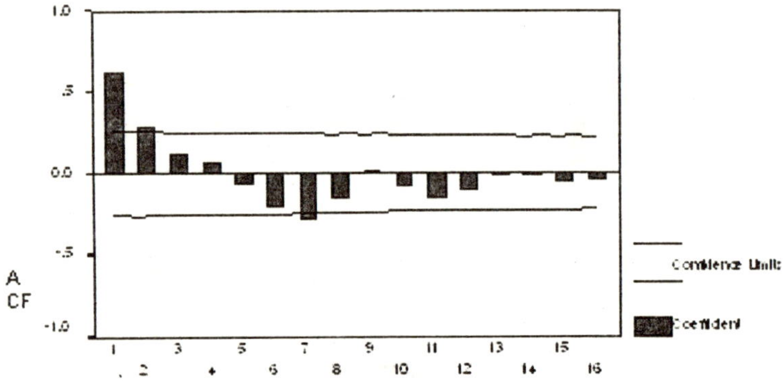

Figure 13
PACF of the Resuduals in Equation (vi)

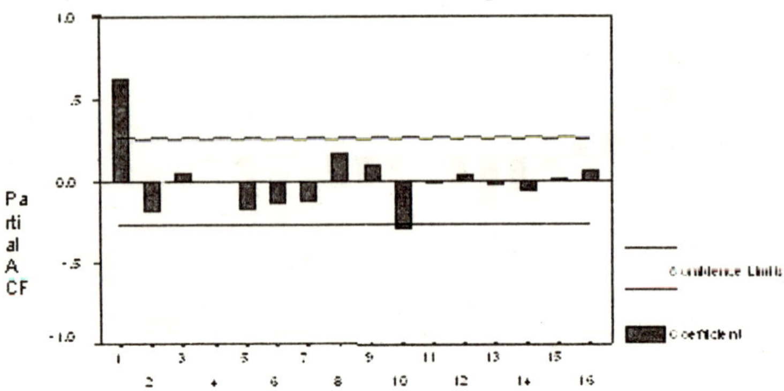

REFERENCES

Anderson, William, Mayler S. Wallace, and J.T. Warner (1986), "Government Spending and Taxation: What Causes What?" *Southern Economic Journal*, Vol. 52, pp. 630 - 639.

Baghestani, H. and R. Mc Nown (1984), "Do Revenue Expenditure Respond to Budgetary Disequilibria?" *Southern Economic Journal* 60, pp. 311 - 322.

Barro, R.J., (1979), "On the Determination of Public Debt", *Journal of Political Economy* 81, pp. 940 - 971.

Barro, Robert J. (1989), "The Ricardian Approach to Budget Deficits", *Journal of Economic Perspective*, Vol. 3 (Spring), pp. 37 – 54.

Bhat, S. K., V. Nirmala, and B. Kamajah (1993), "Causality Between Tax Revenue and Expenditure of Indian States", *Indian Economic Journal.*

Blackley, P.R. (1986), Causality Between Revenue and Expenditures and Size of the Federal Budget", *Public Finance Quarterly* 14, pp. 139-156.

Buchanan, J. and R. Wagner (1977), *Democracy in Deficit: The Political Legacy of Lord Keynes*, (New York: Academic Press).

Buchanan, James M., and Richard E. Wagner, ed., 1978, Fiscal Responsibility in Constitutional Democracy (Leiden, Netherlands: Martinus Nijhoff Social Sciences Division)

Chaudhury, A.R., (1988), "Expenditure and Receipts in state and Local Government Finances: Comment", *Public Choice* 59, pp. 277-285.

Darrat, A.F. (1998), "Tax and Spend, and Spend and Tax? An Enquiry into the Turkish Budgetary Process", *Southern Economic Journal* 64, pp. 940 - 956.

Das A and Sangeeta (1998-1999), "Temporal Causality Between Government Taxes and Spending: An Application of Error Correction Models", *Prajnan*, Vol. XXVII, No.1

Dhanasekaran, K., (1977), "Co-integration and Causality Models: Temporal Causality Between Government Revenue and Expenditure in India", *Prajnan*, Vol. XXIV, No. 1, pp. 25-41.

Dhanasekaran, K., (2001), " Government Tax Revenue, Expenditure and Causality: The Experience of India", *Indian Economic Review*, Vol. XXXVI. No. 2. pp. 359-379.

Dickey, D. A., D.A. Fuller (1981), "The Likelihood Ratio Statistics For Autoregressive Time Series With A Unit Root", *Econometrica*, Vol. 49 No.4, pp 1057-72.

Engle, R.F. and C.W.J. Granger, (1986), "Co-integration and Error Correction: Representation Estimation and Testing", *Econometrica*, Vol. 55, No. 2, March, pp.81-111.

Friedman, Milton, 1978, "The Limitations of Tax Limitation," *Policy Review*, summer, pp. 7 – 14.

Granger, C.W.J., (1986), "Developments in The Study of Co-integrated Variables", *Oxford Bulletin of Economic and Statistics*, Vol. 48, pp. 213-228.

Granger, C.W.J., (1991), "Developments in the Study of Co-integrated Economic Variables, in Engle R.F. and Granger, C.W.J., (Eds.) *Long – run Economic Relationships: Readings in Co- integration*, Oxford; Oxford University Press, pp. 65-80.

Joulfinian, D and R. Mookerjee, (1990), "The Government Revenue Expenditure Nexus: Evidence from a State", *Public Finance Quarterly*, Vol. XVIII, No. 1, January, Pp. 92-103.

Manage, Neela, and Michael L. Marlow (1986), "The Causal Relationship Between Federal Expenditures and Receipts", *Southern Economic Journal*, Vol. 52 (January), pp. 617-29.

Meltzer, Allan, and Richard, Scott (1991), "A Rational Theory of the Size of Government", *Political Economy* (New York: Oxford University Press).

Musgrave, Richard A. (1969), "Priencipals of Budget Determination, in the Public Economy", *An Introduction to Government Finances*, ed. By William Henderson and Helen Cameron (New York: Random House).

Naidu, C. R., Md. Mohsin and V. J. Naidu (1994-95), "Government Expenditure in Andra Pradesh: An Analysis of Growth and Determinants", *Prajnan*, Vol. XXIII, No. 3, pp. 332-352.

Peacock, Alan T., and Jack Wiseman, (1961), "The growth of Publick Expenditure in the United Kingdom" (Princeton, New Jersey: Princeton University Press).

Phillips, P.C.B. (1986), "Understanding Spurious Regression in Econometrics", *Journal of Econometrics*, December, pp. 311-340.

R. Rati (1988), "Additional Evidence on Causality Between Government Revenue and Government Expenditure", *Southern Economic Journal*, Vol. 54, No. 3 (Jan., 1988), pp. 763 – 769.

Regmi, U. R. (2006), "Causal Link between Tax Revenue and Government Expenditure in Nepal", *The Journal of Economic Society*, Vol. 7, No. 1, pp. 1-11.

Sham Bhat, K. V. Nirmala and B. Kamajah, (1991), "Causality Between Revenue and Expenditure of Indian States," *Arthavijnana*, December, pp. 335-344.

Kanak Kanti Bagchi & Subhabrata Chakrabarti

6 THE STRUCTURAL CHANGE OF SIKKIM AND OTHER NORTH-EASTERN STATES: A BRIEF REVIEW

INTRODUCTION

North East (NE) of India constitutes the eight 'sister states' of Arunachal Pradesh, Assam, Manipur, Meghalaya, Mizoram, Nagaland, Sikkim and Tripura. These states cover an area of 2.62 lakh sq. kms, which is 7.9 per cent of the total area of the country. As per census report 2001 the eight states together constitute 3.8 per cent of the total population of the country with literacy rate 68.7 per cent, higher than national average of 65.3 per cent. The north-east India's economy is generally identified by low per-capita income, low capital formation, inadequate infrastructure facilities, geographical isolation and communication bottleneck, inadequate exploitation of natural resources like mineral resources, hydropower potential, forests etc., lack of industrial base and investment opportunities. Per capita income of the states in the NE region is on the average Rs.12918 against the national average of Rs. 17,947/- at current (2001-2002) prices.

Eight states in the NE region are considered as 'special category (SC) states'. The 'Gadgil Formula' during Fourth Five Year plan has made the division of the states into special and general category states. The common identities of Special Category states are preponderance of hilly and difficult terrain, a low population density, strategic location and economic and infrastructure backwardness. Under the Gadgil Formula the SC states get 90 per cent of the central assistance as grants and10 per cent as loans. Why the question of 'assistance' is much more relevant in NE states may be clear if we observe the development experiences of these states. Due to ecological constraints both agriculture and manufacturing sector have not flourished properly. 'Jump' of the economy from primary to territory sector is the common phenomena of almost all NE states. At the end of March 2004, the credit -deposit ratio for NE region was only 29.82 against national average of 58.71. In one sense the chronological order of the stages of development has not been maintained in the NE states. The average values of government expenditure multiplier are generally low due to high import intensity of expenditure. This is why NE states are generally highly dependent on external world. Import substitution is not possible due to low profile industrial base and lack of investment opportunities. As a result state money does not generate income and employment within the state and the development experience of NE states may be defined as jobless growth process. The continuous leakage of money to import goods and services may bring macro economic instability in the long run. During 1987-2000 not even one state has shown a continuous trend of fiscal surplus as percentage of Gross State Domestic Product (GSDP). In comparison with the general category states the performances of SC states are highly insignificant. From the record of Eleventh Finance Commission report it is evident that during 1987-2000 the ranges of pre-devolution non-plan revenue deficit (NPRD) as percentage of GSDP were (-6.76 per cent to -13.90 per cent) for Assam, (-51.19 per cent to 14.97 per cent) for Arunachal Pradesh, (-22.19 per cent to -28.48 per cent) for Manipur, (-16.10 per cent to-21.08 per cent) for Meghalaya, (-22.08 per cent to -59.81per cent) for Mizoram, (-24.28 per cent to -54.87 per cent) for Nagaland and (-21.00 per cent to -27.99 per cent) for Sikkim. Some states like Arunachal Pradesh, Mizoram and Nagaland have shown improvements in pre-devolution (NPRD). But for all the NE states the figure is much higher than other general category states. Even for some low-income states, like Bihar, the pre-devolution NPRD as per cent of GSDP fluctuates in between 3.92 per cent to 12.25 per cent during 1987-2000.

Among other low-income states this range is (1.95 per cent - 6.09 per cent) for Madhya Pradesh. For Orissa (5.08 per cent - 10.47 per cent), and for Uttar Pradesh (3.66 per cent -8.92 per cent). Performance of states regarding own tax effort is an important indicator of financial efficiency. Taking two period averages 1993-96 and 2000-03, overall increase of own tax revenue-GSDP ratio was 0.69 per cent for general category states and it was 0.66 per cent for SC states.

From the very first day of civilization there was a continuous adjustment between economic activities of mankind and the given status of nature. This is Ecological Economics. By definition Ecological Economics means a relationship between eco-systems and economic systems in the broadest sense. With all diversities of climate, altitude, soil quality and topography, north-eastern experience is not an exception in that way. The given set of natural factors has influenced the history of development of this region. Relevance of so-called stage theories of development and the dynamics of shares within the sectors are re-examined in the context of development experience of North-East India.

STRUCTURAL CHANGE FROM 1980 TO 2000

From the Table-1 it cannot be concluded that the continuous fall in the share of NSDP of primary sector has brought a significant rise in the share of secondary sector. On the other hand, in terms of statistical figure, service sector has been flourished at the cost of decline in the share of primary sector, not of industry. In many research papers the figure of the share of secondary sector has been mentioned as statistical jugglery. But the fact of bypassing secondary sector may be explained by the disappointing performance of manufacturing sector. During 1990-2000 the growth rate of manufacturing sector in Arunachal Pradesh was negative (-4.18 per cent). For Assam the share of manufacturing sector in total NSDP has declined from 6.53 per cent to 4.97 per cent during 1980-98. This figure in Meghalaya lies in between 2 per cent to 4.2 per cent, for Mizoram it is only 1.22 per cent (1999-2000), for Tripura the range is 0.94 per cent to 3.8 per cent (1980-2000) and that for

Table-1

The Percentage of Primary Sector (Ps) Secondary Sector (Ss) and Tertiary Sector (Ts) in Total Nsdp NSDP

	Arunachal Pradesh	*Assam*	*Manipur*	*Meghalaya*	*Mizoram*	*Nagaland*	*Sikkim*	*Tripura*
PS	47.28 (1980)	48.07(1980)	49.10(1980)	41.88(1980)	33.23(1993)	42.68(1980)	48.09(1980)	60.22(1980)
	46.19(1990)	40.85(1997-98)	38.02(1990)	35.14(1990)	23.78(2000)	29.07(1990)	44.16(1988)	43.21(1990)
	35.28(2000)		31.35(2000)	32.59(2000)		27.59(1997-98)	24.30(2000)	30.82(2000)
SS	22.21(1980)	11.54(1980)	7.65(1980)	14.55(1980)	9.45(1993)	14.86(1980)	20.4(1980)	8.55(1980)
	21.56(1990)	11.38(1997-98)	10.20(1990)	10.65(1990)	13.46(2000)	12.14(1990)	18.06(1988)	6.98(1990)
	21.88(2000)		26.82(2000)	12.26(2000)		20.38(97-98)	20.27(2000)	13.93(2000)
TS	30.51 (1980)	40.39(1980)	43.25(1980)	43.56(1980)	57.32(1993)	42.26(1980)	32.5(1980)	31.28(1980)
	32.25(1990)	47.76(1997-98)	51.78(1990)	54.21(1990)	62.76(2000)	58.77(1990)	38.71(1988)	49.81(1990)
	42.84(2000)		41.83(2000)	55.15(2000)		52.03(1997-98)	56.81(2000)	55.25(2000)

Source: Das, Gurudas (ed) (2004).
Note: Figures mentioned within brackets indicate respective years

Sikkim is 4.4 per cent to 6.3 per cent (1980-2000). Construction has taken a dominant role in the secondary sector in all north-eastern states.

Disappointing role of secondary sector raises the question of resource-industry linkages in the perspective of north-eastern economy. It is commonly said that an economy is poor because it is poor. But in case of north-eastern economy this is not true. In every corner of north-east region we can observe the affluence of natural resources which may be utilized for economic development. The percentage of total cultivable land in total geographical area of north-east region is 24.17per cent and that of forest area is 45.82per cent along with total hydro-electricity potential of 31857 MW. Besides the entire north-east region is a store house of crude oil (70.46 mt in Assam), natural gas (48000 mcm in Assam and Tripura), coal (1043mt in Assam, Meghalaya, Arunachal Pradesh, and Nagaland), clay (28.5 mt in Meghalaya and Tripura), dolomite (247 mt in Arunachal Pradesh), and graphite (85 mt in Arunachal Pradesh).

Instead of keeping in mind the ecological characteristics in favor of industrialization mentioned above, we cannot deny also, the ecological constraints, which take a negative role against industrialization. For example, mechanization or establishment of heavy industry is almost impossible due to sloppy hilly terrain. It is already mentioned that among the components of secondary sector contribution of "construction" has always remained highest. Constructions of road bridge buildings come under this component. But the prospect of growth through the forward and backward linkages of the economic activities under the item construction has not been proved feasible in the north-east region. In this region roads are in continuous need of repair, due to frequent landslides and erosion. Income is generated several times on a same road within a short period. The cycle of construction and deconstruction is supported by abundant supply of village poor workers and a labor-intensive production process. Sikkim allots 2 workers per kilometer of road to maintain against the national standard 0.3 workers per kilometer. On the other hand, due to typical geographical nature, construction of roads, buildings cannot take place in a limitless manner. Altogether there is a problem of stagnancy with less impact of growth through its forward and backward linkage effects, some of the ecological constraints are responsible partially for the falling contribution of primary sector. These have again restricted the purchasing power of agriculture related people and demand for consumer or capital goods. The net effect is that the secondary sector has not received sufficient inspiration from primary sector through its demand side due to ecological adversities. North-east being basically a hilly region, soil erosion, deforestation, landslides and other natural calamities create problems for cultivation. Irrigation in the hills is difficult. The springs and small rivers become over-flooded in the summer but get dry during rabi season. Again the capillary movement of soil moisture is horizontal in the hills unlike vertical in the planes. Once the soil gets dry there are no means of irrigation unless there is a rain. On the other hand mechanization in the hills is almost impossible due to sloppy hill terrain.

It is true that some of these ecological factors are not helpful to create an industry-friendly atmosphere in the north-east region. One may argue that these factors have influenced the policy making decisions in the development process. Researchers have found many such dimensions of planning process, which are responsible for weak resource-industry linkages and industrial backwardness. (Bhuimali & Bagh 2004) These are: a) Lack of infrastructural facilities like transport, communication, power, banking facility, schooling, health and medical care etc., b) lack of investment, c) absence of appropriate technology which is ecologically suitable and cost effective for small sector industries, d) insufficient demand and improper market structure, e) restrictions of outsiders in property right and land use, f) lack of local interest in entrepreneurship and g) socio-political status. A low profile of credit-deposit ratio or a low rate of return over investment is the reflections of the presence of these factors. As on March 2002 the credit-deposit ratio of India was around 58. In case of north-eastern states it was 15.78 for Arunachal Pradesh, 31.39 for Assam, 25.33 for Manipur, 18.04 for Meghalaya, 25.90 for Mizoram, 12.55 for

Nagaland, 15.97 for Sikkim, and 22.34 for Tripura. Starting from 1960 upto 2002-03 total amount of dividend of all government statutory corporations, companies and co-operative societies etc. is Rs. 17592498 against the amount of total investment of Rs. 695627176 in Sikkim. So the rate of return is only 2.5 per cent. The government has reduced the amount of investment gradually due to this meager rate of return on investment. The share of industrial sector in total plan outlay is reduced from 6.6 per cent (in the 5th plan) to 1.8 per cent (in the 10th plan).

It is already argued that secondary sector has not received sufficient inspiration from primary sector through its demand side due to some ecological factors. From a different angle this fact may be established and perhaps it may be said that industrial sector has maintained a separate and independent identity from the agricultural sector in the structural change of north-east region. It may be noted that north-east is an underdeveloped region and like any developed economy this region is not suffering from the problem of consumption saturation at the macro level. Inspite of a high prospect of business, the return on investment is low. We have already seen that over the years the share of agricultural sector in total GSDP is gradually falling for all NE states. But the proportion of agricultural workers has not decreased significantly. Most of these agricultural workers are coming from rural area. On the other hand the proportion of rural people in the NE region was 84.5 per cent as per census report 2001, which is much higher than national average (73 per cent as per census report 2001). For some states like Assam and Sikkim this figure is much high (87 per cent and 89 per cent respectively). So the simple fact is that a large percentage of population in the NE region is dependent for their livelihood on primary sector of which the share in total GSDP is gradually falling. We can easily conclude that primary sector is the main source of the below poverty line group of people with low per capita income and consumption levels. Thus primary sector has been ineffective to create a market demand for industrial product and to provide an impetus for secondary sector. In the absence of proper marketing facility money economy has not been flourished in the rural areas through the selling of marketable surplus. Actually money economy and the expansion of peasant export product can be interlinked in the following two ways:

(a) Bringing an increasing number of peasant families into export production. (b) There may be specialization in export sector through devotion of whole resources and thus setting up a cash demand for goods and services produced locally or in outside.

Many industrial products like handicrafts, handloom products, agarbatti, tribal jewellary, metal ware; bamboo articles, etc. carry a traditional style. A group of people from the very beginning was engaged to produce these goods in search of their livelihood. Their economic activities were not influenced by the activities associated with primary or tertiary sector. Thus a part of industrial world is not an outcome of any structural change. Actually traditional system was partly responsible for the trend of secondary sector in an independent manner with other sectors.

It is observed that the richer a nation the greater is the variation in the range of services its population enjoys. This is why a rich nation generally has a strong industrial base and most sophisticated forms of services are likely to be concentrated around industrial centers, for example information technology. Since the industrial base of north-east has no potential of diversity, the interdependency between industrial and service sector is absent. In this way also secondary sector has its own separate identity from other sectors.

Table-1 exhibits the dominating role of service sector and it can also be seen from this Table that among the components of this sector public administration is the major one. Actually Himalayan regions are identified by a great demand for government service. With a cultural and traditional background, these communities have no saving-investment based money market. As a result public expenditure has a natural tendency to flow into salaries and current income. During 2001-02 the ratios of number of government employee to the number of total workers were 0.08 for Arunachal Pradesh, 0.05 for

Meghalaya, 0.04 for Assam, 0.08 for Tripura, and 0.14 for Sikkim. This ratio for other general category states was 0.04 for Punjab, 0.03 for Haryana, 0.02 for Rajasthan, 0.01 for Gujarat, 0.01 for Maharashtra, 0.01 for Andhra Pradesh, 0.02 for Karnataka and 0.01 for Uttar Pradesh.

STRUCTURAL CHANGE AND JOBLESS GROWTH

Data reveal that structural change in NE region is characterized by a jobless growth process. For all NE states except Assam, Manipur and Tripura the work participation rates are falling over the period 1971-91. The main reasons behind this fact are high population growth rate and low rate of labour absorption in secondary sector. In 1971 the percentage of main workers engaged in secondary sector for all NE states was only 4.93 per cent against national average of 10.69 per cent and in 1991 for NE states it was 5.78 per cent against national average of 12 per cent. The increase in the percentage points of main workers engaged in secondary sector during 1971-91 was only 1.36 for Assam, -2.58 for Manipur, 0.40 for Meghalaya, 3.31 for Mizoram, 1.10 for Nagaland and 2.16 for Tripura. North-Eastern economy is compelled to import goods and services from outside to meet indigenous demand due to poor performance of both manufacturing and agricultural sectors. Also the common tendency of flowing of current expenditure into government investment and salaries is mentioned before. This implies state income does not generate sufficient additional income and employment within the state. The conception of missing multiplier takes place in this way. During 1993-2000 the magnitudes of the ratio of the increase in the NSDP to the increase in aggregate government expenditure are too low. For example, it is 1.59 for Arunachal Pradesh, 1.56 for Manipur, 1.18 for Mizoram, and .40 for Sikkim. Continuous leakage of money may bring macro-economic instability through the conflict between demand and supply side. To solve this problem north-east is heavily dependent on the injection of central resources into its economy. At the very beginning the trend of pre-devolution non-plan revenue deficit as a percentage of GSDP has been mentioned. As per the population of 2001 per capita transfer during 2000-05 for NE states was Rs. 21047 for Arunachal Pradesh, Rs. 4993 for Assam, Rs. 13982 for Manipur, Rs. 12339 for Meghalaya, Rs. 31690 for Mizoram, Rs. 23420 for Nagaland, Rs. 27232 for Sikkim, and Rs. 13628 for Tripura. Among the general category states Bihar has received the highest amount (Rs.6835). There appears to be a high correlation between the usual trend of GSDP and the Central transfer every year in all NE states and on the question of the sustainability of north-eastern economy with its usual pattern of structural change the contribution of central resource is essential.

Table 2
Changes in the Shares of Primary, Secondary & NSDP Tertiary Sectors in Total 1 and Respective Employment Shares During 1971-91
(A) in percentage points

	1	2	3	4	5	6
ARUNACHAL PRADESH	-13	-13	+1.22	+8.22	+11.78	+4.78
ASSAM	-13.68	-3.66	+1.14	+.46	+12.53	+2.6
MANIPUR	-9.97	-1.29	-6.62	-2.57	+16.59	+3.86
MEGHALAYA	-31.53	-7.03	+9.95	+.44	+21.58	+6.59
NAGALAND	-19.02	-5.94	+1.6	+.36	+17.54	+5.58
TRIPURA	-32.01	-12.5	+1.19	+2.12	+30.82	+10.38
INDIA	-13.7	-5.3	+5.40	+1.5	+8.21	+3.8

1=> Change in the percentage points of the share of primary sector in total NSDP

2=> Change in the percentage points of the employment share of primary sector

3=> Change in the percentage points of the share of secondary sector in total NSDP

4=> Change in the percentage points of the employment share of secondary sector

5=> Change in the percentage points of the share of tertiary sector in total NSDP

6=> Change in the percentage points of the employment share in tertiary sector.

Source: Source: Das, Gurudas (ed) (2004).

Table 2 suggests that the reduction of the share of primary sector in total NSDP over the period 1971-91 is much more higher than the reduction of the employment share in primary sector for all NE states. Throughout the period no state except

Meghalaya has achieved a significant increase in the share of secondary sector. On the other hand the change of employment share in tertiary sector is highly insignificant compared to the change in the share of this sector in total NSDP. This means the structural change in north-east has brought a trend of concentration of economic power in favor of the workers associated with tertiary sector. The other side of this fact is that, economic status of the village based agricultural workers has been worsened gradually. Kuznet curve assumes that at the initial stage in any economy, growth will be accompanied with growing disparity. But this disparity in northeast is not brought at the cost of growth exactly along with poor manufacturing sector and government job based service sector. Actually northeastern economy and its agents are not confident to play the necessary expansionary roles of growth. During 1981-2001 the proportion of rural population steadily increased from 83.5 per cent to 89.9 per cent in Sikkim. Corresponding to growth rates of rural population by 94 per cent during 1971-91 and 30 per cent during 1991-2001, growth rates of agriculture based rural workers are 14 per cent and 38 per cent respectively. This means some of the workers who migrated from agriculture to other field, came back again to their origin and restarted a rural agri-based life. It is also possible that new generation is less interested to switch over from primary to secondary or tertiary sector. The logics are supported also by the steady decline of proportion of urban population after 1981.

Some other factors like process of urbanization etc. may determine the direction of economic concentration through structural change. A test by Dani Rodrick proved that urbanization is positively associated with inequality. Simple reason behind this is the circulation of money at a higher level in urban area due to concentration of economic activities in trade and commerce, public sector undertakings, tourism, education, health sector etc. Consumerism is a by-product of urbanization, which accelerates expenditure on semi-essential purpose, and thus provide a higher income velocity of money in urban area than rural area. The disparity through urbanization involves two elements: (a) the multiplication of points of concentration and (b) the increase in the size of individual concentrations. Ecological constraint has been considered as a major determinant factor in a study of Datta on educational status of Sikkim (Datta, 1991). The strength of this factor is reduced by the increasing process of urbanization. We have seen before that a continuous shift of labor from primary to other sectors has taken place in all NE states. Without sufficient upgradation of technology used in primary sector, the shift of labor from primary to other sectors by rural-urban migration, may simply bring reduction in output of primary sector. Actually the reduced supply of labor is supposed to push up agricultural wage rate and encourage the adoption of labor-saving technology. Introduction of labor-saving technology by heavy machines is almost impossible. So marginal productivity of labor is heavily dependent on the quality of labor itself. In a study of Choudhuri (1979) it has been shown that growth of productivity in agriculture sector in Punjab and Haryana is highly correlated with the secondary education of cultivators.

Wages among landless agricultural laborers are positively influenced by the secondary education. This in turn influenced demand for education in the long run. Among the four districts of Sikkim (North, East, West and South) percentage of people with secondary education (and higher education) in East district always remained higher than other districts. This may explain the experience of significant share in agricultural output with insignificant number of workers in East district of Sikkim over a long period and a greater access into the service sector, dominated by government jobs. A research by Theodore W. Schultz and Rati Ram proved that the increase in life span improves the rate of schooling. In that study during 1951-71 the growth of agricultural output in India had an unexplained residual part. The existence of this part was explained by the assumption that improvements in the health of adults increase the quality of labor force and its productivity. The residual during 1951-61 was larger than the residual during 1961-71. Actually by a massive drive against tuberculosis at the end of 1959 nearly 48 millions were vaccinated.

Lama (2001) has shown the trend of highest educational attainment and life expectancy index of East district over the last decade in the case of Sikkim. We can say that, with highest number of towns, maximum expansion of education, health service, and other facilities, East district has been able to receive maximum benefit from the structural change of Sikkim.

The last of the above analysis is basically based on the development experience of Sikkim. This can be extended in the perspective of NE states. The main purpose of this paper was to build-up a connection between the trend of structural change and some common development parameters. If the structural change can bring the regional disparity through economic concentration, it can also influence other development parameters and these development parameters in turn again can determine the direction of structural change. Our intuitions, our practical experiences are not against this assumption. Harbison and Myres formed a composite index with respect to the enrolment at second and third level of education. It is could be found that the index is highly influenced by GNP per capita and the correlation co-efficient obtained is 0·888.

RESEARCH ISSUES FOR THE NE STATES

So, the entire analysis presented above raises the following research issues for the NE states: a) Pattern and implications of structural changes in the NE states, b) causes of weak resource-industry linkage and trend of lesser contribution of secondary sector (mainly manufacturing sector) in total NSDP of all NE states, c) reasons for an automatic growth of service sector and trend of significant contribution of public administration (dominated by government jobs) in GDSP, d) causes of regional disparity or economic concentration through the employment share in primary, secondary and tertiary sector, e) the impact of significant contribution of Central resource in the State domestic product on the sustainability of north-eastern economy with its usual pattern of structural change, and f) searching the role of urbanization and its various dimensions behind structural change and their interrelationships.

REFERENCES

Bhuimali, Anil & K. K. Bagchi (2004), 'Resource-Industry Linkages in Sikkim: Strategy of Development in the Context of Structural Change', in Das, Gurudas (ed)(2004), *Structural Change and Strategy of Development: Resource-Industry Linkages of North-East India*, M/S Akansha Publications, New Delhi.

Choudhuri, D. P. (1979), *Education, Innovation and Agricultural Development*, Croom Helm Publication, London.

Costanza, Robert (1997), *An introduction of Ecological Economics*, St. Lucie Press, Florence.

Das, Debasis (1998),'Agriculture in Sikkim', in *Sikkim: Perspective for Planning and Development*, Sikkim Science Society Press, Gangtok.

Dasgupta, Manas (1992), *Sikkim: Problem and Prospects of Development*, Indus Publishing Company, New Delhi.

Datta, Amal (1991), *Sikkim since Independence*, Mittal Publications, New Delhi.

Department of Development of North-East Region (DONER), Annual Reports 2001-02 & 2004-05.

George, N. D. (2005), 'Plan Investments and Growth', *Yojana*, December.

Government of India (various years), 9th, 10th, 11th and 12th Finance Commission Reports.

Government of India (various years), Census Report 1971, 1981, 1991, 2001

Government of Sikkim (2002), *Sikkim: A Statistical Profile*, Directorate of Economics, Statistics, Monitoring & Evaluation.

Government of Sikkim (2003), *Finance Account 2002-03: Comptroller and Auditor General Report 2003.*

Government of Sikkim (2001), *Sikkim and the North-Eastern States: A Statistical Abstract*, Planning & Development Department.

Hauser, Philip M. and Leo F. Schnore (eds)(1965), *The Study of Urbanization*, John Willey Publisher, New York.

Joshi, P.C. and C.H. Hanumanth Rao (eds) (1980), *Reflections on Economic Development and Social Change*, Allied Publishers, New Delhi.

Lahiri, Ashok, Soumen Chattopadhya and Anuradha Vasin (2001), *Sikkim: The People's Vision*, Indus publishing Company, New Delhi.

Lama, M.P. (ed)(2003), *The Glory of New Sikkim*, Information and Public Relations Department, Government of Sikkim, Newstech Publishing, New Delhi.

Lama, M.P. (2001), *Sikkim Human Development Report 2001*, Social Science Press, Delhi.

Madhab, Jyanta (2005), 'Enabling the North East', *Yojana*, December.

Myint, H. (1973), *The Economics of Developing Countries*, Hutchinson Publication, London.

NEDFi Databank Quarterly Journal (2004), Issue IV, October.

NEDFi Databank Quarterly Journal (2005), Vol.4, April.

Oberoi, A.S. & H.K. Manmohan Singh (1983), *Causes and Consequences of Internal Migration*, Oxford University Press Delhi.

Pradhan, H.R. (1998),'Economic Structure of Sikkim', in *Sikkim: Perspective for Planning and Development*, Sikkim Science Society Press, Gangtok.

Rao, C.H. Hanumanth (1994), *Agricultural Growth, Rural Poverty and Environmental Degradation, Oxford University Press*, New Delhi.

Sarkar, R.L. & M.P. Lama (eds)(1986), *The Eastern Himalaya: Environment and Economy*, Atma Ram Publications, Delhi.

Sen, A.K. (1996), 'Economic Approaches to Education and Manpower Planning' *The Indian Economic Review, Vol-1.*

Sigh, Manmohan ((2005), 'North East 2020', *Yojana*, December.

Singh, Amar Kaur Jasbir (1988), *Himalayan Triangle: Historical Survey of British India's Relations with Tibet, Sikkim and Bhutan*, 1765-1950, British Library, London.

Streeten, Paul Patrick (1997), *Thinking About Development*, Cambridge University Press.

Subba, J.R. (1998),'Vegetable Crops in Sikkim', in *Sikkim: Perspective for Planning and Development*, Sikkim Science Society Press, Gangtok.

Tanzi, Vito & Ke-Young Chu (eds.) (1998), *Income Distribution and High-Quality Growth*, MIT Press, Cambridge.

Anil Bhuimali & Sidhartha Sankar Laha

7

EXAMINING INDO-BANLADESH BILATERAL TRADE PATTERN

INTRODUCTION

The South Asian Association for Regional Cooperation (SAARC) was established at the First Summit in Dhaka on December 7-8, 1985. Its members are Bangladesh, Bhutan, India, Maldives, Nepal, Pakistan and Sri Lanka. Among the SAARC countries India and Bangladesh are two major countries having long common historical past and similar cultural and social evolutions. As for trade relation is concerned, India is the 2nd largest trading partner of Bangladesh just after USA in 2003. India's position is at the top in Bangladesh's imports from the world (IMF, Direction of Trade Statistics, June 2004). This paper mainly deals with the issues of bilateral trade relationship between India and Bangladesh. This paper has been divided into four parts: Section 1 describes the charactertics, economic indicators and main objectives of the SAARC region. Section 2 highlights the India trade with SAARC as a trade blocks, Section 3 looks at the trend, structure and current picture of India-Bangladesh trade and Section 4 summaries and concludes.

CHARACTERISTICS AND ECONOMIC INDICATORS

There are geographical, human resources and economic asymmetry and wide disparity between India and other member countries of SAARC. Indian population is approximately three times the combined population of the remaining SAARC States, with its area and GDP constituting

70 percent and 78 percent respectively of the entire SAARC. India is 50 times of the size of Sri Lanka, 1000 times richer than Bhutan and has 4000 times as many people as Maldives. The SAARC region had once been unified by British rule which had built up a railway system, similar laws, an efficient system of post and telegraph communication and much more besides. It is the largest English speaking area and has the largest irrigation network in the world. Relevant particular of SAARC countries are as under:

Table 1
Particular of SAARC Countries

Country	**Area (000.Sq. K.M.)*	*Population* (Year 2000) (Million)*	*G.D.P. (Year 1999)# (U.S.$. Billion)*
Bangladesh	144	130	46
Bhutan	47	0.8	0.4
India	3288	1016	447.3
Maldives	0.3	0.3	0.4
Nepal	141	24	5
Pakistan	796	138	58.2
Sri Lanka	66	19	16

Source: *World Development Report 2002
UNDP Report 2000

OBJECTIVES

The objectives of SAARC are listed below:-

(i) To promote the welfare of the people of South Asia and to improve their quality of life.

(ii) To accelerate economic growth, social progress and cultural development in the region and to provide all individuals the opportunity to live in dignity and to realize their full potentials.

(iii) To promote and strengthen collective self-reliance among the countries of South Asia.

(iv) To contribute mutual trust, understanding and appreciation of one another's problems.

(v) To promote collaboration and mutual assistance in the economic, social, cultural, technical and scientific fields.

(vi) To strengthen cooperation with other developing countries.

(vii) To cooperative with international and regional organization with similar aims and proposes.

Thus, the ultimate objective of regional cooperation is accelerating the pace of economic, social and cultural growth of SAARC countries with the principle of social justice and improving the welfare of the people of the region.

INDIA-SAARC TRADE RELATIONS

In the SAARC region, many attempts have been made to encourage regional trade under the regulation of SAARC and the SAPTA. Despite constant attempt, it still could not take an effective shape as a regional trade body because of political problems between Pakistan and India. It indeed hampers the regional interests. Despite official declarations to transform the SAPTA into a FTA in this region by 2001, the idea seems to be unrealistic. India has had problems with RTAs since her neighbors don't want free trade with a giant neighbor they don't trust or like. Hence multilateralism will remain India's only choice. (Sarita, A. & Tanvi, P. 2000). During the ten year pre-SAARC (1975-1985) Period, India's exports increased from US$ 160 million in 1975 to US $ 315 million in 1984 registering a compound growth rate of 7.8%. Compared to it, during the ten years post-SAARC period. India's exports increased from US $ 277 million in 1986 to US $ 1532 million in 1995 i.e., from 8% the exports increased to 30% constituting an additional growth of 22%. This reveals the fact that the formation of the SAARC as a bloc has encouraged India's exports to SAARC countries. Since 1991 the liberalization impact also has a positive impact giving rise to further increase in India's exports to SAARC countries. From US $ 622 million in 1991, the exports have touched a peak level of US $ 2005 million in the year 2000 thus indicating an additional of 9% decadal growth in comparison to the pre liberalization period (1980-90) of 5%. Similarly India's exports to the World during the pre and post liberalization periods have witnessed an upward trend. On the other hand India's imports from the SAARC counties are quite low. It was just US $ 56 million in 1975 and rose to only US $ 105 million during 1984 and further to only US $ 182 in 1995. In fact the immediate reform period has shown a decline in India's imports from SAARC registering a low level of US $ 96 in the year 1993 and later picked up only to the extent of US $ 363 million in 2000. They have grown at a constant rate of 7% throughout the pre liberalization and post liberalization periods. This shows that India is not a good importer for its neighboring countries. While in 1985 and further to US $ 2368 million in 2000. The trend exhibits that there is a spectacular rise in India's trade with SAARC as compared to the increase in the India's global trade, which increased from US $ 24594 million in 1985 to only US $ 94018 million in 2000.

Table 2
India's Linear Growth Rate of Exports, Imports and Volume of Trade with SAARC Countries

(In per cent)

Item	*Bangladesh*	*Maldives*	*Nepal*	*Pakistan*	*Srilanka*	*Total SAARC Bloc*
Exports :						
(1980-1990)	16.3	8.37	4.79	24.97	1.85	8.61
(1991-2002)	10.67	18.86	21.13	14.49	10.63	12.43
Imports:						
(1980-1990)	-2.0	0	-1.6	-7.05	-12.03	-5.51
(1991-2002)	14.72	0	27.58	3.82	15.46	15.11
Trade volume:						
(1980-1990)	13.55	8.37	2.96	1.38	-0.91	4.49
(1991-2002)	10.89	18.86	22.96	9.91	11.03	12.81

Source: Linear growth rate computed from IMF, Direction of Trade Statistics Yearbook (Various Years) data

From table 2, it is clear that during the pre liberalization period India exported mostly to Pakistan followed by Bangladesh and Maldives. But after the liberalization the direction of exports changed and Nepal and Maldives became the major exporting destination. In fact the growth rate of exports to Pakistan has fallen down considerably. The tremendous decline may be attributed to the political disturbances with the two nations. But its export growth to the entire bloc as such has increased from 8.61% in pre-liberalization period to 12.43% in the post-liberalization period and positive in the later period. Nepal is the major exporter of India indicating a high growth rate of about 27.5% followed by Sri Lanka (15.4%) and Bangladesh (14.7%). The total volume of trade with the bloc although has increased, still India does not have good trading patterns with the bloc. Except Nepal, all other nations have registered a very low growth rate. Overall the growth of India's exports and imports clearly reveal the growing trade imbalance between India and its neighboring South Asian countries.

Table 3 presents the coefficients of variation indicating the stability of export and import relations of India with SAARC region. The variation in terms of exports is high in the case of Pakistan, Bangladesh and Maldives and it has been reversed in the post liberalization period except in the case of Maldives and Nepal. The low coefficients with respect to entire SAARC bloc obviously makes out that India's export relations is quite high. On the other side there is no constant import trade. Although India's export relation is quite impressive, the overall trade is not stable since it does rely on her neighbours for its imports thus contributing to a low intra trade with in the SAARC region.

Table 3
Trade Stability between India and SAARC countries

(In per cent)

Item	Bangladesh	Maldives	Nepal	Pakistan	Srilanka	SAARC
Exports:						
(1980-1990)	85.19	84.4	45.5	92.69	21.49	40.29
(1991-2002)	38.84	79.67	70.36	51.49	33.37	39.37
Imports:						
(1980-1990)	53.36	0	48.85	43.19	66.49	28.61
(1991-2002)	60.91	0	92.35	78.58	48.64	57.20
Trade volume:						
(1980-1990)	71.89	84.4	32.45	34.62	20.41	24.53
(1991-2002)	39.96	-9.67	76.46	44.69	34.40	40.77

Source: Calculated from IMF, Direction of trade statistics Yearbook (Various Years)

*Data on Bhutan are not available

TREND, STRUCTURE AND CURRENT PICTURE OF INDIA-BANGLADESH TRADE

One of the important features of Indo-Bangladesh bilateral trade to be mentioned is that a large volume of informal or unrecorded trade, both in commodities and services, occurs every year and it is growing despite unilateral or regional or multilateral trade liberalization in these two countries (Pohit and Taneja. 2003, Eusufzai 2000).Due to non-availability of data on illegal trade. We concentrate our discussion on official data.

In this section, data on trend, structure and current state of Indo-Bangladesh trade are presented.

Table 4
Share of India and Bangladesh in Intra-SAARC trade, (1990-2002)

(Million of US dollars)

Year	*Intra -SAARC (I)*	*IndiaTrade (II)*	*Bangladesh Trade (III)*	*I+B * (IV)*
1990	1590	584(36.73)	310(19.5)	894(56.23)
1991	1914	718(37.51)	331(17.29)	1049(54.8)
1992	2488	913(36.7)	423(17.0)	1336(53.7)
1993	2458	920(37.43)	532(21.64)	1452(59.07)
1994	2937	1151(39.19)	635(21.62)	1786(60.81)
1995	4263	1742(40.86)	1230(28.85)	2972(69.71)
1996	4928	1848(37.5)	1368(27.76)	3216(65.26)
1997	4447	1648(37.06)	967(21.74)	2615(58.8)
1998	6001	2549(42.48)	1376(22.93)	3925(65.41)
1999	5511	2370(43.00)	1206(21.88)	3576(64.88)
2000	3884	2400(40.79)	1138(19.34)	3588(60.15)
2001	6537	2783(42.57)	1383(21.16)	4166(63.73)
2002	6246	2739(43.85)	1290(20.65)	4029(64.5)

Source: Calculated from IMF, Direction of Trade Statistics Yearbook (Various Years) data

Note: Numbers within the parentheses indicate percentages to total

* I +B = India + Bangladesh

Share India-Bangladesh trade in SAARC Perspective

As mentioned earlier, both India and Bangladesh are two major partners in the SAARC region: Their combined share in the SAARC trade demonstrates their importance and high in the regional trade. Table 4 shows that the trade share of both counties was 56.23 percent of the intra-SAARC trade in 1990. This share increased to 64.5 percent in 2002. India's share is, more or less, double of Bangladesh's share in intra-SAARC trade with limited exception for some years. However, India's exports share is much higher than imports share in the regional trade. On the other hand, Bangladesh's position is just opposite; its imports share is much higher than exports share in the SAARC trade. This is shown in Table 5.

Table 5
Export and Import Share of India and Bangladesh in Intra-SAARC trade, (1990-2002)

(In Percent)

Year	*India's Export Share*	*India's Import Share*	*Bangladesh's Export Share*	*Bangladesh's Import Share*
1990	30.63	6.10	3.77	15.72
1991	33.52	4.96	4.18	13.11
1992	28.90	7.80	1.81	15.19
1993	33.40	4.03	2.24	19.40
1994	34.80	4.39	1.70	19.92
1995	36.21	4.64	1.95	26.92
1996	33.48	4.02	1.18	26.58
1997	32.92	4.14	1.84	19.90
1998	34.23	8.25	1.72	21.21
1999	36.04	6.97	1.47	20.41
2000	34.31	6.48	1.50	17.84
2001	35.90	6.67	1.39	19.76
2002	33.34	9.51	1.19	19.47

Source: Calculated from IMF, Direction of Trade Statistics Year Book (Various Years) and Direction of Trade Statistics Yearbook for Asia and the Pacific (Various Years) data

Trade Intensity Indices

The trade intensity indices on both imports and exports demonstrate the bilateral trade Orientation of a country with its trading partners. The import intensity index can be defined as (Venkatsubbulu 1996, Kojima 1964):

$$m_{ij} = \frac{\dfrac{M_{ij}}{M_i}}{\dfrac{X_j}{X_W - X_i}}$$

Where

m_{ij} = import intensity index of trade of country i with country j,

M_{ij} = Imports of a country i from trading partner j.

M_i = Total imports of country i,

X_j = Total world exports,

X_i = Total exports of country i.

Export intensity index can also be defined in the same way; that is:

$$x_{ij} = \frac{\dfrac{X_{ij}}{X_i}}{\dfrac{M_j}{M_W - M_j}}$$

Where

X_{ij}= Export intensity index of trade of country i with country j,

X_{ij} = Export of country i to trading partner j,

X_i= Total exports of country i,

M_j = Total imports of country j,

M_w= Total world imports,

M_i= Total imports of country i.

Exports and import intensity indices have been calculated for India's trade with Bangladesh and Bangladesh's trade with India for some selected years from 1980 to 2003. The results are noted in Table 6 and Table 7.

It is observed that India's export intensity with Bangladesh is very high for all those years under study. This indicates that India was exporting extremely high to Bangladesh all the time than what it ought to export. The highest index, 130. 11230, was observed in the year 2001. (Due to rupee depreciation along with further trade liberalization, tariff reductions, and more further to foreign investment in export-oriented sector like information technology in Indian economy). After that the index was declining and reached to 97.33020 in the year 2002, though it increased slightly in 2003.

Table 6
India's Export and Import Intensity Indices with Bangladesh

Year	m_{ij}	x_{ij}
1980	1.00231	99.72132
1985	0.98235	105.73250
1990	0.73231	97.33672
1995	0.83129	120.66731
2000	0.34114	109.67329
2001	0.30121	130.11230
2002	0.21329	97.33020
2003	0.07291	101.00213

Source: Calculated from IMF, Direction of Trade Statistics Yearbook (Various Years) data

Where
m_{ij} = India's import intensity index with Bangladesh.
x_{ij} = India's export intensity with Bangladesh.

Compared to export intensity indices, India's import intensity indices with Bangladesh are very low. However, it is still far bellow the desired level of 100. The index value decreased tremendously in 2003 and reached to 0.07291. During 2000-2003, the index values were less than 0.5.

Therefore, it is revealed from the discussion that India imported much less from Bangladesh than its exported to Bangladesh.

Table 7
Bangladesh's Export and Import Intensity Indices with India

Year	$^*m_{ij}$	$^*x_{ij}$
1980	4.88552	1.41491
1985	4.62714	3.47303
1990	8.746103	1.90698
1995	25.35823	1.67226
2000	17.00011	1.36479
2001	20.10860	1.60816
2002	18.81877	1.00087
2003	21.61386	0.799651

Source: Calculated from IMF, Direction of Trade Statistics Yearbook (Various Years) data

Where

$*m_{ij}$ = Bangladesh's import intensity with India.

$*x_{ij}$ = Bangladesh's export intensity with India.

The result from table 7 shows Bangladesh's export intensities with India were far below 100 for all those years. The highest index was 3.47303 in the year 1985. After that, it was cautiously declining and reached 1.36479 in 2000.

Bangladesh's import intensity indices with India are quite high than export intensity indices. The index value almost doubled in 1995 compared to 1980 or 1985. The index value increased tremendously in 1995 reaching to 25.35823.

The data indicates that Indo-Bangladesh trade was not as high as it should be. So there is a scope for trade expansion for both the countries.

The Importance of India in Bangladesh's Trade

India plays an important role in Bangladesh's trade since the independence, and recently, especially in 1990s the trade of Bangladesh trade with India increased tremendously. The table 8 compares the growth rates of Bangladesh's trade with India, SAARC countries and world for selected years from 1980 to 2003. It is observed from the table that the average annual growth rate of Bangladesh's trade with India during 1980 to 1995, were much higher than those with the SAARC and the world. For example, during 1980 to 1985, while average annual growth rates of Bangladesh's trade with the World and SAARC countries were 2.46 percent and 0.11 percent respectively, this figure was 9.72 percent with India. During 1985-1990 the growth rates with the world, SAARC countries and India were 7.94 percent, 18.68 percent and 20.63 percent respectively. The growth rate with the world and SAARC countries were 16.70 percent and 57.85 percent respectively and the growth rate with India was 87.29 percent. Though the growth rates with SAARC countries and India were slightly negative during 1995-2000; those figure turns into positive in 2001. The overall performance was negative in 2002 following the 9/11 incident in 2001 in USA. The overall growth performance in 2003 was positive.

Table 8
Growth of Bangladesh's Trade with India in SAARC and Global Perspectives

(Million of US $)

Year	BTWI	Annual growth rate	BTWS	Annual growth rate	BTWW	Annual growth rate
1980	63.6	-	164.8	-	3358	-
1985	94.5	9.72	163.9	-0.11	3771	2.46
1990	192	20.63	317	18.68	5269	7.94
1995	1030	87.29	1234	57.85	9670	16.70
2000	995.6	-0.67	1146	-1.43	13147	7.19
2001	1256.3	26.91	1391	21.38	13176	0.22
2002	1185.2	-5.66	1294	-6.97	12480	-5.28
2003	1541.6	30.07	1681	29.91	16744	34.17

Source: Calculated from IMF, Direction of Trade Statistics Yearbook (Various Years) data

Where
BTWI = Bangladesh's trade with India
BTWS = Bangladesh's trade with SAARC
BTWW = Bangladesh's trade with World.

India's share is not convincingly high in Bangladesh's trade although it has been increasing over the years. Table 9, it is observed that India's share in Bangladesh's global trade has increased to 10.7 percent in 1995 from 3.6 percent in 1990. This share has slightly decreased in recent years. But India's share in Bangladesh's global import has been increasing over the years. India's share in Bangladesh's global import increased to 15.5 percent in 2003 from 4.7 percent in 1990. On the other hand, India's export share decreased to 0.7 percent from 1.3 percent during the same period.

India's contribution to Bangladesh's export to SAARC countries increased to 53.5 percent in 2003 from 36.6 percent in 1990. India's share in Bangladesh's total trade with the SAARC countries increased from 60.6 percent to 91.7 percent during the same period of time.

Table 9
India's Share in Bangladesh, Global and SAARC Trade

(Million of US $)

Item	*1990*	*1995*	*2000*	*2001*	*2002*	*2003*
Global Exports of Bangladesh	1671	3173	4786	4826	4566	7167
Global Imports of Bangladesh	3598	6497	8360	8350	7914	9577
Exports to SAARC	60	83	89	92	73	99
Imports from SAARC	257	1151	1057	1299	1221	1582
Exports to India	22	36	50	61	39	53
Imports from India	170	994	945	1195	1146	1489
(I/W)T	3.6	10.7	7.6	9.5	9.5	9.2
(I/W)X	1.3	1.1	1	1.2	0.8	0.7
(I/W)M	4.7	15.3	11.3	14.3	14.5	15.5
(I/S)T	60.6	83.5	86.8	90.2	91.6	91.7
(I/S)X	36.6	43.3	56.1	66.3	53.4	53.5
(I/S)M	66.1	86.3	89.4	91.9	93.8	94.1

Source: Calculated from IMF, Direction of Trade Statistics Yearbook (Various Years) data

(I/W)T = India's share in Bangladesh's global trade (per cent)
(I/W)X = India's share in Bangladesh's global exports (per cent)
(I/W)M= India's share in Bangladesh's global imports (per cent)
(I/S)T = India's share in Bangladesh's global imports (per cent)
(I/S)X = India's share in Bangladesh's exports to SAARC Countries (per cent)
(I/S)M = India's share in Bangladesh's imports from SAARC Countries (per cent)

India was the fourth largest importing source in Bangladesh in 1990 just after Japan. But in 2003, India is the largest importing source (1489 million of US $) for Bangladesh.

The Importance of Bangladesh in India's Trade

In India's global trade, Bangladesh's contribution was 0.74 percent in 1990. This share rose to 1.59 percent (Table. 10) in 1995. After that, though this figure decreased marginally, it was still 1.13 percent in 2003.This is the official record of trade; if unofficial trade is also considered, this ratio would be double or even more.

With regard to exports, Bangladesh's contribution to Indian global exports is significant. In 1990, India's export to Bangladesh was 297 million US dollar, i.e. 1.67 percent of India's global exports. Within 5 years of time, i.e. in 1995, this ratio increased to 3.14 percent. In 2002 and 2003, Bangladesh's share in India's global exports was 2.11 percent and 2.42 percent respectively.

India imported from Bangladesh only 0.06 percent of its global imports in 1990. This ratio remained more or less the same over the years except 1995 and 2001. It was 0.23 in 1995 and 0.13 percent in 2001.

In the context of India's trade with SAARC Countries, Bangladesh's Contribution is significant. Bangladesh contributed 40.91 percent of India's total trade with the SAARC countries in 2003 (Table. 10). Bangladesh share of India's export to SAARC countries was 49.64 percent in 2003. In 2002, it was 52.57 percent. In 1990 and 1995, this ratio was higher i.e. 60.98 percent and 62.17 percent respectively. However Bangladesh's share of India's imports from SAARC countries was not convincing. It is only 8.42 percent in 2003.

Table 10
India's Trade in Global and SAARC Perspective

(Million of US $)

Item	*1990*	*1995*	*2000*	*2001*	*2002*	*2003*
Global Exports of India	17813	30537	44313	44613	49312	57080
Global Imports of India	23990	34484	52773	51562	56517	71238
Exports to SAARC	487	1544	2018	2347	1982	2786
Imports from SAARC	97	198	381	436	492	748
Imports from Bangladesh	15	79	55	67	43	63
(B/W)T	0.74	1.59	0.94	1.2	1.02	1.13
(B/W)X	1.67	3.14	1.94	2.44	2.11	2.42
(B/W)M	0.06	0.23	0.1	0.13	0.07	0.08
(B/S)T	53.42	59.64	38.14	41.47	43.86	40.91
(B/S)X	60.98	62.17	42.61	46.31	52.57	49.64
(B/S)M	15.46	39.9	14.43	15.36	8.73	8.42

Source: Calculated from IMF, Direction of Trade Statistics Yearbook (Various Years) and United Nation's, Statistical Yearbook (Various Years) data

Where

(B/W)T = Bangladesh's share in India's global trade (per cent)

(B/W)X = Bangladesh's share in India's global exports (per cent)

(B/W)M = Bangladesh' share in India's global imports (per cent)

(B/S)T = Bangladesh' share in India's global trade in SAARC countries (per cent)

(B/S)X = Bangladesh' share in India's exports to SAARC countries (per cent)

(B/S)M = Bangladesh' share in India's import from SAARC countries (per cent)

From Table 11, it is realized that India's largest export market in the SAARC region is Bangladesh all the time (1990 to 2003).

Table 11

Direction of India's Exports of SAARC Countries for Selected Years

(Percent of Total Share)

Country	*1990*	*1995*	*2000*	*2001*	*2002**	*2003**
Bangladesh	1.67	3.14	1.94	2.44	2.11	2.42
Bhutan	—	0.04	0.03	0.04	0.01	0.01
Maldives	0.03	0.04	0.09	0.01	0.05	0.08
Nepal	0.22	0.35	0.89	0.97	0.35	0.38
Pakistan	0.24	0.23	0.37	0.49	0.3	0.32
Sri Lanka	0.57	1.25	1.23	1.23	1.2	1.68
SAARC	2.73	5.05	4.55	5.27	4.02	4.89
World	100	100	100	100	100	100

Source: Calculated from IMF, Direction of Trade Statistics Year book (Various Years) data

Intra-Industry Trade Indices

Recent decades have witnessed an upsurge in Intra-Industry Trade i.e, trade in similar but differentiated products. Various theoretical arguments have been advanced for explaining this phenomenon. According to Grubel-Lloyd (1975), differences in the level of technology and human capital can lead to intra-industry trade even in products with identical factor input requirements. Krugman (1981) emphasizes the role of monopolistic competition and increasing return to scale in generating intra-industry trade. More precisely, Krugman argues that industries in which increasing returns are achieved at a fairly low level of output each producing a different brand.

This section focuses on the extent of Intra-Industry Trade between India Bangladesh, SAARC and the World. The following section discusses the Grubel-Lloyd indices of Intra-Industry Trade at the bilateral level.

The Grubel-Lloyd index to measure two-way trade may be defined as:

$$\text{IIT} = 1 - \frac{|X_i - M_i|}{(X_i + M_I)}$$

Where X_i = Exports of country i
M_i = Imports of country i

The intra-industry trade index ranges between 0 and 1 with larger values indicating a grater degree of intra-industry trade.

The importance of India-Bangladesh Intra-Industry Trade can also be examined. In 1990, IIT was 0.096 (Table 12). After that, though this figure increased to 0.152 in 1995 which was the highest index value of IIT. The IIT index was continuously declining and reached to 0.087 in 2003. In the chemical and related products category, the bilateral intra-industry trade between India and Bangladesh largely consisted of inorganic chemical insecticides and herbicides. The intra-industry trade between India and the World, shown in table.12 displays a more upward trend, starting at a lower value of 0.852 in 1990 and increasing up to about the same share as intra-industry with the world.

India's trade with the SAARC countries the height IIT is 0.423 in 2003. In 1990, this value was 0.331. The rate of growth of Intra-Industry Trade increased 28 percent in the study period. The historical pattern of intra-industry trade amongst the South Asian countries is highly erratic, and there are only a few products in which intra-industry trade occurred on a sustained basis. With few exceptions, leather products, textiles and clothing, and some basic machinery and tools have dominated the intra-industry trade profiles of the South Asian Countries. On average, the proportion of intra-industry trade to total has been very low for most of the products implying a low intensity of intra-industry trade in the region.

Table 12
India's Intra-Industry Trade with Bangladesh, Global and SAARC

Item	*1990*	*1995*	*2000*	*2001*	*2002*	*2003*
Global Exports of India	17813	30537	44313	44613	49312	57080
Global Imports of India	23990	34484	52773	51562	56517	71238
Exports to SAARC	487	1544	2018	2347	1982	2786
Imports from SAARC	97	198	381	436	492	748
Imports to Bangladesh	297	960	860	1087	1042	1383
Exports to Bangladesh	15	79	55	67	43	63
IIT between India and World	0.852	0.939	0.959	0.928	0.932	0.890
IIT between India and SAARC	0.331	0.227	0.318	0.313	0.398	0.423
IIT between India and Bangladesh	0.096	0.152	0.121	0.116	0.079	0.871

Source: Calculated from IMF, Direction of Trade Statistics Yearbook (Various Years) data

CONCLUSIONS

This study highlights the importance of bilateral trade relationship between India and Bangladesh. Currently India is the 2nd largest trading partner of Bangladesh, and India's position is at the top for Bangladesh's import trade.

India and Bangladesh are very important trading partner in the SAARC region. India along provided 94.1 percent of Bangladesh's imports from SAARC Countries in 2003. India's share in Bangladesh's total trade with the SAARC countries was 91.7 percent, and Bangladesh's share in India's total trade with the SAARC countries was 40.91 percent in 2003, India's largest export market is Bangladesh in the SAARC region.

Among the SAARC countries, India is relatively placed at an advanced position and it is trying to diversify its exports. Consequently, the share of manufactured goods to total exports of India is increasing. This gives scope for other SAARC Countries to imports manufactured goods from India. This is the major reason for India's favourable balance of trade with SAARC countries. This is a healthy sign in intra-regional trade.

There is a scope for mutual trade expansion between India, Bangladesh and SAARC countries. There are various possibilities like counter-trade, off shore trade fairs and exhibitions, market sharing arrangements and reduction of tariff and non-tariff barriers and utilize and existing potential for the expansion of SAARC region.

REFERENCES

Adiseshiah Malcom, S. (1987), *"The Economic Rationale of SAARC"* South Asian Journal. Vol. 1 No. 1 Jun-Sep.

Bhattacharya, B. and Pal, P (1998), *"Trade Related Joint Ventures between India and Bangladesh"* Indian Institute of Foreign Trade, New Delhi-110016.

Balassa, Bela (1965), *"Trade Liberalization and Revealed Comparative Advantage"* The Machester School of Economic and Social Studies" Vol. 33.

CPR. (1995), *"Indo Bangladesh Dialogue-Economic and Trade Cooperation"* Report, Prepared by Centre for Policy Research (CPR), New Delhi and Centre for Policy Dialogue (CPD), Dhaka.

Dasgupta, B. (2000), "International Institutions for Global Trade: The Case for South Asian Free Trade Association". In Dutta, D. (ed.) Economic Liberalization and Institutional Reform in South Asia: Recent Experiences and Future Prospect. Atlantic Publisher.

Das Gupta, A.K. (1977), "The Problem of International Economic order", International Studies, April June, Vol. 16.

Despande, G.P.(1981), "Long Shadow over South Asia" Economic and Political weekly, No. 21.

Donges, J.B. (1977), "The Third World Demand for a New International Economic Order" Kykios, Vol. 30.

Eusufazi, Zaki. (2000), "Liberalization in the Shadow of a Large Neighbor: A Case of Bangladesh-India Economic Relations" Centre for Policy Dialogue, The University Press Limited, Dhaka, Bangladesh.

Edelman, J.A. (1977), "Aid and Income Distribution" in J.N. Bhagwati (ed.), The New International Economic Order, MIT, Harvard University Press.

Frank Andre Curdar. (1980), "Development Crisis and Crisis of Development-Living in the Real World", Economic and Political Weekly, Vol. XV, 5,6 and 7 Feb.

George Skorov. (1978), "Developing Nations in the Struggle for Economic Equality", Social Sciences, Vol. 9 No. 3.

Grubel H. and Lloyd, P. (1975), "Intra-Industry Trade: The Measurement of International Trade Differentiated Products". New York.

Gupta, Sisir. (1964), "Regional Integration in South Asia" Asia Publishing House, New Delhi.

Halder, A. (1976), "India's Export Pattern Analysis on Potential Diversification, Minerva Association Pvt. Ltd, Calcutta.

Hassan, M.K. (2002), "Trade with India and Trade Policies of Bangladesh" in Cook son, Forrest and Alam A.K.M.S. 2002 (ed.) Towards Greater Sub-regional Economic Cooperation, chapter 10.

Haq. M.U. (1980), "Beyond the Slogan of South-South Co-operation", World Development, Vol. 8.

Harrison, S. (1965), "Troubled India and her Neighbours", Foreign Affair, January.

Hariharan, S.V. (1998), "Growth of India's Export in Asian Region", Indian Economic Panorama, Vol. 8. No. 1.

Hassan, M.K. (2001), "Is SAARC a viable Economic Block? Evidence from Gravity Model", Journal of Asian Economics, Vol. 12, No. 2 North-Holland.

Jagdish, N. Bhagwati. (1972) ed, "Economic and World Order" New Delhi.

Jha, L.K. (1982), "North South Debate", Chanakya Publications, New Delhi IMF, Various Years. Direction of Trade Statistics Year Book. Washington.

Kelegama, J.B. (1994), "Will the SAARC Preferential Trading Arrangement Expand Mutual Trade in South Asia", Economic Review, May-June.

Kumar Rajiv. (1988), "Co-operation of Economic Policies" South Journal, Vol. 1 No. 3, Jan-March.

Krugmen, P.R. (1981), "Intra-Industry Specialization and the Gain from Trade" Journal of Political Economy Vol. 89. No. 5.

Kemal et al. (2002), "A plan to strength on Regional Trade Cooperation in South Asia" in T.N. Srinivasan (ed), Trade Finance and Investment in South Asia, Social Science Press, New Delhi.

Kojima, K. (1964), "The Pattern of International Trade among Advanced Countries" Histosubashi, Journal of Economic. Vol.5 No.1 June.

Maddan, D.K. (1996), "Indo-Bangladesh Economic Relations and SAARC", Deep and Deep Publications. New Delhi – 110059'.

Mayer, Jorg & Wood. A. (2001), "South Asia's Export Structure in a Comparative Perspective" Oxford Development Studies, Vol. 29, No. 1.

Munsi, S.D. (1979), "India's Beneficial Bilateralism in South Asia" India Quarterly, Oct-Dec.

Mahendra P. Lama (2000), "SAARC: Shallow Regionalism Political Abstinence and Economic Advocacy" BIISS, Vol. 21. No. 1.

Pohit, S and Taneja, N (2003), "India's Informal Trade with Bangladesh: A Qualitative Assessment", The World Economy, Vol. 26, No. 8. Blackwell Publishing.

Rahaman, M (2000), "Bangladesh – India Bilateral Trade: An Investigation into Trade in Service", Draft Report, Prepared under South Asia Network of Economic Research Institutes (SANEI) Study Programme, CPD, Dhaka.

Rahaman, M. (1998), "Bangladesh-India Bilateral Trade: Current Trends, New Perspectives, New Challenges" BIISS journal, Vol. 19, No.1.

Rahaman M. (1998), "Intra-Regional Trade in South Asia: Current Status, Emerging Opportunities and Future Challenges", in Sadrel A.L. Reza (ed.) Export led Growth Strategy for South Asia: Prospects and Challenges, Asian and Pacific Development Centre.

Satreta Aiyar and Tanni Popal (2001), "WTO and Regional Trade Agreements", WTO monthly Digest.

Sharma, A and P.K. Mehata (1997), "Indian Exports to the Europeans Union in the Emerging Economic Environment" Asia-Pacific Development Journal, Vol. 4, No. 1. UNDP-2002

United Nations: Statistical year book for Asia and the pacific(various years).

Taneja, N. (2001), "Informal Trade in the SAARC region" *Economic and Political Weekly*, 17 March.

Venkatasubbuler, T. (1996), "India's Trade with SAARC Countries. Discovery Publishing House. New Delhi. 110002.

World Bank (2001), "World Development Indication" Washington D.C.

World Bank: World Development Report (Various Years), Oxford University Press.

Yeats, Alexander J. (1998), "Just How Big Global Production Sharing" World Bank Policy Research Working Paper 1817, The World Bank, Washington, D.C.

Anil Bhuimali, Md. Gholam Kibria
Sidhartha Sankar Laha

8

BANGLADESH JUTE MILLS AND TRADE UNION IN REFORMED REGIME

INTRODUCTION

The most important task before the economy of Bangladesh in the post-reformed era has been the restructuring of public sector industries including jute mills. The Government has initiated reform process in the prime sector. The main thrust has been shifted towards industrialisation under private sector initiative along with the invitation of foreign direct investment. Tax exemption has been offered to exported-oriented industries. This has encouraged new enterprises to under take production activities of export-oriented goods. The present paper deals with the detailed analysis of two private sector jute mills, a comparison of nationalised and private mills in terms of production, growth rate of output, export, growth rate of export, and manpower position. For this part of analysis we rely on secondary data collected from different sources. Field survey has been conducted with two private sector jute mills especially to study the socio-economic background of trade union members of the two separate mills. For our purpose an opinion survey has been conducted with the workers, employees, trade union leaders and the management as a whole. Concluding observations have been made at the end.

PRIVATE JUTE MILLS

We present here the short history of two private jute mills, viz, Ajax Mill and Mohsen Mill. The Ajax Mill was established at

Mirerdanga, Daulatpur and Khulna in 1964. Production was started in 1965. It is a medium-sized enterprise offering regular employment to1320 workers. Of this 1080 are permanent workers and 240 are temporary workers. Apart from the workers the total number of employees and officers are 190 and 59 respectively. It was basically a privately-managed enterprise. After liberation in 1971, 80 percent of the private enterprises were nationalized including the Ajax Jute Mill. After nationalisation the enterprise started experiencing losses. Due to Government policy changes and subsides offered by the Government the financial health of the mills improved substantially and it gradually started making profit. Due to a policy of the Government this enterprise was again denationalised in 1982. After denationalization the position of the industry further deteriorated. Due to mounting losses the workers are not provided with wage and other benefits properly and timely. The employment absorption capacity has also been reduced.

The other jute mill, viz, Mohsen Jute Mill was established in 1969. The production process began in 1970. It was set up at Shiromoni in Khulna with its head office at Nasim Chamber, Dil-Khusa and Dhaka as a private jute industry. The production was started with sixty five broad looms equivalent to 250 narrow looms. The industry was nationalized in 1972. Ten years later it was again denationalised in 1982. The Mohsen Jute Mill is relatively smaller than the Ajax Jute Mill in terms of production, export, employment absorption etc.

COMPARING TWO DIFFERENT MILLS

In this section comparative description of production and export of jute product of two different types jute mills, viz, nationalised and privately-managed jute mills of Bangladesh has been presented. Man-power position and wage-differentials of the mills have also been shown. The data for this analysis have been collected from Bangladesh Bureau of Statistics. Tables 1 and 2 show the production and growth rate of output of both the public and private sector jute mills respectively.

Table 1
Production of Jute Goods in Public Sector Mills

(In 000 M.T.)

Year	*Quantity Produced*	*Growth Rate*
1986-87	334	-
1987-88	326	-2.39
1988-89	317	-2.76
1989-90	332	+4.73
1990-91	261	-21.38
1991-92	244	-6.51
199-93	283	15.98
1993-94	271	-4.24

Source: Compiled from Bangladesh Bureau of Statistics (various years)

Table 2
Production of Private Sector Jute Mills

Year	*Production (in M.T.)*	*Growth Rate*
1990-91	173438	-
1991-92	172280	-0.66
1992-93	162865	-5.46
1993-94	150657	-7.49

Source: Compiled from Bangladesh Bureau of Statistics (various years)

Comparative picture of production of nationalised and private jute mills is portrayed in table 3 and the growth rate of output in table 4.

Table 3
Production of Nationalised and Private Jute Mills

	Year-wise Production			
Jute Mills	*1996-97*	*1997-98*	*1998-99*	*1999-2000*
Nationalised Jute Mills	271.53 (66.1)	255.29 (62.43)	236.19 (64.13)	234.9 (69.27)
Private Jute Mills	239.22 (33.9)	153.59 (37.57)	132.06 (35.87)	104.2 (30.73)

Source: Annual Jute Goods Statistics, 1999-2000, Vol. 89, Bangladesh
Note: *Figures within the parentheses indicate percentages to total*

Table 4
Growth Rate of Output

	Growth Rate	
Year	Nationalised Mills	Private Mills
1996-1997	-	-
1997-1998	-5.98	+10.32
1998-1999	-7.48	-14.01
1999-2000	-0.54	-21.09

Source: Calculated from table 3 above

Table 3 shows that nationalised jute mill's contribution were 66.1, 62.43,64.13 and 69.27 percent in 1996-97, 1997-98, 1998-99, and 1999-2000 respectively, whereas the contribution made by the private jute mills were 33.9, 37.57 35.87 and 30.73 percents respectively during the above mentioned periods. A dismal picture of growth rate of jute output is noticed in both the nationalised and the private jute mills (see table 2). The growth rate of jute output was -5.98 percent in nationalised jute mills in 1997-98. This reduced to -7.48 percent in 1998-99 and also in 1999-2000 it was not good enough (- 0.54 percent). The conditions of the private jute mills were equally bad. The only exception was 1997-1998 when the private jute mills experienced a positive growth rate in output (+10.32 percent). In 1998-99, the growth rate of private mills was again negative (-14.01 percent). This negative trend also continued in 1999-2000 (-21.09 percent).

An idea of export of jute goods and their growth rates in both nationalised and private jute mills has been presented in tables 5 and 6.

Table 5
Export of Jute Goods

(In 000 M.T)

	Export			
June Mills	*1996-97*	*1997-98*	*1998-99*	*1999-2000*
Nationalised	192.85	160.27	223.84	201.6
	(67.92)	(67.77)	(73.92)	(74.91)
Private	91.06	76.20	78.97	67.5
	(32.07)	(32.22)	(26.07)	(25.08)

Source: Compiled from Annual Jute Goods Statistics, 1999-2000, Bangladesh
Note: *Figures within the parentheses show percentages to total*

Table 6
Growth Rate of Export

	Export Growth Rate	
Year	*Nationalised Mills*	*Private Mills*
1996-1997	-	-
1997-1998	-16.89	-16.31
1998-1999	+39.66	+3.63
1999-2000	-9.93	-14.52

Source: Calculated from table 5

Man-power position of nationalised and private jute mills of Bangladesh is shown in table 7.

Table 7

Man-power Position of Nationalised and Private Jute Mills.

(As on 30.06.2000)

Category of Mills	*Employees*				*Workers*				*Attendance*			
	Officers	*Clerical Staff*	*Non-Clerical Staff*	*Total*	*Permanent*	*Adhoc*	*Badli*	*Total*	*Permanent*	*Badli*	*Casual*	*Total*
Public	2475	3889	3779	10143	71116	1119	27834	100069	52237	17237	331	699.35
	(56.45)	(61.97)	(58.79)	(59.36)	(67.63)	(100)	(52.0)	(62.62)	(80.68)	(64.17)	(14.18)	(74.29)
Private	1909	2886	26.48	6943	34026	-	25688	59714	12502	9696	2003	24201
	(43.55)	(39.03)	(41.21)	(40.64)	(32.37)		(48.0)	(37.38)	(19.32)	(35.83)	(85.82)	(25.71)
Total	4384	6275	6427	17086	105142	1119	53522	1597	64739	27063	2334	94134
	(100)	(100)	(100)	(100)	(100)	(100)	(100)	(100)	(100)	(100)	(100)	(100)

Source: Compiled from Bangladesh Economic Review, 2000

Note: Figures within the parentheses indicate percentages to total.

Table 7 shows that public sector jute mills are the largest employment providers in Bangladesh jute industry. This sector altogether provides 59.36 percent employment of total employment opportunity available in this industry.

Wages provided to both nationalised and private jute mills workers vary greatly. Data show that nationalised jute mill workers receive greater wages and other benefits relative to private jute mill workers. This is shown in table 8.

Table 8

Wage Differentials between Nationalised and Private Mills

Position	*Basic Pay of Nationalised Mills (in Taka)*	*Basic Pay of Private Mills (in Taka)*
Helper	1550-2270	560-860
Cleaner	1550-2270	560-860
S/Feeder	1600-2410	590-920
T/Feeder	1600-2410	590-920
B/Feeder	1600-2410	590-920
F/Feeder	1600-2410	590-920
Reliever	1600-2410	590-920
B/Shifter	1600-2410	590-920
D.S.O.	1600-2410	590-920
B.M.O.	1600-2410	590-920
Sli Feeder	1650-2970	620-980
Spinner	1800-2970	620-980
Reliever Grade	1800-2970	730-1180

Source: Compiled From Data Received from Nationalised and Private jute Mills (2002)

FIELD SURVEY ON PRIVATE JUTE MILLS

We analyse here the socio-economic background of trade union members of two private jute mills. An opinion survey has been conducted with the workers, employees, trade union leaders and the management. We have collected information of 80 workers from Ajax Jute Mill and 50 workers from Mohsen Jute Mill workers. All the socio-economic data thus collected from these private jute mills have been presented in tables 9, 10, 11, 12, 13, 14, 15, 16, 17, 18, 19, 20, 21, 22, 23, 24, 25, 26, 27, 28, 29, 30, 31 and 32. We have shown the classification of workers on –

the basis of age in table 9, classification on the basis of education in table 10, parental occupation in table 11, workers encouragement to join the union in table 12, role of unions in table 13, management's attitude towards workers in table 14, ways of placing demands by the workers in 15, negotiation process in 16, causes of disputes in 17, value of disputes in 18, ways of workers facing disputes in 19, nature of workers cooperation in 20, nature of demand in 21, workers' reaction in 22, legal provision followed in the jute mills in 23, impact of non-complacence with legal provisions in 24, ways of increasing productivity in 25, major problems faced by the mills in table 26, major causes of problems faced by the mills in 27, solutions prescribed by the workers in 28, nature of working of collective bargaining association in 29, causes of conduct between trade unions in 30, suggestions for removing the conflict in 31 and worker's suggestions to management for developing trade union in table 32.

Table 9
Classification of Workers on the Basis of Age

Class Internal	*Mill-I*		*Mill-II*	
(Year)	*Frequency*	*%*	*Frequency*	*%*
21-25	Nil	Nil	03	6.00
26-30	02	2.50	08	16.00
31-35	05	6.25	08	16.00
36-40	07	8.75	07	14.00
41-45	10	12.50	10	20.00
46-50	15	18.75	08	16.00
51-55	15	18.75	06	12.00
56-60	26	32.50	Nil	Nil

Table 10
Classification on the Basis of Education

Level of	*Mill-I*		*Mill-II*	
(Year)	*Frequency*	*%*	*Frequency*	*%*
Up to class v	37	46.25	17	34.00
Class vi-ix	39	48.75	26	52.00
SSC & Above	04	5.00	07	14.00
Graduation level	Nil	Nil	Nil	Nil

Table 11
Parental Occupation

Type of Occupation	*Mill-I* Frequency	%	*Mill-II* Frequency	%
Agriculture	43	53.75	27	54.00
Business	24	30.00	13	26.00
Service	13	16.25	10	20.00
Total	80	100.00	50	100.00

Table 12
Workers Encouragement to Join the Unions

Sources of Encouragement	*Mill-I* Frequency	%	*Mill-II* Frequency	%
Encouraged by the colleagues	40	50.00	26	52.00
As the union works for the workers	09	11.25	04	8.00
Influenced by union leaders	23	28.75	14	28.00
As appointed by trade union leaders	08	10.00	06	12.00
Total	80	100.00	50	100.00

Table 13
Role of Trade Unions

Role	*Mill-I* Frequency	%	*Mill-II* Frequency	%
Alright	09	11.25	04	8.00
Not Satisfactory	35	43.75	23	46.00
Pro-management	15	18.75	12	24.00
Somehow Satisfactory	21	26.25	11	22.00
Total	80	100.00	50	100.00

Table 14
Management's Attitude towards Workers

Attitude	*Mill-I* Frequency	%	*Mill-II* Frequency	%
Not sympathetical	15	31.29	22	44.00
Not so much sympathetic	26	32.50	11	22.00
Sympathetic	12	15.00	09	18.00
Management not considerate to the workers getting union support	17	21.25	08	16.00
Total	80	100.00	50	100.00

Table 15
Ways of Placing Demands by the Workers

Ways	Mill-I		Mill-II	
	Frequency	%	Frequency	%
Trough union leader	33	41.25	22	44.00
Through direct discussion	17	21.25	11	22.00
Through internal communication	14	17.50	10	20.00
Written ultimatum	16	20.00	07	14.00
Total	80	100.00	50	100.00

Table 16
Negotiation Process

Process of Negotiation	Mill-I		Mill-II	
	Frequency	%	Frequency	%
Through CBA leader	32	40.00	20	40.00
Through departmental heads	15	18.75	08	16.00
Written ultimatum	17	21.25	10	20.00
Though strikes	16	20.00	12	24.00
Total	80	100.00	50	100.00

Table 17
Volume of Disputes in Last Five Years

(Survey conduced in 2002)

Volume of Disputes	Mill-I		Mill-II	
	Frequency	%	Frequency	%
Cannot say the exact number	35*	43.75	26	52.00
So many disputes take place	27	33.75	14	28.00
It take several times	18	22.50	10	20.00
Total	80	100.00	50	100.00

Table 18
Ways of Workers Facing Disputes

Ways of Facing Disputes	Mill-I		Mill-II	
	Frequency	%	Frequency	%
Through negotiation communicable settlement between union leaders of management	18	22.50	20	40.00
Negotiation through CBA	30	37.50	23	46.00
By giving pressure through strikes	32	40.00	07	14.00
Total	80	100.00	50	100.00

Table 19
Causes of Disputes

Causes	*Mill-I*		*Mill-II*	
	Frequency	%	*Frequency*	%
Wage and other benefits	34	42.50	23	46.00
Financial and non-financial benefits	22	27.50	11	22.00
Wage and other facilities	24	30.00	16	32.00
Total	80	100.00	50	100.00

Table 20
Nature of Cooperation from Workers

Workers Cooperation	*Mill-I*		*Mill-II*	
	Frequency	%	*Frequency*	%
Workers cooperate at the time of necessity	23	28.75	17	34.00
Cooperative unconditionally	14	17.50	13	26.00
Cooperative without hampering their interest	21	26.25	13	26.00
When management seeks cooperation they go ahead	22	27.50	07	14.00
Total	80	100.00	50	100.00

Table 21
Nature of Demand in Last Five years
(Survey Conducted in 2002)

Demands	*Mill-I*		*Mill-II*	
	Frequency	%	*Frequency*	%
Demanding new scale	22	27.50	12	24.00
Higher wages and benefits	24	30.00	18	36.00
Better housing and other benefits	17	21.25	13	26.00
Considering price level and scale of play demanded	17	21.25	07	14.00
Total	80	100.00	50	100.00

Table 22
Workers' Reaction

Reaction on Non-fulfilment	*Mill-I*		*Mill-II*	
	Frequency	%	*Frequency*	%
Go for movement	29	36.25	17	34.00
Ultimatum for greater movement	17	21.25	13	26.00
Give demonstration	16	20.00	09	18.00
Go for strike	18	22.50	11	22.00
Total	80	100.00	50	100.00

Table 23
Legal Provisions Followed in the Mills

Provisions followed	*Mill-I*		*Mill-II*	
	Frequency	%	*Frequency*	%
To some extent	18	22.50	20	40.00
Not always	22	27.50	17	34.00
Try to follow somehow	28	35.00	09	18.00
No idea about that	12	15.00	04	08.00
Total	80	100.00	50	100.00

Table 24
Impact of Non-Compliance with Legal Provisions

Impact	*Mill-I*		*Mill-II*	
	Frequency	%	*Frequency*	%
Personal or industrial relations will be disturbed	22	27.50	21	42.00
Personal problem will come up	26	32.50	13	26.00
Legal environment will be threatened	15	18.75	08	16.00
Labour problem will emerge	17	21.25	08	16.00
Total	80	100.00	50	100.00

Table 25
Ways of Increasing Productivity

How to Increase Productivity	*Mill-I*		*Mill-II*	
	Frequency	%	*Frequency*	%
By giving training and proper wages and other benefits to the workers	27	33.75	16	32.00
By supplying raw materials, proper wages and other benefits	22	27.50	19	38.00
By careful observations and timely payment of wages	31	38.75	15	30.00
Total	80	100.00	50	100.00

Table 26
Major Problems Faced by the Mills

How to Increase Productivity	*Mill-I*		*Mill-II*	
	Frequency	%	*Frequency*	%
Production has gone down due to shortage of raw materials and working capital	13	16.25	07	14.00

Contd.....

How to Increase Productivity	*Mill-I*		*Mill-II*	
	Frequency	*%*	*Frequency*	*%*
Unhealthy alliance between management and CBA leader	23	28.75	08	16.00
Financial, administrative and personal problem.	23	28.75	20	40.00
Inefficient management and corrupt CBA leaders not concerned about financial crisis	21	26.25	15	30.00
Total	80	100.00	50	100.00

Table 27
Major Causes of Problems Faced by the Mills

Causes	*Mill-I*		*Mill-II*	
	Frequency	*%*	*Frequency*	*%*
Management's consistent negligence to the problems after denationalization	22	27.50	13	26.00
Main causes are administrative and poor industrial and financial relations	18	22.50	13	26.00
Management's negligence to the official business and poor wage	12	15.00	12	24.00
Main causes are corruption with the help of CBA leaders for lowering wages and other benefits	28	35.00	12	24.00
Total	80	100.00	50	100.00

Table 28
Nature of Working of CBA

Working	*Mill-I*		*Mill-II*	
	Frequency	*%*	*Frequency*	*%*
Works nicely	06	7.50	09	18.00
Not up to the mark	28	35.00	18	36.00
Not satisfactory	29	36.25	17	34.00
They serve the purpose of the management	17	21.25	06	12.00
Total	80	100.00	50	100.00

Table 29
Solution by the Workers

Causes of the Problems	*Mill-I*		*Mill-II*	
	Frequency	%	*Frequency*	%
Management should look after the problems of the mill management and should try to minimize corruption and try to look after interest of the workers	30	37.50	11	22.00
Management should have to ensure logistic problems of the mill and should pay wages timely	08	10.00	03	06.00
Management should look after the problems of the mill and should try to minimize corruption	35	43.75	13	26.00
Management should try to follow the provision to minimize losses through management audit and should be more careful to make it a profitable organization	07	8.75	23	46.00
Total	80	100.00	50	100.00

Table 30
Causes of Conflict between Trade Unions

Causes of Conflict	*Mill-I*		*Mill-II*	
	Frequency	%	*Frequency*	%
Due to political reason	20	25.00	18	36.00
Due to leadership conflict	35	43.75	15	30.00
Due to personality class	25	31.25	17	34.00
Total	80	100.00	50	100.00

Table 31
Suggestions for Removing Conflict

Suggestion	*Mill-I*		*Mill-II*	
	Frequency	%	*Frequency*	%
We should try to minimize politicisation of unions.	28	35.00	13	26.00
Early settlement of disputes	24	30.00	16	32.00
Worker's participation in management and union activities	16	20.00	11	22.00
Direct negotiation with union	12	15.00	10	20.00
Total	80	100.00	50	100.00

Table 32
Workers Suggestion to Management for Developing Trade Unions

Suggestion in Management for Developing Trade Union	*Mill-I*		*Mill-II*	
	Frequency	*%*	*Frequency*	*%*
Training for trade union members	20	25.00	10	20.00
Motivation of trade union members	28	35.00	17	34.00
Close cooperation between management and workers	32	40.00	23	46.00
Total	80	100.00	50	100.00

CONCLUSIONS

Since the initiation of liberalisation process in Bangladesh the major thrust has been towards denationalisation of major industries including the jute industry. The reasons for adopting such a policy, among others are to overcome havoc losses incurred by the jute mills, increase efficiency, reduce average cost, and overcome strain relations between the employers and the employees. Even after completing 25 years after denationalisation it was not possible to improve the condition of the industry substantially. Of 45 private jute mills 30 have been closed. In all, some 45 jute mills which include public jute mills too are now defunct. The industries are closed due to continuous losses. One of our two sample jute mills namely the Ajax Jute Mill also once stopped production, but later on started production. The golden days of Bangladesh Jute Industry have gone and it seems that those days would not roll back again. Jute industries (both public and private) fail to cope up with the international competitive conditions, because the jute industry has not gained any benefit from the advantage of devaluation. The price of jute goods in Bangladesh is not fixed on the basis of costs incurred (average variable cost and intrinsic cost). The sales price instead is determined on the basis of sales price of competitors in the international market. The other reason for weak performance of this industry is that internal market for jute goods is too small. The substitute goods especially the polithin bags have partially replaced the demand for jute goods in Bangladesh. Home consumption of jute goods is less than 15 percent of the total goods produced in

Bangladesh. Jute goods production and consumption data show that jute goods production countries of the world consume a substantial portion of their self-produced jute goods. India, for instance, consumes almost 90 percent of its total jute goods produced. It is thus necessary to enhance the multiple use of jute goods.

The liberalization policy has an impact on industrial relations especially the relation between the management and the workers. Broadly speaking, the liberalisation policy throughout the world has three types of impacts, viz, (a) it has intensified economic inequality globally, (b) it has adverse impact on employment and wages of unskilled or low-skilled workers, and (c) there has been a change in policy orientation on labour relations i.e. relation between the management and the workers. In Bangladesh too casualisation of workforce in jute sector has increased, increasing the helplessness among the workers in this sector. This again has weakened the collective bargaining power of trade unions. Trade union activities are very weak in private jute mills. Naturally, they cannot motive the management to enhance their wages and other benefits.

REFERENCES

Bangladesh Bureau of Statistics (2000), Quarterly Jute goods statistics, 1993-94, Dakha, Bangladesh.

Bangladesh Jute Mills corporation (2000), Annual Jute Goods Statistics, 1999-2000, Vol. 89.

Finance Ministry, Government of Bangladesh (2000), Bangladesh Economic Review 2000 Bangladesh Economic Survey, 1985-1986.

Government of Bangladesh (1994), Bangladesh Economic Survey, 1993-1994.

Gorlier (1999), Encyclopedia No. 31 of Knowledge, Vol.2, USA.

Hafiz, M.A. (1980), "Trade Union Movement in Bangladesh", Bangladesh.

Janardhan, V. (2003), "Arguing for Industrial Relations: Journey to a lost World" Economic and Political Weekly, Vol. XXXVIII, No. 31, August 2-6.

Kaushal, G. (2001), Economic History of India 1757-1966, Kalyani Publishers.

Kibria, M.G., Anil Bhuimali and Kanak Kanti Bagchi (2006), Trade Union Movement in Bangladesh, Serials Publications.

Official Records of Ajax Jute Mills.

Official Records of Mohsen Jute Mills.

Rashid, H. (2003), "Bangladesh Jute Industry: Problems and Prospects" Bangladesh Observer, March 7.

Seth, N.R. (2001), "Trade Unions in Word and Deed". Indian Journal of Industrial Relations. Vol. 37, No. 2, October.

Srinivasan, T.N. (2002), Eight Lectures on India's Economic Reforms. Oxford India.

The Hindu (2002), India Book of the Year 2002.

Vijay, G. (2003), "Changing Policy Regime and Labour: A Case Study." Economic and Political Weekly, Vol. XXXVIII, August, 2-6.

Chandan Kumar Mukhopadhyay
Shyam Charan Barma

9

MONEY AND PRICE RELATIONSHIP IN THE ECONOMY OF PAKISTAN

INTRODUCTION

Empirical analysis of money price relationship has received greater importance in recent years. It arises from the fact that maintaining price stability is considered to be the main task of the central bank of any country. The central bank can effectively contribute to maintenance of price stability provided it understands the empirical relationship between money and price.

The empirical issue of money-price relationship is important for Pakistan because Pakistan has undertaken economic reforms since the early 1990s with outward orientation of the economy. With the change in economic policies, money-price relationship may also be expected to undergo changes. This indicates a structural shift in money-price relationship. The estimation of money-price relationship, therefore, may present an account of dynamic relations between these two variables.

REVIEW OF THEORETICAL RELATIONSHIP BETWEEN MONEY AND PRICE

One of the most important issues in macroeconomics constitutes a quiry into the relationship between money, price and income. The quiry has been continuing since the days of classical economists until today. A brief review is presented below.

The Quantity Theory of Money

The Quantity Theory of Money specifies the direct and

proportional relationship between money and price level. According to Fishers equation of exchange

$$M_tV_t + P_tY_t$$

Or $$P_t = \frac{M_tV_t}{Y_t} \qquad (i)$$

Where

M_t = Money supply
V_t = Velocity of money
P_t = Price level

and

Y_t = real output level

Consequently,

$P_t = f(M_t)$

and change in money supply causes proportional change in price level.

Keynesian Postulates

Keynesians advocate Phillips curve approach and hold that there exists a trade off between inflation and unemployment. Increase in money wage may raise inflation level and also reduce unemployment. With increase in money supply, employment output and prices rise. Keynesians, therefore, assume a direct relationship between money supply and price level. However, this relationship is not proportional.

Friedman- Phelp Approach

Friedman and Phelp argue that Phillips curve exists in the short run only. In the long- run the Phillips curve is a vertical straight line. Consequently, increase in money supply leads to proportional rise in price level without having any effect on output level and employment in the long-run.

Rational Expectation Hypothesis

According to rational expectationists Phillips curve does not exist even in the short run. Consequently, there exists no trade off between employment and price level. Change in money supply leads to change in price level even in the short-run.

However, rational expectationists distinguish between anticipated and unanticipated part of the money supply. They hold that output level is affected by unanticipated part of the money supply, while anticipated part of the money supply affects price level only.

From (1) we have

$$m_t + v_t = p_t + y_t \qquad (ii)$$

Where

m_t = log of the money supply
v_t = log of the (constant) velocity of money
p_t = log of the price level
y_t = log of the real out put

The aggregate supply curve is given by the Lucas supply equation (iii) where

y_t = log of the real out put

$$Y_t = y_{p+} \beta (p_t - {}_{t-1} p^e_t) \qquad (iii)$$

Where

y_p = log of full employment output ${}_{t-1} p^e_t$ = log of the price level that the public expects will occur in time t viewed from period t-1.

Let the monetary rule used by the policy authorities be

$$M_t = a_1 y_{t-1} + \varepsilon_t \qquad (iv)$$

Where $E(\varepsilon_t / I_{t-1}) = 0$

Under rational expectations, the price expectations are determined within the model in the light of past and present developments of the money supply. This can be expressed as

$${}_{t-1} p^e_t = E(p_t / I_{t-1}) \qquad (v)$$

This equation asserts that people's subjective and psychological expectation of the price level ($t\text{-}1p^e_t$) equals the mathematical expectation of the price level, given both the structure of the model and the information available.

From (ii) and (iii) we have

$$m_t + v_t - p_t = y_p + \beta(p_t - {}_{t-1} p^e_t) \qquad (vi)$$

Taking the mathematical expectation of both sides of the equation (v) as of time t-1 gives

$$\alpha_1 y_{t-1} + v - {}_{t-1} p^e_t = y_p \qquad (vii)$$

Or, $\quad {}_{t-1}P^e_t = \acute{a}_1 y_{t-1} + v - y_p$ *(viii)*

Substituting equation (viii) into equation (6) we have

$$P_t = \alpha_1 y_{t-1} + \bar{v} - y_p + \frac{\varepsilon_t}{I+\beta} \qquad (ix)$$

Therefore, the gap between the actual price and the expected price is

$$P_t - {}_{t-1}P^e_t = \frac{\varepsilon_t}{1+\beta} \qquad (x)$$

Using the Lucas supply equation, we find that output will equal

$$Y_t = y_p + \frac{\beta_{\varepsilon t}}{1+\beta} \qquad (xi)$$

Equation (ix) and (xi) show that both the anticipated and unanticipated parts of money supply affect price level and not the output level. Equation (xi) shows that only unanticipated part of money supply (ε_t) affects output level.

The Objective of the Study

This present study seeks to enquire into the following issues.

(i) The state of short-run and long-run relationship between money supply and prices in Pakistan.

(ii) The direction of causality between money supply and price level

The Data

The wholesale price index is used for the study and the base period is 2000. Two measures of money supply are available for Pakistan. One is narrow money M_1 which includes currency held by non-bank public and demand deposits held by commercial banks sector. M_2 consists of M_1 and time deposits held of commercial banks. Both types of money supply have been used in the present study in order to investigate into their effects on price level.

The data have been collected from different issues of International Financial Statistics (IFS). Again quarterly data have been used in the study. The data range from first quarter of 1973 through the fourth quarter of 2005.

FORMS OF ESTIMABLE EQUATIONS

The estimable equation follows from the quantity theory of money. From equation (ii) we have

Equation (12) shows that

$$p_t = m_t + v - y_t \qquad (xii)$$

Therefore, $P_t = f(m_t, v_t, y_t)$

Consequently, the estimable equation becomes

$$P_t = a + b_1 m_t + b_2 v_t - b_3 y_t + u_t \qquad (xiii)$$

However, is any macroeconomic study the rate of change in price level is more important than the price level itself to the policy makers. This is done through first differencing of the price level such that

$$\Delta p_t = a + b_1 \Delta m_t + b_2 \Delta v_t - b_3 \Delta y_t + u_t \qquad (xiv)$$

Money demand function is assumed stable for Pakistan so that v_t and y_t are taken to be constant. Consequently, equation (xiv) can be written as

$$\Delta p_t = a + b_1 \Delta m_t + u_t \qquad (xv)$$

The impact of money supply on prices may not be instantaneous. In that case

$$\Delta p_t = a + \Sigma b_i \Delta m_{t-i} + u_t \qquad (xvi)$$

II

TEST OF UNIT ROOTS

In the case of time series analysis, unit root tests are important since these tests detect the stationarity and non- stationarity of the time series data used for the study. A stationary time series data set has three basic properties.

First, it has a finite mean, which implies that a stationary series fluctuates around a constant long run mean.

Second, a stationary time series has a finite variance. This implies that variance is time invariant.

Third, a stationary time series data set has finite auto-covariances.

This reflects that theoretical autocorrelation co-efficients decay fast as lag length increases. Regression runs on non-stationary time series produce a spurious relationship. Hence, to avoid a spurious relationship, there is a need to perform a unit root test on variables. The Dickey-Fuller (DF) and Augmented Dickey –Fuller (ADF) tests are widely used for performing unit root tests. The ADF test involves the autoregressive AR (1) process. For this we consider the following equation.

$$Y_t = a + \rho Y_{t-1} + \zeta_t$$

In case ρ carries the value $-1<P<1$ the variable Y is stationary. If the value of ρ is one, the variable Y is non-stationary. Hence, the unit root null hypothesis is:

$$H_o : \rho = 1$$

While testing the null hypothesis of unit root, the following equation is used.

$$\Delta (Y_t) = \alpha + \gamma Y_{t-1} + \zeta_t \qquad (xvii)$$

where, $\gamma = \rho - 1$ and $\Delta(Y)$ is the first difference of the series Y. Here the unit root null hypothesis is:

$$H_{0:}\ \gamma = 0$$

If the variable is stationary at level, the variable is said to be integrated of order zero, I(0). If the variable is non- stationary at level, the ADF test can be utilized and the first difference of the variable can be used for testing a unit root. In this case, the variable is said to be co-integrated of order one, i.e I (1). Likewise, one can test for the higher order of co-integration of the variables. It must be noted that a larger negative t-statistic suggests rejection of the hypothesis of a unit root and implies that the series is stationary.

AUGMENTED DICKEY-FULLER TESTS FOR UNIT ROOTS

The results of the Augmented Dickey-Fuller Tests for the presence of unit roots in the series concerned are being presented through the table-1.

Table -1
Augmented Dickey Fuller Test (Unit Root Test)

Variable	*ADF Test Statistic*	*Mackinnon Critical Value* 1%	5%	10%
Log (WP-Pak)	-1.536941	-3.480818	-2.883579	-2.578601
Log (WP-Pak)With C and trend	-2.500496	-4.029595	-3.444487	-3.147063
ΔLog (WP-Pak)With C and trend	-11.00895	-4.030157	-3.444756	-3.147221
Log (M1)	0.746786	-3.482035	-2.884109	-2.578884
Log (M1) with C and trend	-2.769857	-4.030157	-3.444756	-3.147221
ΔLog (M1)	-10.05892	-3.482035	-2.884109	-2.578884
Log (M2)	-0.334430	-3.481217	-2.883753	-2.578694
Log (M2) with C and trend	-2.268375	-4.030157	-3.444756	-3.147221
ΔLog (M2)	-18.19738	-3.481217	2.883753	-2.578694

The results for the unit root test, present the following features:-

First, the results show that all the variables in the log level-forms contain unit roots Consequently, the series are non-stationary in the log levels.

Second, according to the unit root tests the variables are trended.

Third, wholesale price of Pakistan (WPI-Pak), M_1 and M_2 are integrated of order one I(1).That is, the first difference log WPI-Pak , logM_1 and logM_2 are stationary.

PHILLIPS-PERRON UNIT ROOT TEST:

The Table 2 presents the results of Phillips- Perrone unit root tests on variables concerned.

CORRELOGRAM ANALYSIS FOR STATIOARITY

The stationarity of the variables has been confirmed through the study of their Auto Correlation functions (ACFs) and Partial Auto-correlation functions (PACFs). Figure 1-3 present the ACFs and PACFs of the variables concerned. It is observed from these functions that the series for M1, M2 and wholesale price Index are non-stationary and, therefore, contain unit roots.

Table: 2
Phillips-perron Unit Root Test

Variable	*ADF Test Statistic*	*Mackinnon Critical Value* 1%	5%	10%
Log (WPI-Pak)	5.78694	-2.582734	-1.943285	-1.615099
Log (WPI-Pak)With C and trend	-2.883118	-4.029595	-3.444487	-3.147063
ΔLog (WPI-Pak)With C and trend	-11.10146	-4.030157	-3.444756	-3.147221
Log (M1)	9.029067	-2.582734	-1.943285	-1.615099
Log (M1) with C and trend	-4.486144	-4.029595	-3.444487	-3.147063
ΔLog (M1)	-13.55634	-2.582872	-1.943304	-1.615087
Log (M2)	9.584169	-2.582734	-1.943285	-1.615099
Log (M2) with C and trend	-3.579871	-4.029595	-3.444487	-3.147063
ΔLog (M2)	-13.35074	-2.582872	-1.943304	-1.615087

It also corroborates the results of ADF tests. It is observed that M_1, M_2 and WPI series are non-stationary. It is further observed that WPI, M_1 and M_2 series are stationary first difference.

The ACFs and PACFs of the first differenced series of the variables concerned are being presented through the figures 4-6. These functions also testify for the stationarity of the series concerned.

COINTEGRATION: THEORETICAL BASIS

Co-integration is the study concerning the stability of long run, equilibrium relationships among variables. The study allows for the researcher to describe the existence of an equilibrium or stationary relationship among two or more time series, each of which is individually non-stationary. According to Engle and Granger (1987) the variables will be co-integrated when the linear combination of the non-stationary variables is stationary. Co-integration provides a method for elimination of the cost of differencing by rationalizing terms in levels but only in linear combinations which are stationary.

For example, if there are two variables X(income) and Y(non-durable consumption), the following equation can be considered for cointegrating test.

Figure 1

Correlogram of LOGWPRICEPAK

Included observations: 132 Sample: 1973:1 2005:4

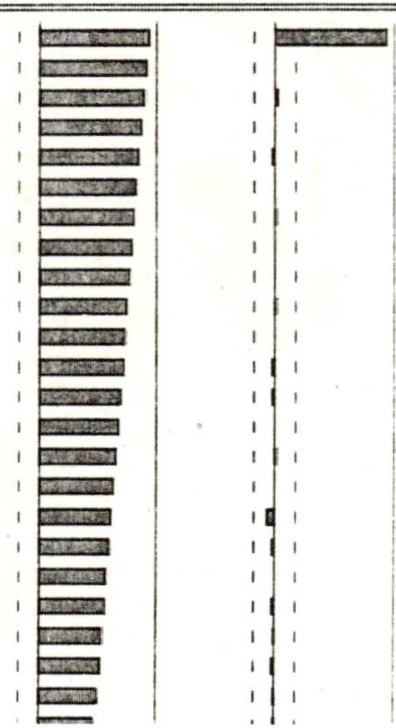

Autocorrelation / Partial Correlation (lag)	AC	PAC	Q-Stat	Prob
1	0.975	0.975	128.25	0.000
2	0.950	-0.002	250.97	0.000
3	0.927	0.025	368.73	0.000
4	0.904	0.002	481.76	0.000
5	0.881	-0.022	589.97	0.000
6	0.859	-0.004	693.53	0.000
7	0.837	0.009	792.75	0.000
8	0.817	0.006	887.90	0.000
9	0.797	0.005	979.20	0.000
10	0.778	0.016	1067.0	0.000
11	0.760	-0.004	1151.4	0.000
12	0.741	-0.021	1232.3	0.000
13	0.721	-0.019	1309.6	0.000
14	0.702	-0.007	1383.5	0.000
15	0.684	0.009	1454.1	0.000
16	0.666	-0.002	1521.7	0.000
17	0.645	-0.070	1585.6	0.000
18	0.623	-0.026	1645.8	0.000
19	0.602	-0.008	1702.5	0.000
20	0.580	-0.026	1755.6	0.000
21	0.558	-0.015	1805.2	0.000
22	0.536	-0.021	1851.4	0.000
23	0.514	-0.013	1894.2	0.000

Figure 2

Correlogram of LOGM1PAK

Included observations: 132 Sample: 1973:1 2005:4

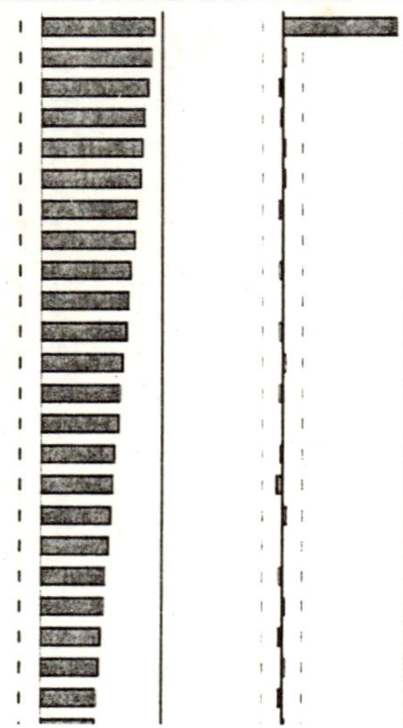

Autocorrelation / Partial Correlation (lag)	AC	PAC	Q-Stat	Prob
1	0.974	0.974	128.05	0.000
2	0.949	0.020	250.69	0.000
3	0.923	-0.046	367.55	0.000
4	0.897	-0.008	478.82	0.000
5	0.873	0.015	584.94	0.000
6	0.850	0.015	686.32	0.000
7	0.825	-0.042	782.69	0.000
8	0.802	0.006	874.40	0.000
9	0.778	-0.024	961.35	0.000
10	0.754	0.005	1043.9	0.000
11	0.730	-0.025	1121.9	0.000
12	0.708	0.020	1195.8	0.000
13	0.685	-0.030	1265.7	0.000
14	0.663	0.005	1331.6	0.000
15	0.641	-0.011	1393.8	0.000
16	0.617	-0.052	1451.9	0.000
17	0.596	0.034	1506.6	0.000
18	0.575	0.007	1557.9	0.000
19	0.554	-0.025	1606.0	0.000
20	0.535	0.009	1651.1	0.000
21	0.513	-0.040	1693.1	0.000
22	0.493	0.018	1732.2	0.000
23	0.473	-0.033	1768.5	0.000

Figure 3

Correlogram of LOGM2PAK

Included observations: 132 Sample: 1973:1 2005:4

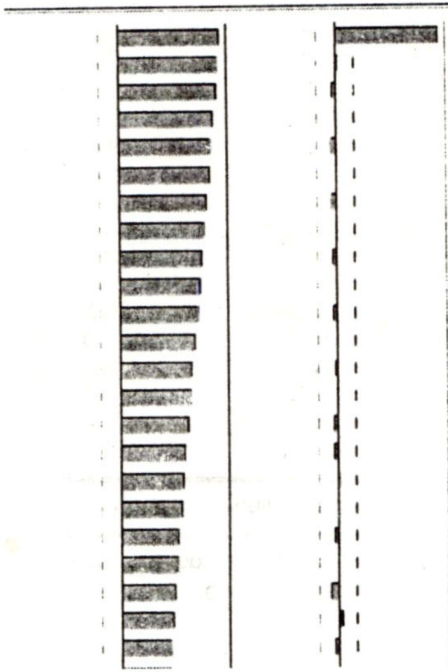

	AC	PAC	Q-Stat	Prob
1	0.976	0.976	128.73	0.000
2	0.954	0.018	252.63	0.000
3	0.931	-0.031	371.51	0.000
4	0.909	0.000	485.60	0.000
5	0.885	-0.044	594.57	0.000
6	0.861	0.002	698.71	0.000
7	0.837	-0.041	797.73	0.000
8	0.813	0.007	891.99	0.000
9	0.789	-0.018	981.48	0.000
10	0.766	0.001	1066.5	0.000
11	0.742	-0.022	1146.9	0.000
12	0.719	0.004	1223.1	0.000
13	0.696	-0.015	1295.1	0.000
14	0.674	0.003	1363.1	0.000
15	0.651	-0.018	1427.2	0.000
16	0.628	-0.025	1487.4	0.000
17	0.606	0.010	1543.9	0.000
18	0.585	0.006	1597.1	0.000
19	0.564	-0.026	1646.9	0.000
20	0.543	0.005	1693.5	0.000
21	0.520	-0.062	1736.6	0.000
22	0.500	0.035	1776.8	0.000
23	0.479	-0.020	1814.0	0.000

Figure 4

Correlogram of D1LOGWPRICEPAK

Included observations: 131 Sample: 1973:2 2005:4

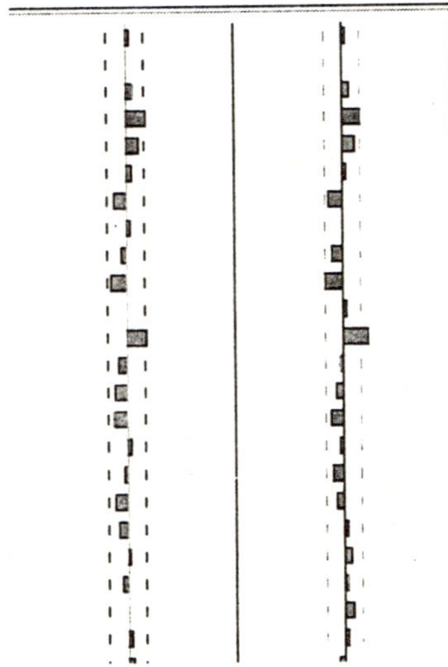

	AC	PAC	Q-Stat	Prob
1	0.038	0.033	0.1917	0.661
2	0.003	0.001	0.1926	0.908
3	0.068	0.063	0.8200	0.845
4	0.183	0.179	5.4392	0.245
5	0.130	0.123	7.7357	0.170
6	0.051	0.045	8.1281	0.229
7	-0.103	-0.132	9.6048	0.212
8	0.041	-0.007	9.8413	0.276
9	-0.046	-0.107	10.149	0.339
10	-0.149	-0.179	13.350	0.205
11	0.006	0.034	13.354	0.271
12	0.185	0.241	18.350	0.105
13	-0.090	-0.027	19.537	0.107
14	-0.113	-0.062	21.438	0.091
15	-0.127	-0.127	23.865	0.067
16	0.042	-0.043	24.135	0.087
17	-0.024	-0.104	24.225	0.113
18	-0.098	-0.061	25.721	0.106
19	-0.083	0.039	26.799	0.109
20	0.023	0.065	26.883	0.139
21	-0.048	0.022	27.250	0.163
22	-0.004	0.079	27.252	0.202
23	0.037	0.039	27.469	0.237

Figure 5

Correlogram of D1LOGM1PAK

Included observations: 131 Sample: 1973:2 2005:4

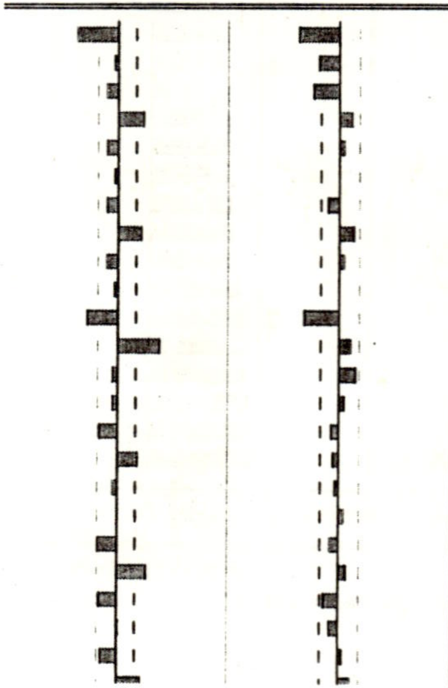

	AC	PAC	Q-Stat	Prob
1	-0.382	-0.382	19.569	0.000
2	-0.021	-0.195	19.627	0.000
3	-0.111	-0.238	21.314	0.000
4	0.248	0.122	29.742	0.000
5	-0.096	0.045	31.026	0.000
6	-0.025	-0.007	31.116	0.000
7	-0.095	-0.101	32.387	0.000
8	0.237	0.134	40.342	0.000
9	-0.106	0.037	41.932	0.000
10	-0.017	0.001	41.972	0.000
11	-0.281	-0.330	53.410	0.000
12	0.396	0.106	76.391	0.000
13	-0.057	0.144	76.867	0.000
14	-0.050	0.053	77.235	0.000
15	-0.158	-0.063	80.992	0.000
16	0.183	-0.050	86.043	0.000
17	-0.041	-0.034	86.294	0.000
18	0.005	0.036	86.298	0.000
19	-0.182	-0.080	91.476	0.000
20	0.267	0.065	102.64	0.000
21	-0.163	-0.138	106.87	0.000
22	0.028	-0.095	106.98	0.000
23	-0.145	0.028	110.38	0.000

Figure 6

Correlogram of DLOGM2PAK

Included observations: 131 Sample: 1973:2 2005:4

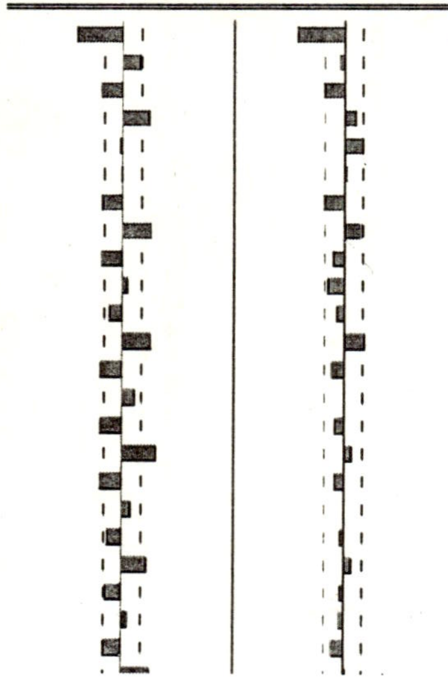

	AC	PAC	Q-Stat	Prob
1	-0.440	-0.440	25.991	0.000
2	0.164	-0.037	29.628	0.000
3	-0.208	-0.185	35.492	0.000
4	0.239	0.104	43.308	0.000
5	-0.019	0.173	43.358	0.000
6	-0.014	0.026	43.385	0.000
7	-0.182	-0.192	48.017	0.000
8	0.268	0.146	58.227	0.000
9	-0.204	-0.091	64.169	0.000
10	0.048	-0.151	64.504	0.000
11	-0.131	-0.060	66.979	0.000
12	0.264	0.194	77.155	0.000
13	-0.214	-0.101	83.904	0.000
14	0.099	0.002	85.374	0.000
15	-0.219	-0.087	92.567	0.000
16	0.314	0.068	107.51	0.000
17	-0.219	-0.078	114.85	0.000
18	0.087	-0.006	116.01	0.000
19	-0.145	-0.029	119.26	0.000
20	0.232	0.060	127.69	0.000
21	-0.166	-0.024	132.08	0.000
22	0.056	-0.035	132.57	0.000
23	-0.174	-0.114	137.48	0.000

$\varepsilon_t = Y_t = a - \beta X_t$ (*xviii*)

where ε_t is the residual. It ε_t the residual is stationary, the series Y and X are said to be cointegrated.

RESULTS OF COINTEGRATION STUDY

The Table 3 presents the results of study on the co-integrated relationship of variables concerned.

Table 3

Variables Dependent	*Independent*	*Constant*	*Trend*	*Orderof Co-integration*	*Dickey Fuller Test*
LogWP-Pak	Log (M1)	No	No	I(0)	-2.232185*
LogWP-Pak	Log (M2)	No	No	I(0)	-2.542921**

*Significant at five percent
** Significant at one percent

It is observed from the Table 3 that

(i) Log(wp pak) and log(M_1) are co-integrated of order zero i.e I(0). The co-integrating vector vector is significant at five percent.

(ii) Log(wp pak) and log(M_2) are also co-integrated of order zero i.e I(0). In this case the co-integrating vector is significant at one percent.

Granger Causality Tests

In the regression analysis, we regress dependent variable on independent variables by which we obtain a statistical relationship between the dependent variable and independent variables. Therefore, before regressing dependent variable on independent variables, we must establish a direction of causality. The 'Granger- Approach to Causality uses the past information of both variables. To test this causality, two-regression equations are set. To conduct the causality test between the money and price, we have used the following two equations both for narrow money as well as for broad money.

Dlog(W-price - pak)t = $\alpha+\beta_1$dlog(W price – pak)$_{t-1}$ + β_2 dlog(W price- price)$_{t-2}$ + $\beta_3$dlog(W price – pak)$_{t-3}$ + β_4 dlog(W price – pak)$_{t-4}$ +$\beta_t$dlogM_t + $\gamma_1$dlogm_{1t-1} + $\gamma_2$dlogM_{1t-2} + $\gamma_3$dlogM_{1t-3} +$\gamma_4$dlogM_{1t-4} +u_{1t}

And dlogM_{1t} = θ+$\delta_1$dlogM_{1t-1} + $\delta_2$dlogM_{1t-2} + $\delta_3$dlogM_{1t-3} + $\delta_4$dlogM_{1t-4}+$\pi_0$dlog(W price-pak)$_t$ + π_1 dlog(W price-pak)$_{t-1}$ + $\pi_2$dlog(W price-pak)$_{t-2}$ + $\pi_3$dlog(W price-pak)$_{t-3}$ +$\pi_4$dlog (W price-pak)$_{t-4}$ +u_{2t}

Similarly, the other equation used for the Granger Causality tests are

Dlog(W price-pak)$_t$= α_1 + $\psi_1$dlog(W price-pak)$_{t-1}$+ $\psi_2$dlog(W price-pak)$_{t-2}$ + $\psi_3$dlog(W price-pak)$_{t-3}$ + $\psi_4$dlog(W price-pak)$_{t-4}$ + $\eta_0$dlogM_{2t} + $\eta_1$dlogM_{2t-1} + $\eta_2$dlogM_{2t-2} + $\eta_3$dlogM_{2t-3} + $\eta_4$dlogM_{2t-4}+ u_{3t}

And dlogM_{2t} = α_2+$\psi_1$dlog M_{2t-1} + $\psi_2$dlogM_{2t-2}+ $\psi_3$dlogM_{2t-3}+ $\psi_4$dlogM_{2t-4} + $\rho_0$dlog(W price-pak)$_t$ + $\rho_1$dlog(W price-pak)$_{t-1}$ + $\rho_2$dlog (W price-pak)$_{t-2}$ + $\rho_3$dlog (W price-pak)$_{t-3}$+ $\rho_4$dlog (W price-pak)$_{t-4}$+u_{4t}

The null hypotheses and the test results are given below: -

Null Hypothesis:	Obs	F-Statistic	Probability
DLOGMT$_1$PAK does not Granger Cause DLOGWPRICEPAK	129	0.05472	0.94677
DLOGWPRICEPAK does not Granger Cause DLOGMT$_1$PAK		0.28468	0.75275

The above test presents the estimations for the model of Granger causality test. The F-statistic and its corresponding probability value show that the null hypothesis has been rejected with lag 2 for the series dlog w-price (pak) and dlogM_1 (narrow money). This indicates that price level and M_1 supply Granger cause each other. Similarly, Granger Causality Test has been conducted for M_2 money supply and price level. The results of the test are presented below.

Null Hypothesis:	Obs	F-Statistic	Probability
DLOGMT$_2$PAK does not Granger Cause DLOGWPRICEPAK	129	0.23376	0.79190
DLOGWPRICEPAK does not Granger Cause DLOGMT$_2$PAK		0.06949	0.93290

It is observed that F statistics in both the cases are insignificant. Consequently, the null hypotheses are rejected in both cases. This indicates that both M_2 and price level Granger Cause each other over the period concerned.

CONCLUSION

It is therefore, observed from our study that

(i) M_1, M_2 and price series display non-stationarity at the level and therefore, the relevant series contain unit roots.

(ii) M_1, M_2 and price level datasets attain stationarity upon first difference. The co-integrating ACFs and PACFs plots testify for stationarity.

(iii) M1 and price level datasets are co-integrated of order zero. The co-integrating vector is significant at five percent.

(iv) M_2 and price level datasets are also co-integrated of order zero. However, the co-integrating vector is significant at one percent. This indicates that M_2 money supply has stronger relation with price level in Pakistan than M_1 money supply.

(v) Both M_1 and Price level Granger cause each other.

(vi) Both M_2 money supply and price level also Granger cause each other. Consequently, there exists no unidirectional causality between M_1 and price level or M_2 money supply and price level.

REFERENCES

Enders, Walter. *Applied Econometrics Time series,* Singapore; John Wiley and sons, Inc. (1995).

Fuller, W. *Introduction to Statistical Time Series.* New York: John Wiley & Sons (1976).

Gujurathi, D.N. *Basic Econometrics,* Singapore: Mc Grow-Hill, Inc. (1995).

Garbade, K. " Two Methods for Examining the Stability of Regression Coefficients." *Journal of the American Statistical Association,* 72 (March 1977), 54-63.

Lee, S., and W. Li (1983), Money, Income, and Prices and Their Lead-lag Relationship in Singapore. *Singapore Economic Review,* April 73-87.

Pakistan, Government of (1998), 50 Years of Pakistan in Statistics.Islamabad: Federal Bureau of Statistics.

Pakistan, Government of (Various Issues) *Monthly Statistical Bulletin.* State Bank of Pakistan.

Phillips, R., and P. Perron (1998), Testing for a Unit Root in Time Series Regression. *Biometrika,* June 335-346.

Schwert, W. (1987), Effects of Model Specification on Tests for Unit Roots in Macroeconomic Data. *Journal of Monetary Economics,* July,73-103.

Sims, C. (1972), Money, Income, and Causality. *American Ecomic Review,* September 540-552.

Williams, W., C. Goodhart, and D. Gowland (1976), Money, Income and Causality: The U.K. Experience. *American Economic Review,* June, 417-423.

——,1981, Some Properties of Time Series Data and Their Use in Econometric Model Specification, *Journal of Econometrics* 16, 121-130.

———1992, Maximum Likelihood Estimation of Stationary Univariate Fractional Integrated Time Series Models, *Journal of Econometrics* 53, 165-188.

Yajima, Yoshihiro, 1988, On Estimation of a Regression Model with Long – Memory Stationary Errors, *Annals of Statistics* 16, 791-807.

Anil Bhuimali & Kamanad Dev

10

WILDLIFE TOURISM IN NEPAL: PROBLEMS AND PROSPECTS

INTRODUCTION

According to Malcom Hunter's lively short history, the term, "wildlife" is less than a century old and was not included in major dictionaries before 1961 in the United State and before 1986 in the United Kingdom (Hunter; 1990). Ominously, its first use was in a book published in 1913 called 'Our Vanishing Wildlife' which foreshadowed the conversation crisis apparent during the second half of the 20th century while this work defined wildlife primarily in terms of game species. It also includes vertebrate species not regarded as game but perceives as subject to human harvesting or culling. Later definition of wildlife often emphases game animals while other includes all non-domesticated verteberate and in some cases, invertebrates and plants. In general, it is used in various senses. Strictly speaking, it should denote the entire flora and fauna of the region aquatic as well as terrestrial, including the whole range of plants from fungi to forest trees and invertebrate as well as vertebrate life (H, Julian, 1961).

In general, Wildlife tourism encompasses all forms and scales of tourism that involves the enjoyment of natural areas and wildlife, e.g., bird watching, wildlife viewing, photographic and walking safaris, reef diving, whale watching, trophy hunting and sport fishing. Wildlife tourism may be achieved through many different forms of transport, including on foot, by vehicle, boat or ballon.

Wildlife tourism is an important component of the international and domestic tourism industry. Overall depending on the region, wildlife tourism accounts for 20 to 40 percent of international tourism (Fillion et al, 1992; Giongo et al. 1993, CEP 1994). The scale of wildlife tourism is even larger if domestic wildlife tourism is taken into consideration. However, statistics are often not available to determine what proportion of wildlife tourism is domestic in origin, but it is likely to be very high in some countries. For example, nationals make up around 15 to 25 percent of wildlife tourists in Canada (Filion et al, 1992), and some 90 percent of visitors to the national park in Thailand, India and South Africa (Ceballos-Lascurian 1996). Wildlife tourism in United States is now the fastest growing sector of the tourism industry with annual growth rate of 25-30 percent (Jackson, 1996). Wild tourism currently accounts for 10 percent of international tourism (Pleymaroni, 1994) with its global value in 1988 estimated as high as US $1 Trillion (Filion et,al 1992)

As with tourism generally, wild tourism is likely to increase in importance and scale (Gingo et al. 1993,). Furthermore, it may also attract an increasing market share, as suggested by a number of surveys indicating an increasing interest in wildlife among tourists. A 1994 Gallup survey found that the employment of wildlife was a priority for 90 percent of UK holiday makers, while a 1992 study for the Canadian wildlife service of a variety of destinations found that wildlife was a prime attraction for 32 percent of tourists to Australia, 80 percent to Kenya and Zimbabwe, 30 to 64 percent to North America; 9 to 60 percent to Latin America (Mexico, Belize, Dominica, Costa Rica and Ecuador) and approximately 50 percent to Europe (Risk and policy analysis Ltd. 1996).

NEPAL, A HOTSPOT IN WILDLIFE

Nepal, a land locked mountain kingdom nestling among the Himalyas, is the lure of tourists and travelers of all kinds. It is located between 26°22′ and 30°27′ North latitude and 80°4′ and 88°12′ East longitude. About 77 percent of total land area is covered bv mountain hills and, rest 23 percent areas lie in the

Terai region (C1BS, 2004). Nepal is one of the richest countries in the world in terms of bio-diversity due to its unique geographical position and latitudinal variation. The elevation of the country ranges from 60m above sea level to the highest point on earth, Mt. Everest at 8,848m all within a distance of 150 km with climatic conditions ranging from subtropical to arctic. The wild variation fosters an incredible variety of eco-systems, the greatest mountain range on earth, thick tropical jungles teeming with a wealth of wildlife, thundering rivers, forested hills and frozen valleys (NTB, 2003).

The country like Nepal has abundant nature based and man made resources to promote wildlife tourism in the country. Though it occupies only 0.1 percent of earth but it shares 2 percent of all the flowering plants in the world; 8 percent of the world's population of birds (more than 848 species); 4 percent of mammals on earth; 11 of the world's15 families of butterflies (more than 500 species); and the home of 600 indigenous plant families and 319 species of exotic orchids (NTB, 2003). Nepal's bio-diversity is a reflection of its unique geographical position, and altitudinal and climate variations. Nepal's location in the centre of the Himalayas makes it a traditional zone between the Eastern and Western Himalayas, representing the palaeoarctic and the Indo-Malayan biographical regions and the major floristic province of Asia. It is also well-known for its greenery as well as natural habitat which attract a large number of biologists and ecologists for study. Tourism is one of the fastest growing industry in Nepal. It is an important source of foreign exchange earning as well as a source of employment opportunity. It was recorded that tourism sector provided direct employment to 80,000 people in 2001 and was contributed 12 percent and 3.1 percent to the total foreign currency earning and in total GDP respectively in the same year(Tenth Plan,2002-2007).

FOREST RESOURCES

The forest is on of the main source of wildlife tourism in Nepal. It can be classified into four major types on the basis of altitude and composition, which comprises about 29 percent of total land area of the country (CBS, 2003).

(a) Tropical Deciduous Monsoon Forest

This includes the Terai and the broad flat valleys or Duns found between successive hill ranges. The dominant tree species of this area are Sal, Semal, Asna, Dalbergla spp and other species, and pinus rosburghi occurring on the higher ridges of the Churia hills, which in places reach an altitude of 1800m. This tropical zone is richest area for wildlife, with gaurs, buffaloes, four species of deer, tigers, leopards and other animals found in the forest areas rhinoceros; swamp deer and hot deer found in the valley grassland and two species of crocodile and the Gangetic dolphin inhabiting the rivers. The principal birds are the peacock, jungle fowl and black partridge, while migratory duck and geese swarm on the ponds and lakes and big river of Terai.

(b) Subtropical Mixed Evergreen Forest

This includes the Mahabharat Lekh, which rises to a height of about 2400m and comprises the outer wall of the Himalayan range. Great River such as the Karnali, Narayani and Sapta kosi flow through this area into the broad plains of the Terai. Among the tree species characteristics of this region are Castenopsis Indica in association with Schima Wallichii, and other species such as Alnus nepalensis. The variety and abundance of the flora and fauna increase progressively with decreasing altitude and increasing luxuriance of the vegetation. This zone is generally poor in wild life. The only mammals, which are at all widely distributed, are wild bear, barking deer, serow, ghoral and bears. Different varieties of birds are also found in this zone.

(c) Temperate Evergreen Forest

Northward, on the lower slopes and spurs of the great Himalayas, Oaks and Pines are the dominant species up to an altitude of about 2400m above which are found dense conifer forests including picea, Tuseg, Larix and Abies spp. The wildlife of this region includes the Himalayan bear, serow, , ghoral, barking deer and wild boar, with Himalayan Tahr sometimes being seen on steep rocky faces above 244m. The red panda is among the more interesting of the mammals found in this zone. It appears to be fairly distributed in suitable areas of the forest above 1800m. The rich and varied avifauna of this region includes several spectacular and beautiful. Theasants, including the Danphe pheasant, Nepal national bird. Nepal, therefore, is unique in being a blend of three distinct types of fauna, which reflects enormous potentiality of wild tourism.

PROTECTED AREAS AND WILDLIFE RESERVES

Protected areas are perhaps the prime sites for wildlife tourism since they offer some guarantee of maintaining their attraction in the long term through a strong legislative regime. Nepal's rich bio-diversity renders to deal as an eco-tourism as well as wildlife tourism destination. The 18.33 percent of the country's total land accounts for its sixteen protected wildlife areas across the country. Among these, nine are designated as national parks three are wildlife reserves, three are conservation areas and one is a hunting reserve (NPWC, 2003)

Royal Chitwan National Park

The Royal Chitwan National Park offers a wilderness of rich ecosystem that includes mammals, birds, reptiles and water animals of several kinds. It is little surprising that this is one of the most popular and most frequented parts of the country. Owing to its rich adornment of nature, the park was declared UNESCO Natural Heritage Site in 1979, covering an area of 932 sq.km, the park includes hilly areas of Shivalik range covered by deciduous forests. One fifth of the park is made up of flood plains of the Narayani,Rapti, and the Renu rivers. There are around 600 plants, 50 mammals, 526 birds and 49 amphibians, reptiles found in the park. The highlights, of course are the 500 Asian one-horned rhinoceros and some 100 nocturnal Royal Bengal tigers that live in the dense forests of the park. Sharing home with these are other animals like rhesus monkey, grey langur, deer, leopards, wild boar, wild dogs and wild cats, the white Sockinged gaur (the world's largest wild cattle) and many other smaller animals. The swampy areas and numerous oxbow lakes of Chitwan provide a home for marsh crocodile. In a stretch of the Narayani river is found one of the few remaining populations of the rare and endangered fish-only eating gharial, or Gangetic crocodile.A rare attraction is world's fresh water dolphinsn variety sometimes seen in river Narayani.

Shey Phoksundo National Park

It is the largest national park and covers 3.555 sq.km. Sitting astride the Dolpa and Mugu districts of Western Nepal. The park was established to protect the trans-Himalayan ecosystem found only in few areas of country. The unique park includes the Kanjiroba Himal, with many peaks of over 6,000m, as well as the famous shey Monastery, the Phoksundo Lake and the Langu Gorge. The wildlife of Shey- phoksundo includes a good population of blue sheep and ghoral, muskdeer, leopard, wild dog, wolf, marmot, weasel, mouse hare, rhesus and langur monkeys. The adjoining Tibetan region is home to such rare animals as the great Tibetan sheep, Tibetan wild ass, Tibetan gazelle and antelope, and wild yak. Bird species of the park include the Impeyan and cheer pheasant, chough, raven, Tibetan snow cock, Tibetan twit, brown dipper, Himalayan griffon and lammergeier.

Langtang National Park

It is one of the most unspoiled national parks of Nepal. Situated to North of Kathmandu, it is the most easily accessible highland sanctuary from the capital. Langtang covers 1.710 sq. km, forming the upper catchment areas of two of Nepal's largest river systems- the Trishuli and khoshi. The animals,common to these forests are wild boar, Himalayan black, bear, ghoral, grey langur monkey and leopard. The rare Himalayan honey guide has been sighted here and the park is also the home for Impeyan, Tragopan and kalij phesants amoung others. Larch, a rare deciduous conifer, is also found in the forest of lower Lantang valley. Further-up, Himalayan tahr, musk deer and snow leopard are also found in this park.

Makalu-Barun National Park and Conservation Area

It is situated in the Sankhuwasabha and Solukhumbu district in West Nepal. The park covers 2,330 sq. kms and on of the prime attractions for visitors to the park is its offer to experience the unique Himalayan bio-diversity. There are 47 varieties of orchids, 67 species of bamboos, 15 oaks including Arkhoulo, 86 species of food fodder trees and 48 species of primrose. Over 400 species of birds have been sighted in the Makalu-Barun area, including two species never before seen in Nepal, the spotted wrenbabbler and the olive ground warbler. Wildlife includes the endangered red panda, musk deer, Himalayan black bear, clouded leopard and possibly Snow leopard, in addition to more substantial populations of ghoral, thar, wild boar, barking deer, Himalayan marmot weasel, common langur monkey and the serow.

Royal Bardia National Park

It is situated on the Eastern banks of the Karnali river, about 400 kms. west of Kathmandu. The park is 968 sq. kms. in area and extends from the Churia hills Southward to the gentle slopes of the 'Bhabhar'. Bardia is the home of a wide variety of animals, many of which live in and around the phants. The most conspicuous of which is the spotted deer. Other ungulates include block buck, hog deer, samber deer, wildboar and barasingha or swamp deer. The park is famous for its small herds of wild elephants which are rarely seen. The park also boasts a small population of the rare gharial, the marsh mugger crocodile and the Gangetic dolphin. The karnali and Babai rivers attract a large number of wintering waterfowl along with resident species such as herons, kingfishers and wall creepers. More than 350 bird species have been recorded in Bardia, truly a bird watcher's paradise.

Sagarmatha Nation Park

This park was declared a world Heritage site in 1979 which includes Mt. Everest (8,848 M.) and other high peaks such as Lhotse Shar Cho oyu Ama Dablam, Pumori Kangtega etc. Sagarmatha National Park is 1,148 sq.km in area and consists of the upper catchment areas of the Dudh Koshi, Bhote Koshi and the Imja Khola rivers. Much of the park lies above 3,000m. Sagarmatha is rugged, with deep gorges, glaciers and unnegotiable ice and rock faces. Tree such as rhododendron, birch, blue pine, juniper and silver are found upto an altitude of 4,000 meters. Wildlife most likely to be seen in Sagarmatha is the Himalaya tahr, ghoral, musk deer, pikka (mouse hare) weasel and occasionally jackal. Other rarely seen animals are Himalayan black bear, wolf, lynx and snow leopard, Birds commonly seen are Impeyan pheasant, blood pheasant, snow cock, snow pigeon, red billed and yellow billed chough, Himalayan griffin vulture and lammergeier.

Khaptad National Park

A newest park area is in the middle hills of the Far-West of the country. The 225 sq. kms. area of the park is situated where the district Bajhang, Bajura, Doti and Achham meet. Khaptad is plateau of grassland and forest cover at an elevation of about 3,000 meters. This habitat provides good cover for bear, leopard, barking and musk deer, as well as birds like the Impeyan, Kokals and Kalij pheasants. At the north eastern corner of the park, a small serene lake and swampy area called khapted Daha is religious site where Hindu pilgrims come to worship Shiva on the full moon of July-August each year.

Rara National Park

This is Nepal's smallest and most scenic national park situated about 370 km. north-west of Kathmandu. It covers the area of 106 sq km. Lies at an altitude of about 3,000 meters forested by conifers. The biggest lake in Nepal, which is known as Mahendra Tal also lie here. The habitat supports animals like the red panda, black bear, yellow-throated martin, ghoral, serow and musk deer. The lake attracts migrant wildfowl like teals, Pochards and mallards. Resident birds include the Impeyan, Kalij and blood pheasant as well as others like chukkor partridge.

Shivpuri National Park

The Shivpuri Park (144 sq. km) is the major watershed supplying drinking water to the capital city of Kathmandu. Lying in the transition between the subtropical and temperate climatic zones, its diverse vegetation is composed of pine, oak, rhododendron and others. The park is rich in wild mushrooms

(129 species). The wildlife found in the national park includes Himalayan black bear, leopard, jungle cat and rhesus monkeys. The park is home to over 177 species of birds including 9 threatend species, over 100 species of butterflies including rare and threatend.

Royal Sukla Phanta Wildlife Reserve

The wildlife reserve is situated in the extreme south-west of Nepal. The name of the park is derived from the largest grassland which is known as Sukla- phanta. The park area is 155 sq. kms. and would be 305 sq. kms. after the completion of its extension.

The reserve now shelters almost 2,000 swamp deer, around 50 wild elephant and 30 tigers. Other animals found here are spotted deer, blue bulls, barking deer, hog deer, wild boars, leopards, jackals, langurs and rhesus monkeys. Among the birds the reserve provides habitat to sarus crane, swamp francolin, grass owl and the endangered Bengal Florican. Reptiles species include marsh mugger, crocodile, cobra and python.

Parsa Wildlife Reserve

The Parsa Wildlife Reserve provides a rare opportunity to experience the nature and culture to Nepal's terai. The reserve covers 499 sq. kms, spread over parts of Chitwan, Makawanpur, Parsa and Bara districts. The vegetation is tropical and subtropical mostly covered with sal forests while the hills are covered with chir, pine, khar, silk cotton are found along water areas. The reserve provides good habitat for animals like wild elephant, tiger leopard, sloth bear, blue bull and wild dog. Other common animals in the reserve are samber, chital, hog deer, jungle cat, langur monkey etc. There are 527 species of birds in the reserve; one being the endangered great hornbill found in certain parts of the forest. Other bird species include peafowl, red jungle fowl, and wood peackers. Birds and animals apart the reserve also habitats snakes like king cobra, common cobra, krait and Python.

Koshi Tappu Wildlife Reserve

This wildlife reserve has carved a place for itself as a birdwatcher's paradise. The reserve covers the area of 175 sq.

kms and spreads over Saptari and Sunsari districts in East Nepal. The reserve had been recognized as a wetland site from 1987. The vegetation of the reserve is mainly grassland with patches of scrub and deciduous reverie forests. The reserve has recorded around 439 species of bird variety, some of which fly all the way from Siberia during winter. A wide variety of ducks, herons, storks, egrets, and ibis are seen on the riverbanks. Koshi Tappu Reserve also has one of the few elephant stables of Asia. Other animals found here are wild buffalo, wild boar, hog deer, spotted deer, blue bell and jackals, Gharial Crocodile and Gangetic dolphin are other attraction.

Annapurna Conservation Area

This conservation area has been claimed as one of the best trekking areas in the world. It is also the most visited trekking area in the country. Beginning 790 meters, the area reaches as high as 8.091 meters of Mt. Annapurna. Ghandruk is the first experience and further down is Ghorepani that provides fantastic panoramic view of the Annapurna ranges. The vegetation in this region includes various species of orchids and rhododendron, wildlife includes around 100 different kinds of mammals including rare snow leopards and blue sheep. The region also boasts of around 478 species of birds including multi coloured Impheyan kokals and blood pheasants. In addition the region is also home to 39 species of reptiles and 22 species of amphibians.

Kanchanjunga Conservation Area

This conservation area belt lies below Mt. Kanchanjunga. The reason with its alpine grasslands, rocky outcrop, low river valleys, temperate and subtropical forests is situated in Taplejung district that borders with the Tibetan Autonomous Region of China. The KCA has been selected as one of the 200 global eco-regions recognized by world wildlife fund. Ten species among Nepal's 20 indigenous gymnosperms species and 15 among Napal's 28 endemic flowering plants are found in this region. Wildlife includes endangered snow leopard, Himalayan black bear, musk deer, red panda, blue sheep and rhesus macow. About 202 species of different birds including

Impheyan pheasant, red billed blue magpie, are found in the area.

Manaslu Conservation Area

The Manaslu area in Gorkha district is a classic setting to experience pristine mountain nature and culture. The conservation area starts at 600 meters and is crowned by the eight highest peak in the world Mt. Manaslu at 8,163 meters. The region is home to 29 species of mammals including snow leopard, musk deer and Himalayan Tahr. There are over 20 species of birds and three species of reptiles. Vegetation includes 200 species of plants, more than 50 of which are useful for various purposes.

Dhorpatan Hunting Reserve

It is the only area in Nepal where licensed hunting is allowed. The reserve adjoins Myagdi district and Baglung district, spreading over an area of 1,325 sq. kilometers, the reserve begins at 3,000 meters reaching as high as 7,000 meters. One of the prime attractions for hunters is blue sheep, which is abundant in the area. Hunters also get pheasants and partridges in viable populations for hunting. Other animals found here are leopard, ghoral, serow, Himalayan black bear, barking deer etc. Endangered animals in the reserve are musk deer, wolf, red panda, cheer pheasant and Danphe.

BIRD WATCHING NEPAL

Nepal, unlike any parts of the world is considered as a paradise for bird lovers and ornithologists. Nepal only accommodates more than 848 species of the birds in the world. It is more than 8 percent of the world total. The Kathmandu valley and the surroundings, which has historic as well as the cultural value has almost 500 species. The major sites popular for bird watching could be counted as shivpuri conservation area, Nagarkot, Phulchoki area, Godavari area, Nahgarjun area, Bagmati River side, Taudaha among others in Kathmandu valley. Among them phulchoki hill, the highest peak of the valley rim situated 20 km southeast of Kathmandu is the most popular bird watching spot with some 265 species recorded.

Regularly recorded species include Besra, Black Eagle, Mountain Hawk-Eagle, Kalij pheasant, common Hill Partridge, Ashy Woodpigeon, Mountain scops owl, Collared owlet, Golden throated Barbet among others and a further 55 species have been known to visit the area as migratory or occasional visitors. Outside of Kathmandu valley, Chitwan National park, Bardia National Park and Makalu Barun National Park & Conservation Area are considered as the best places for the same. Chitwan National Park offers more than 450 species of birds including the endangered birds are the Bengal florican, Giant horn bill, lesser florican, black stork. Moreover, more than 45 species of amphibians and reptiles are visible into park. Chitwan National Park offers many finest lodges for the accommodation inside as well as outside the park area. One can stay as per his requirements to enjoy the bird watching.

Bardia National Park, which is consider as the best National Park after Chitwan National Park, which is truly a bird watcher paradise. Similarly Makalu-Barun National Park & Conservation Area, Shuklaphanta Wildlife Reserve, Koshi Tappu Wildlife Reserve, Shey phoksundo National Park are equally rich in many species of birds. Phewa Tal and Begnas Tal and the surrounding areas in Pokhara are highly famous for the bird lover. Terraced hills and light forest surround the lake. One should spend time on the slopes and wet fields. Birds sighted here are Ducks, Pheasant-tailed jacana; Hoppie Grey Bellied Tesias, common pintail snipe, bulbuls, etc.

PROBLEMS AND CHALLENGES

It is obvious from the above fact that the wildlife and natural habitats of Nepal are major natural resources of the region. Its wildlife, unique in abundance and variety, is the wonder of the rest of the world, but it was gravely affected in the past due to deforestation. So, to make a balance in ecology and to minimize the environment effects, the activities of deforestation should be stopped. Deforestation destroys the natural beauty, climate, rare animals and birds of the economy and, ultimately it will have bad impact on tourism.

Despite this problem some national parks and wildlife reserves are not fully managed as per the requirement of international standard due to which a few national park and conservation areas could have been marketed in Nepal. Data for 2000 indicated that the chitwan National Park attracted about 16.5 percent of total visitors arrived in the country. Annapurna conservation area drew 65 percent followed by Sagarmatha National Park about 9 percent (NTB, 2003104). So, for the promotion and conservation of wildlife tourism in Nepal, all the National Park including wildlife reserve, conservation areas and bird watching resort should have facilitated with all the amenities for visitors. Such as Jungle lodge, safari park and resort and creative enrichment of drinking, feeding, dewelling sites and comping ground and trekking facilities etc. will be helpful to provide wildlife experiences, if possible include photographic darkrooms and information and advice centre is highly desirable. There should have some parks for small animals like reptiles and butterfly that would be a welcome experience for the tourists. National parks should also of course be provided with Modern equipment and with adequate staff enable to carry out their function efficiently. If properly planned and sited, access roads can introduce visitors to new aspects of a country's scenery and natural beauty. The road from the Kenya coast to the Tsavo park was planned to give over the chyulu Hills, with views so beautiful that they aroused enthusiasm among the staff and workers, both African and European. All national parks should also have a museum with maps and relief-models, explanatory diagrams and pictorial charts, study collections, exhibition collection of the main interesting animals and plant, fossils, geological specimens and diagrams, meteorological, historical, archaeological material, and a sector devoted to various aspects of conservation. Such museums, if well arranged, and if a curator or a park warden is available to answer questions and give advice, can be of the greatest service to visitors, and can act as a valuable adjunct to the country's educational and museums system as well as a local base for research. 'Treetops' venture in Kenya is an excellent example of such a venture where visitors can spend the night in a tree shelter with the certainty of seeing and hearing a variety of wildlife at close quarters.

A trained guide or a tour operator is also an important ingredient of successful wildlife tour. Such guides who have been operated tour for the guests in different National Parks and wildlife reserves are ill trained and less skilled in their activities. Most of them do not even recognize wild animals beyond a few common ones. They require six months or one year certificate course supported by a weakened workshop will make them trained guide or tour operator. Their knowledge will make them more confident and more enthusiastic. They may even be taught to make detailed records of animals sighted for creating a research database. Such a database will not only be interesting for tourists, but also help for planning and managing wildlife encounters. The tour guides should also be able to highlight the importance of wildlife in terms of conservation and ecosystem function, interesting features of wildlife natural history. Conservation threats faced by wildlife, current wildlife management issues for important species and day to day activities. Moreover the guides and tour operators should be familiarized with modern technology as it has enhanced dramatically our capacity to provide real life experience to the tourists.

Similarly all park systems should have at least one trained biologist on their staff.They should carryout research themselves and should provide research facilities for visiting scientists. A beginning in this direction is being made in Uganda, where the two National Parks are being provided with small laboratories as field research centres.

One of the major challenges for wild tourism as a whole is how to ensure that protected areas are financially self-sufficient without detracting from their primary function of preserving biodiversity and natural value (child, 1996) to achieve this. It is usually necessary to encourage private sector investment and provide local communities with a vested interest in wildlife tourism. Increasingly, it is recognised that effectively local participation is an essential element of sustainable wildlife management, linking wildlife tourism to conservation with development (Giongo et al, 1993, HED, 1994)

Conclusion

Wildlife tourism, in the context of Nepal is a recent phenomenon. Nepal is fortunate in being endowed by nature the unique resources of its wildlife and natural habitats. It is incredibly diverse, its greenery and biodiversity are of international importance. The sixteen protected wildlife areas are designated across the country in a view to conserve them so as it can yield profit in the form of foreign currency. But those National Parks and wildlife reserves except few are either ill managed or not in a way to afford accommodation and basic amenities for the visitors due to the lack of financial resources. If the National Parks and wildlife reserves of Nepal are efficiently managed and intelligently developed, they could become chosen places of world pilgrimage, where people of every race, creed and colour will come to learn, to admire, and to enjoy.

REFERENCES

CEP (1994), *Ecotourism in the wider Caribbean, Region*– An Assessment Caribbean Environment Programme/United Nations Environment Programme, Nairobi.

Ceballos – Lascurain. H. (1996), *Tourism, Ecotourism and Protected Area.* World Conservation Union (IUCN). Gland and Cambridge.

Child. G. (1996), *The wildlife Manager's Perspective of Tourism.* In ODA African Wildlife Policy Consultation. Final Report, London: Overseas Development Administration.

CBS (2004), *Statistical year Book of Nepal,* 2004, HMG, Central Bureau of Statistics, Kathmandu.

Departmental Document (2003), Department of National Park and wildlife conservation, Kathmandu.

Departmenatal Document (2002), Department of Forest and Soil Conservation, Ministry of Forest and Soil Conservation, Kathmandu.

Fillion, F. L, Foley, J. P. and Jacquemot., A. J. (1992), *The Economics of Global Ecotourism,* Paper Presented at the IUCN IVth world

Congress on Parks and Protected Areas, Venezuela, 10-21 February, 1992.

Giongo, E, Bosco – Nizeye, J. and Wallace, G.N. (1993), A study of visitor Management in the world's *National Park and Protected Area,* Colorod State University.

HED (1994), Whose Eden? *An Overview of community Approaches to Wildlife* Management, International Institute of Environmental and Development, London, H,Julian. (1961): *The Conservation of Wild life and Natural Habitats in Central and East Africa,* UNESCO, Place de Fontenoy, Paris.

Joshi, S. (1999), *An Introduction to Nepalese Economy,* 1999. Nabin Prakasan, Bhotahily, Kathmandu

Jackson, J.J, (1996), *An International Perspective on Trophy Hunting,* In N, leader – Williams, J, A. kayera and G.I. overton (Eds), Turist Hunting in Tanzania (P.P. 7-11) World conservation Union (IUCN), Gland and cCambridge.

Lott, D.F, and Mccoy, M. (1995) : Asian Rhinos (Rhinoceros Unicornis) on the Run? *Impact of Tourist on one population, Biological conservation* 73, 23-36.

NIB, (2003104), *Annual operational Plan,* 2003-2004; Nepal Tourism Board, Tourist Service Centre, Bhrikuti Mandal, Kathmandu.

Pleumarom, A. (1994), *The Political Economy of Tourism. The Ecologist,* 24(4), 142-147.

Risk and Policy Analysis Ltd. (1996), Conservation and Development Benajits of the Wildlife Track Report to this Wildlife and Conakry side Directorate Department, London. Website-www.welcomenepal.com

Tenth Plan (2002/2007), National Planning Commission, HMG, Nepal.

Chandan Kumar Mukhopadhyay, Shankar Prasad Acharya & Arjun Kumar Baral

11

TWIN DEFICIT HYPOTHESIS: AN EMPIRICAL INVESTIGATION ON NEPALESE TIME SERIES 1964-2000

INTRODUCTION

Nepal has experienced nearly a five decades of planned economy since 1956. Prior to mid 80s, she had adopted almost controlled economy with decisive government even in fixing day-to-day commodity prices through public enterprises. Government had an influential role not only to the socio-political issues but also to the economic matters too. Thus government had a sole power in promulgating and implementing monetary, fiscal, financial, industrial, pricing, exchange, trade, and other relevant economic policies for the nation. Central bank was not autonomous. Role of the private sector was not recognized and deemed almost negligible.

While, as a severe balance of payment (BOP) crisis appeared in 1989, she had formally started liberalization by devaluating her currency significantly (nearly 15 percent). Afterwards, banks were allowed to quote their rate of return and cost of fund at their own discretion. Exchange rate quoting system had been jumped to partial convertibility regime first to full convertibility regime on current account later on. Economic policies (fiscal as well as monetary) were transformed. Structural adjustment policy (SAP), structural adjustment facility (SAF), extended structural adjustment facility (ESAF) programs were launched in collaboration with IMF and World Bank. Industrial policies were renewed followed by open general license (OGL) system in foreign trade. Now, she has obtained membership of WTO. Despite the efforts of all these reforms, Nepal has been facing almost continuous budget deficit and trade deficit simultaneously.

Referring the macroeconomic phenomenon, budget deficit (BD) had affected trade deficit (TD) to move positively during 1980s and early 1990s in USA and then political economists had given its name as inseparable twins. Martin Feldstein had popularized this behavior first time (1985) in USA. There was a hypothesis there that BD was the cause of TD since its secular type of positive relationship observed empirically too at that period in USA. Afterwards, there had been performed numerous empirical tests across the countries over the world. In Nepal's case, this hypothesis hasn't been tested empirically. So, this research work deems pertinent to verify its presence or non-presence in the Nepalese context.

Derivation of twin deficit symptom normally follows the following path in macroeconomic literature:

(a) $Y = C + I + G + (X - M)$[1]

(b) $Y = C + S + T$

(S stands for Saving & T for Taxes)

(c) $C + I + G + (X - M) = C + S + T$

(By substituting equation a on b)

(d) $(I - S) + (G - T) - (M - X) = 0$

(e) $(I - S) + (G - T) = (M - X)$

(By manipulation)

The three terms in the equation (e) can now be explained as,

(f) $(I - S)$ implies Domestic Saving Deficit

(g) $(G - T)$ implies Budget (Fiscal) Deficit

(h) $(M - X)$ implies External Trade Deficit

If the sign changes in the concerned deficits, the drama turns to a situation of deficits to surpluses. However, excess surpluses are also subjects of other debates because of their demerits. The equation (e) doesn't turn until and unless as like the form of the equation $(I - S) = (M - X) + (T - G)$, budget deficit and trade deficit always behave as twins implying budget deficit being the source of financing of trade deficit where investment and saving are not responsive to policy shocks or where investment and saving have fairly negligible role in the economy due to high level of consumption.

By this assumption, our empirical model forms as –

$$TD = a + bBD + U \qquad (i)$$

TDH had especially been made more popular and gone through series of empirical investigations after the emergence of secular nature of simultaneous movement of the twins in the United States from the early 1980s. In economic literature, lot many researches focused on the inter-link between twin deficits. Research scholar, Mr. Olga Vyshnyak of National University "Kyiv-Mohyla Academy", Ukraine has mentioned following results from literature review in his research paper on *Twin Deficit Hypothesis: the Case of Ukraine.*

Opposing view to TDH has been proposed as Ricardian Equivalence Hypothesis (REH). This proposition conveys that any change in government tax does not affect real interest rates and quantity of investments and current account deficit. It is because of rational expectation of the taxpayers. They assume that present tax cut is a future burden and government would extract it ultimately in the future so that they start saving meeting future burden.

Olga Vyshnyak (2001) for Ukraine, Elif Akbostanci and Gul Ipec Tunk (2002) and Ahmet Zengin (2001) for Turkey; Daniel L. Thornton (2003) for 16 OECD countries, Komerandi (1983) and Carlous Fonseca Marinheiro (2001) for Portuguese data have verified the TDH and found that their econometric models supported TDH for these countries. Mamdouh Alkswani (2000) has found reverse impact for petroleum economy in contrast to TDH and found supported that TD was the source of BD for Saudi Arabia.

Abdulnasser Hatimi-J and Ghaji Shukur (2001) have tested TDH for US data with testing the causality direction between through US twin deficits using quarterly US data from 1975Q1 to 1998Q2 from IFS with multivariate Rao's F test and bootstrap test applying VAR (2)[3] and they found very interesting result that twin deficits do not Granger cause each other for whole sample period. While identifying structural break and using sub-periods data separately, first sub-period time supports BD Granger cause CAD wile second sub-period supports CAD Granger cause BD. Thus it can be inferred that the 'Lucas

Critique' might have been in effect due to internal policy shifts and international economic shocks.

Table 1[2]
Relationship between Twin Deficits

Authors/s	*Sample Countries*	*Results/Findings*
Darrat (1988)	USA	Bi-directional causality between TD & BD.
Bahmani-Oskooee (1989)	USA	Unidirectional causality from BD to CAD.
Latif-Zaman & DaCosta (1990)	USA	Unidirectional causality from BD to CAD.
Enders & Lee (1990)	USA	Positive innovation in government debt is associated with an increase in consumption spending and in the CAD.
Zietz & Pemberton (1990)	USA	BD was transmitted to the TD primarily through the impact on imports.
Bachman (1992)	USA	Unidirectional causality from BD to CAD
Mohammadi & Skaggs (1996)	USA	Maximum effect of an innovation in the budget surplus (BS) on the TD is relatively modest. So, shocks in the BS are not the major factors in determining the behavior of TD.
Laney (1984)	58 countries	Causality form BD to CAD in developing countries. Amongst world's largest economies, Canada & Italy only demonstrate a statistically significant positive relationship between BD and CAD.
Bernheim (1988)	6 countries	$ 1.00 increase in the BD is associated with roughly a $ 0.30 decline in CA surplus for USA, UK, Canada, and West Germany but $ 0.85 decline in CA for Mexico. No effect on CA for Japan.
Kearney & Monadjemi (1990)	8 countries	Causality from CAD to BD in USA. No causality in Australia and France.
Vamvoukas (1997)	Greece	One-way causality from BD to TD.
Khalid & Guan (1999)	10 countries	Unidirectional causality from BD to CAD in USA, France and Canada. No causality between BD & CAD in UK and Australia. Weaker support for bidirectional causality too in Canada. Two-way causality for India. Causality from CAD to BD in Pakistan and Indonesia. Unidirectional causality from BD to CAD for Egypt and Mexico.

Correlogram of BDF Included observations: 37 Sample: 1964 2000

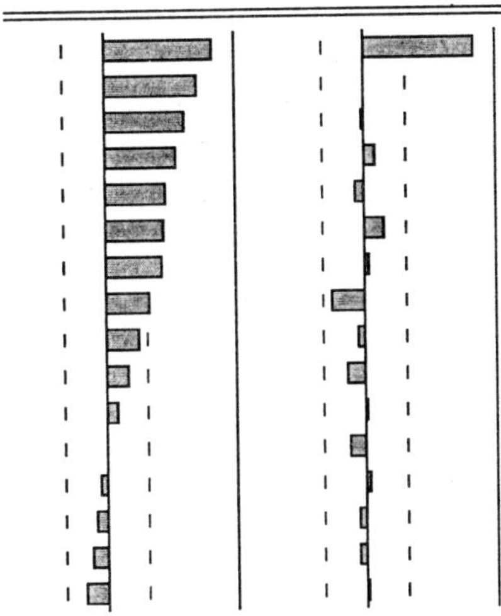

Autocorrelation	Partial Correlation		AC	PAC	Q-Stat	Prob
		1	0.863	0.863	29.871	0.000
		2	0.747	0.005	52.853	0.000
		3	0.640	-0.023	70.224	0.000
		4	0.571	0.090	84.488	0.000
		5	0.495	-0.057	95.515	0.000
		6	0.467	0.149	105.65	0.000
		7	0.445	0.040	115.17	0.000
		8	0.358	-0.268	121.57	0.000
		9	0.269	-0.041	125.31	0.000
		10	0.165	-0.146	126.76	0.000
		11	0.092	0.008	127.23	0.000
		12	-0.002	-0.122	127.23	0.000
		13	-0.043	0.030	127.34	0.000
		14	-0.085	-0.042	127.79	0.000
		15	-0.128	-0.048	128.87	0.000
		16	-0.173	0.014	130.92	0.000

Stilianos Fountas and Christopher Tsukis (1997) for Germany, UK, and Canadian data; Michel Normandin (1994) for US and Canadian data; G. Karras and F. Song for for Australia, Italy, Sweden, UK and the US data have found the mixed results in their empirical findings depending upon the models used and sample periods selected. Amelie Clement (2001) has experimented both the REH and TDH and concluded that neither the REH nor TDH were able to explain correctly the effects of fiscal behavior.

Andrew B. Abel and Ben S. Bernanke have analyzed in their book on Macroeconomics[4] about the relationship between the US government budget deficit and current account deficit for the period 1960-1998. Along this period they found that the twin deficit relation has gone in opposite direction barring the period of whole 1980s and first half of the 1990s (however, this period has shown strong support in favor to twin deficit hypothesis). They also mentioned some evidences on this issue from other countries in the same book referring the paper[5] on 'Investigating U.S. Government and Trade Deficits'. The results for the other countries have observed mixed. For example, revealing the twin deficits idea, Germany's budget deficit and current account deficit both increased in the early 1990s following the reunification of Germany. During mid 1980s, however, Canada and Italy both ran government budget deficits that were considerably larger than those in the United States (as percentage of GDP), without experiencing severe current account problems. Finally the authors conclude for sure that if an increase in the government budget deficit is not offset by an equal increase in private saving, the result must be a decline in domestic investment, rise in the current account deficit or both.

Thus delving into this most widely and rigorously tested TDH, it would have a far reaching policy prescription to this issue in the Nepalese context as it is not empirically verified before.

METHODOLOGY OF THE STUDY

Data and Variables

The sample data of BD and TD incorporated in the study holds for the period 1964 to 2000 of annual observation. The data are obtained from various issues of International Financial Statistics, a publication of IMF. The two measures of budget deficit and trade deficit have been used to verify their influences on each other. The data are transformed into growth form to minimize the problem of heteroscedasticity. The model has been formed on the basis of widely tested and verified empirical works of TDH, with bi-variate simple modeling to avoid the multi-co-linearity effects in the model.

Unit Root Test

Most of the time series data have been found non stationary for several reasons. So, prior to establish the relationship between the variables, it is pertinent to check them whether they are stationary. To determine the stationarity, Augmented Dickey Fuller unit root test has been run on each variable. The ADF test is based on the following equation,

$$\Delta Xt = \gamma + \alpha X_{t-1} + \sum_{j=2}^{k} \theta_j \, \Delta \, X_{t-j+1} + e_t \qquad (ii)$$

Alternative method of testing unit root is Phillip-Perron Model that satisfies following equation:

$$\Delta Xt = \alpha + p^{o} X_{t-1} + e_{t} \quad (iii)$$

The PP test is the t value associated with the estimated coefficient of ρ^*. The series is stationary if ρ^* is negative and significant. The test is performed for TD and BD where both the original series and difference of the series are tested for stationarity.

Co-Integration and Vector Error Correction Modeling

Co-integration establishes long run relationship between modeled variables. Engle Granger and Johansen's co-integration technique have been used in verifying the co-integration of the data. Engle-Granger technique uses the following equation in co-integration test.

$$\mu = TD_{t} - \alpha - \beta BD_{t} \quad (iv)$$

Vector Error Correction Modeling presents important information on the short run relationship between any two co-integrated variables. The Engle-Granger method for vector error correction modeling is based on the following equations:

$$\Delta TD_{t} = \gamma_{1} + \rho_{1} z_{t-1} + \alpha_{1} \Delta TD_{t-1} + \alpha_{2} \Delta TD_{t-2} + \alpha_{3} \Delta BD_{t-1} + \alpha_{4} \Delta BD_{t-2} + \varepsilon_{1t} \quad (v)$$

$$\Delta BD_{t} = \gamma_{2} + \rho_{2} z_{t-1} + \beta_{1} \Delta BD_{t-1} + \beta_{2} BD_{t-2} + \beta_{3}'' TD_{t-1} + \beta_{4} \Delta TD_{t-2} + \varepsilon_{2t} \quad (vi)$$

Structural Break

The idea of Chow Breakpoint test is to fit the equation separately for each sub sample and to see whether there are significant differences in the estimated equations. A significant difference indicates a structural change in the relationship. This test can be used with least squares and two- stage least squares regressions also. In order to carry out this test, the data should be divided into two or more sub samples. Each sub sample must contain more observations than the number of coefficients in the equation so that the equation could be estimated. The

Chow Breakpoint test compares the sum of squared residuals obtained when separate equations are fit to each sub sample of the data. E-Views 4.1 edition econometric software package provides two test statistics i.e. F-statistic and Log Likelihood Ratio Statistic for the Chow Breakpoint test. The F-statistic is based on comparison of the restricted and unrestricted sum of squared residuals and in the simplest case involving a single breakpoint is computed as:

$$F = \frac{[u'u-(u_1'u_1+u_2'u_2)]/k}{(u_1'u_1+u_2'u_2)/T-2k}$$

Where u'u is the restricted sum of squared residuals, $u_i'u_i$ is the squared residuals from sub sample i, T is the total number of observations, and k is the number of parameters in the equation. This formula can be generalized normally to more than one breakpoint. The F-statistic has an exact finite sample F-distribution if the errors are independent and identically distributed normal random variables.

Table 2

Augmented Dickey Fuller Unit Root Test on Variables

Exogenous: Constant ***Null Hypothesis: The variable has a unit root*** **MAXLAG=9) [Sample 1964-2000]**

Lag length (Automatic based on SIC,

variable	*ADF test statistic*	*Prob* value*	*Lag length*	*Test 1%*	*critical 5%*	*values 10%*
BD	1.754455	0.9995	0	-3.626784	-2.945842	-2.611531
"BD	-5.996160	0.0000	0	-3.632900	-2.948404	-2.612874
BDG	-6.089555	0.0000	0	-3.632900	-2.948404	-2.612874
TD	8.187428	1.0000	5	-3.661661	-2.960411	-2.619160
"TD	3.931980	1.0000	8	-3.699871	-2.976263	-2.627420
"²TD	1.461102	0.9986	9	-3.724070	-2.986225	-2.632604
TDG	-3.993513	0.0040	0	-3.632900	-2.948404	-2.612874

* MacKinnon (1996) One-sided P-values

EMPIRICAL FINDINGS

As per the set methodology and fitting the above stated formulae, we have derived following findings in the corresponding tests like unit root, co-integration, VAR – error correction and structural break point.

Stationarity Test

The stationarity test of the variables (BD and TD) has been performed by using ADF and PP test and following results have been obtained.

Correlogram of D(BD) Included observations: 36 Sample: 1964 2000

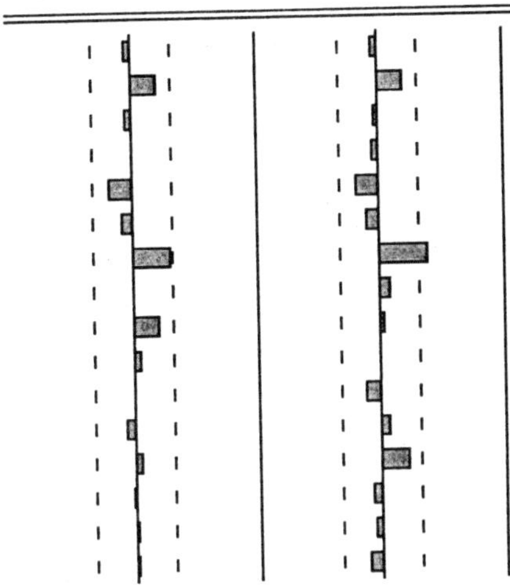

	AC	PAC	Q-Stat	Prob
1	-0.056	-0.056	0.1227	0.726
2	0.208	0.206	1.8685	0.393
3	-0.054	-0.035	1.9912	0.574
4	0.000	-0.049	1.9912	0.737
5	-0.192	-0.185	3.6199	0.605
6	-0.097	-0.114	4.0473	0.670
7	0.307	0.409	8.5015	0.290
8	0.001	0.085	8.5015	0.386
9	0.199	0.030	10.517	0.310
10	0.053	0.004	10.668	0.384
11	0.000	-0.124	10.668	0.472
12	-0.074	0.066	10.976	0.531
13	0.050	0.226	11.122	0.601
14	-0.021	-0.078	11.149	0.674
15	0.010	-0.050	11.155	0.742
16	0.023	-0.111	11.191	0.798

The result of ADF has indicated that the variables are non stationary at level. The BD has been found stationary in its first difference but the TD hasn't been found stationary at first difference and even in second difference too.

Table 3
Phillips-Perron Unit Root Test on Variables

Exogenous: **Constant** *Null Hypothesis*: **The variable has a unit root**
Bandwidth: (Newey-West using Bartlett Kernel) [Sample: - 1964 - 2000]

Variable	*PP test statistic*	*Prob**	*Bandwidth value*	*Test critical values* 1%	5%	10%
BD	2.508130	1.0000	4	-3.626784	-2.945842	-2.611531
"BD	-5.996191	0.0000	1	-3.632900	-2.948404	-2.612874
BDG	-6.094820	0.0000	3	-3.632900	-2.948404	-2.612874
TD	0.131974	0.9639	2	-3.626784	-2.945842	-2.611531
"TD	-6.449641	0.0000	2	-3.632900	-2.948404	-2.612874
TDG	-3.732370	0.0078	13	-3.632900	-2.948404	-2.612874

* MacKinnon (1996) One-sided P-values

While running the PP test for the same data, both of the variables have been found non stationary at level and stationary at first differences. Growth rates of both the variables have also been found stationary at level for both the tests of ADF and PP.

orrelogram of TD ==Included observations: 37==Sample: 1964 2000

Autocorrelation Partial Correlation

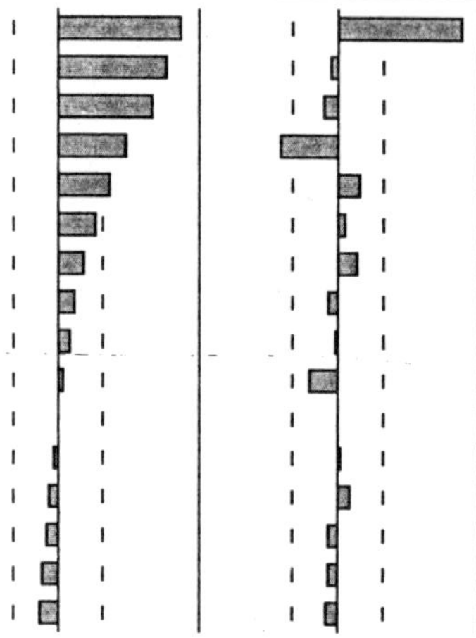

	AC	PAC	Q-Stat	Prob
1	0.900	0.900	32.497	0.000
2	0.802	-0.048	58.994	0.000
3	0.692	-0.111	79.334	0.000
4	0.516	-0.424	90.976	0.000
5	0.387	0.152	97.733	0.000
6	0.275	0.054	101.27	0.000
7	0.183	0.146	102.88	0.000
8	0.127	-0.059	103.69	0.000
9	0.085	-0.021	104.06	0.000
10	0.037	-0.200	104.13	0.000
11	0.000	0.004	104.13	0.000
12	-0.032	0.021	104.19	0.000
13	-0.064	0.095	104.44	0.000
14	-0.092	-0.069	104.97	0.000
15	-0.116	-0.061	105.86	0.000
16	-0.138	-0.087	107.17	0.000

Co-integration Test (Engle-Granger)

This test has been performed using ADF and Phillips-Perron test on residual part of the regression equation $TD = a + bBD + U$. The residual part is stationary at 5 percent level of significance for ADF while it is stationary only at 10 percent level of significance for PP test. The co-integration test using Engle-Granger method has suggested that the variables (TD and BD) are co-integrated. The results of the tests have been presented in the following Table 4.

VAR Model for Vector Error Correction Estimates

Vector error correction estimates have presented the short run dynamics of two co-integrated variables. The following table (Table 5) has depicted vector error correction estimates of the TD and BD which are co-integrated variables according to both methods.

Table - 4
Unit Root Test on Residual

***Exogenous*: Constant** ***Null Hypothesis*: The residual has a unit root**
Lag length: (Automatic based on SIC, MAXLAG=9)

Residual	ADF test statistic	Prob.* value	Lag length	Test 1%	critical 5%	values 10%
$\grave{\imath}_t$	-3.464629	0.0172	9	-3.699871	-2.976263	-2.627420

Bandwidth: (Newey-West using Bartlett Kernel)

Residual	PP test statistic	Prob.* value	Band width	Test 1%	critical 5%	values 10%
$\grave{\imath}_t$	-2.670827	0.0889	1	-3.626784	-2.945842	-2.611531

* MacKinnon (1996) One-sided P-values

Correlogram of D(TD) Included observations: 36 Sample: 1964 2000

Autocorrelation Partial Correlation

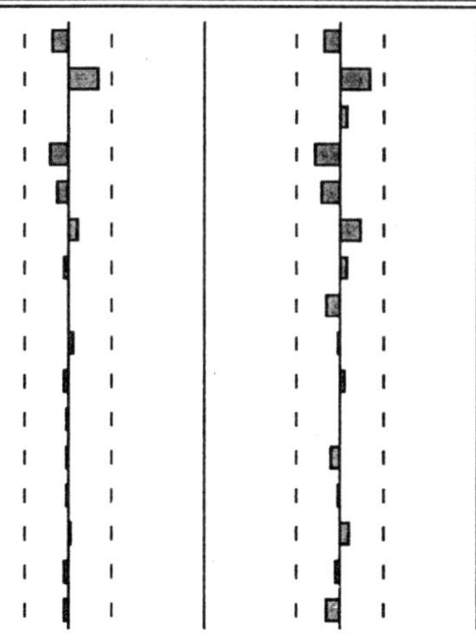

	AC	PAC	Q-Stat	Prob
1	-0.121	-0.121	0.5708	0.450
2	0.234	0.223	2.7730	0.250
3	-0.006	0.046	2.7743	0.428
4	-0.132	-0.193	3.5172	0.475
5	-0.084	-0.138	3.8250	0.575
6	0.079	0.155	4.1101	0.662
7	-0.040	0.053	4.1848	0.758
8	0.002	-0.101	4.1849	0.840
9	0.031	-0.025	4.2339	0.895
10	-0.031	0.037	4.2847	0.934
11	-0.024	-0.008	4.3164	0.960
12	-0.021	-0.066	4.3404	0.976
13	-0.024	-0.022	4.3753	0.987
14	0.021	0.063	4.4027	0.993
15	-0.026	-0.025	4.4455	0.996
16	-0.035	-0.099	4.5311	0.998

The significant value of the coefficient of co-integrating equation $(\tilde{n}_1)$ indicates that the system is in the state of the short run dynamics. The negative sign show that the change in the value of TD depends inversely on the past error (deviation of actual value from its long run equilibrium path). The insignificant value of the coefficient of co-integrating equation $(\tilde{n}_2)$ indicates that short run disequilibrium is insignificant in second equation. The estimates of the model also present the Granger causality between BD and TD. In the present case z_t

Granger causes TD since lagged value of the Z_t entering equation (4) is statistically significant.

Table 5
Vector Error Correction Estimates (TD_t & BD_t)

Dependent variable	*Explanatory variables*	*Coefficient*	*'t'- statistics*	*Standard errors*
"TD	Constant ($\tilde{a}_1$)	-3547.984	[-2.86082]	(1240.20)
	z_{1t-1}	-0.257856**	[-3.67081]	(0.07024)
	"TD_{t-1}	-0.086207	[-0.54583]	(0.15794)
	"TD_{t-2}	0.137823	[0.85894]	(0.16046)
	"BD_{t-1}	-1.981125	[-2.02074]	(0.98040)
	"BD_{t-2}	-2.665209*	[-2.83503]	(0.94010)
"BD	Constant ($\tilde{a}_2$)	-212.2422	[-0.71879]	(295.278)
	Z_{1t-1}	0.009775	[0.58445]	(0.01672)
	"BD_{t-1}	0.056373	[0.24151]	(0.23342)
	"BD_{t-2}	0.394343	[1.76182]	(0.22383)
	"TD_{t-1}	0.018176	[0.48336]	(0.03760)
	"TD_{t-2}	0.060861	[1.59311]	(0.03820)

*(**) Indicates statistical significance at the 5% (1%) level.

Chow Test for Identifying Structural Break

In order to identify the structural breaks, following models have been applied and the results are displayed accordingly in the corresponding Tables 6 and 7 respectively in the Table 6.

Table 6
Chow Break Point Test on Equation ($TD_g = \tilde{a}_1+\tilde{a}_2BDg+ z_t$)

year	F-statistic	Probability	year	F-statistic	Probability
1967	5.177361**	0.011271	1984	0.168761	0.845457
1968	13.85107*	0.000046	1985	0.293235	0.747830
1969	14.13338*	0.000040	1986	0.284971	0.753924
1970	2.797666***	0.075903	1987	0.241006	0.787250
1971	2.419534	0.105066	1988	0.196496	0.822588
1972	1.849805	0.173694	1989	0.184688	0.832244
1973	2.650423	0.086080	1990	0.217472	0.805729
1974	1.544067	0.229000	1991	0.208981	0.812510
1975	0.815336	0.451472	1992	0.429169	0.654742
1976	0.772147	0.470437	1993	0.447319	0.643277
1977	0.778319	0.467676	1994	0.444947	0.644763
1978	0.503970	0.608842	1995	0.357582	0.702124
1979	0.314372	0.732477	1996	0.366459	0.696056
1980	0.306147	0.738411	1997	1.052620	0.360796
1981	0.095431	0.909239	1998	1.117838	0.339420
1982	0.197408	0.821848	1999	0.057784	0.943953
1983	0.109018	0.897046			

*, **, *** indicates significant at 1%, 5% and 10%

The F-statistic for the Chow test in the model TD$_g$ = ã$_1$ + ã$_2$ BDg + z$_t$ shows that the structural breaks have occurred in the year 1967 to 1970. After 1970 it is completely stable. (Please refer Table 6 above). Table 7 describes the F-statistic for the Chow test in the model ÄTD = ã$_1$+ ã$_2$ ÄBD + z$_t$. The results present that the economy is stable up to 1984 and the structural breaks have been seen after 1985.

Table 7

Chow Break Point Test on Equation (ÄTD = ã$_1$+ ã$_2$ÄBD+ z$_t$)

year	*F-statistic*	*Probability*	*year*	*F-statistic*	*Probability*
1967	0.180737	0.835501	1984	2.834126***	0.073585
1968	0.282810	0.755527	1985	3.492577**	0.042463
1969	0.396607	0.675859	1986	3.823827**	0.032428
1970	0.496676	0.613164	1987	4.120293**	0.025572
1971	0.611800	0.548596	1988	4.245635**	0.023154
1972	0.733049	0.488336	1989	4.420766**	0.020173
1973	0.875334	0.426463	1990	4.723594**	0.015940
1974	1.005496	0.377130	1991	6.177673*	0.005386
1975	1.149612	0.329497	1992	7.514327*	0.002112
1976	1.346162	0.274578	1993	9.579277*	0.000549
1977	1.524516	0.233122	1994	8.353544*	0.001205
1978	1.699914	0.198784	1995	8.345611*	0.001211
1979	1.913345	0.164094	1996	5.134073**	0.011646
1980	2.207749	0.126421	1997	16.87915*	0.000010
1981	2.322422	0.114339	1998	11.42443*	0.000180
1982	2.785345***	0.076703	1999	0.663936	0.521769
1983	2.833646***	0.073616			

*, **, *** indicates significant at 1%, 5% and 10%

SUMMARY AND CONCLUSION

Widely tested TDH has been tested for Nepalese time series of 1964 through 2000. Popular methods of testing like unit root test, co-integration, vector error correction and stability test has been performed. TD and DB has been found non stationary at level and stationary at first differences. There is long run relationship between the two variables that has been supported by Engle-Granger co-integration test. VEC model suggests that there is unidirectional causality from BD to TD. The stability test based on Chow break point test indicates that the economy has structural breaks after 1984. In fact Nepal has been following liberalized and open economic policy since 1985 and this might have caused in the economy structural shifts in the economic from 1985. Causality from BD to TD suggests that there is a of need for efficient use of government finance towards investment activities and export promotion for mitigatins the TDH dilemma.

Notes

1. Y stands for output (income), C stands for consumption, G stands for government expenditure, X stands for export and M stands for import.
2. Refer Mr. Olga Vyshnyak, Twin Deficit Hypothesis: The case of Ukraine, National University 'Kyiv Mohyla Academy', Department of Economics Ukraine, 2001.
3. For detail, vide Abdulnasser Hatimi-J and Ghaji Shukur, Multivariate – Based Causality Tests of Twin Deficits in the US, International School, Jonkoping University, Sweden, JEL classification, C32, H62.
4. Andrew B Abel (The Wharton School of the University of Pennsylvania) and Ben S Bernanke (Woodrow Wilson School of Public and International Affairs, Princeton University) have written very excellent book i.e. Macroeconomics, Pearson Education Inc., 2001 (First Indian Reprint, 2003).
5. Ellis Tallman and Jeffery Rosenweig, Investigating U.S. Government and Trade Deficits, Federal Reserve Bank of Atlanta, Economic Review, May/June 1991, pp. 1-11.
6. The Wharton School of the University of Pennsylvania.
7. Woodrow Wilson School of Public and International Affairs, Princeton University.
8. Mr. Christ is a Professor of Economics at the Johns Hopkins University.
9. Assistant Vice President, Federal Reserve Bank of Saint Louis, USA.
10. Department of Economics, University of Victoria, P.O. Box 1700, Victoria BC, Canada, V8W2Y2.
11. Ottawa, Canada
12. Ottawa, Canada

13. London Business School
14. University of Cyprus and Union Bank of Switzerland
15. With the assistance of Shihua Lu, PhD candidate at Georgetown.
16. Martin Eichenbaum is a Professor of Economics at Northwestern University and a Senior Consultant to the Federal Reserve Bank of Chicago.

REFERENCES

Abdulnasser Hatemi-J and Ghazi Shukur, *The Causal Nexus of Government Spending & Revenue in Finland: A Bootstrap Approach,* Applied Economics Letters 1999, JEL Classificaiton C32.

Andrew B Abel[6] Ben S Bernanke[7] *Macroeconomics,* Pearson Education Inc., 2001 (First Indian Reprint, 2003).

Abdulnasser Hatemi-J and Ghazi Shukur, *Multivariate Based Causality Tests of Twin Deficits in the U.S.,* International Business School, Jonkoping University, Post Box 1026, SE-551 11 Sweden.

Ahmet Zengin, *The Twin Deficits Hypothesis (The Turkish Case),* Zonguldak Karaelmas University, Department of Economics, Zonguldak, Turkey, azengin@karaelmas.edu.tr

A. Koutsoyannis, *Theory of Econometrics: An Introductory Exposition of Econometric Methods,* 2nd Edition, ELBS with McMillan, 1993.

Alan McLean, *On the Nature of Hypothesis Tests,* Monash University, Department of Econometrics, Australia, Working Paper 4/2001, June 2001.

Apostolos Papadhilippou, *An Econometric Estimation of Import Demand in in Moldova,* Moldovan Economic Trends, Pages 91-98.

Bank of England, *Vector Auto Regression Models,* Economic Models at the Bank of England, Chapter-5. (Web Based Article)

Benjamin Friedman, *What We have Learned from the Disappearance of the Deficits?* Copy Right 2000 M.E. Sharpe, Inc., Copy Right 2000 Gale Group, USA, Issue- July 2000.

Carig Burnside, Martin Eichenbaum and Sergio Rebelo, *On the Fiscal Implications of Twin Crises,* NBER Working Paper No-W8277, May 2001.

Carlos Fonseca Marinheiro, *Ricardian Equivalence: An Empirical Application to the Portuguese Economy,* Faculty of Economics of the University of Coimbria and Katholieke Universiteit Leuven, Portugal, March 2001.

Carl F. Christ[8], *Asseing Applied Econometric Results*, Federal Reserve Bank of Saint Louis, March/April 1993.

Chung-Ming Kuan, *Lecture on Basic Time Series Models*, Istitute of Economics, Academia Sinica, Taiwan, March 4, 2003.

C. R. Kothari, *Research Methodology, Methods and Techniques*, Wishwa Prakashan, India, 1998.

Daniel L. Thornton[9], *Do Government Deficits Matter?* Reserve Bank of Saint Louis, USA, 2003.

David E. A. Giles, *Causality Between the Measured and Underground Economies in New Zealand*, Department of Economics, University of Victoria, Canada, V8W 3P5, February 1996.

David E. A. Giles[10], Lindsay M. Tedds[11] and Gugsa Werkneh[12], *The Canadian Underground and Measured Economies: Granger Causality Results*, JEL Classification, C53, H26, June 1999.

Doug Noland, *Ominous Return of the Twin Deficits*, The Credit Bubble Bulletin, June 21, 2002.

Douglas S. Meade, *Twin Deficits and Balances in QUEST and LIFT*, Simulation Presented at INFORUM Seminar, USA, 1995.

Edward Shapiro, *Macroeconomic Analysis, Fifth Edition*, Galgotia Publications (P) Ltd., New Delhi, 1996.

Elif Akbostanici and Gul Ipek Tunc, *Turkish Twin Deficits: An Error Correction Model of Trade Balance*, (Middle East Technical University, Departments of Economics), Turkey 2002. (JEL Classification: F30, F32, F41).

Emmanuel Anoruo (Coppin State College, Maryland) and Yusuf Ahmad (The World Bank, Washington), *Openness and Economic Growth: Evidence from Selected ASEAN Countries*, The Indian Economic Journal, Volume 47, Number 3, and Pages 110-117.

Eric DOR and Alan DURRRE, *Investigating the Forecasting Performance of Co-integrated VAR Models for Quarterly Macroeconomic Variables in Belgium*, Le Bulletin de L'LRES accueille des communications scientifiques de sources tant internes qu'externes a L'LRES, Belgium, No-11, 1998.

G. Karras and F. Song, *Government Spending and the Current Account: Some Evidence*, International Economic Journal, Volume 9, Number 4, winter 1994, Pages 45-56.

Gerard Jackson, *Twin Deficit Bogey Returns*, The Australian, No-10, 21-27, October 1996.

Guglielmo Maria Caporale[13] and Nikitas Pittis[14], *Efficient Estimation of Co-integrating Vectors and Testing for Causality in Vector Autoregressions,* Journal of Economic surveys, Vol. 13, No. 1, 0950-0804/98/05 0001-35, © Blackwell Publishers Ltd. 1999, 108 Cowley Rd., UK, and 350 Main St., Malden, USA.

H. Robert Heller (Fed Governor), *Trim Twin Deficits, Hold Line on Prices,* Southeastern Economic Insight, Federal Reserve Bank of Atlanta, Research Department, Volume 7, Number 2, April 1, 1987.

Jarko Fidrmuc, *Twin Deficits: Implications of Current Account and Fiscal Imbalances for the Accession Countries,* Foreign Research Division, Oesterreichische National Bank, Vienna, Austria, JEL F15, F41

John Fox, *Lectures 14 and 15: Hypothesis Testing,* Sociology 3H06, 2003.

John Maynard Keynes, *The General Theory of Employment, Interest and Money,* McMillan and Co. Ltd. 1970.

John S. Atlee, *The Federal Budget's Twin Deficits and Balanced Budget Amendments,* IEA Home Page, Written at December; Revised at March 1995 and July 1997.

John T. Cuddington[15], *Analyzing the Sustainability of Fiscal Deficit in Developing Countries,* Economics Department, Georgetown University, Washington D.C, USA, September 3, 1999.

Jack Johnston and John DiNardo, *Econometric Methods,* Fourth Edition, McGraw Hill International Editions, Economics Series, 1997.

Jordan Shan, and Fiona Sun, *Domestic Saving & Foreign Investment in Australia: Granger Causality Tests,* International Economic Journal Volume 12, Number 4, winter 1998.

Jose Ricardo da Costa e Silva, *Currency Crises in Emergent Markets and Minsky Financial Fragility Theory: Is There a Link?* Department of Economics, Washington University at Saint Louis, September 19, 2002.

Kawai Masahiro and Maccini Louis J., *Twin Deficits versus Unpleasant Fiscal Arithmetic in a Small Open Economy,* Journal of Money, Credit and Banking, Vol: 27, august 1995, Pages 639-58.

Kenneth Kasa, *Finite Horizons and the Twin Deficits,* Federal Reserve Bank of Sanfrancisco, Economic Review, 1994, Pages 19-28.

Lex Oxley and David Greas, *Vector Autoreression, Cointegration and Causality: Testing for Causes of the British Industrial Revolution,* Applied Economics, 1998, 30, 1387-1397.

Martin Eichenbaum[16], *Some Comments on the Role of Econometrics in Economic Theory*, Economic Perspective, Federal Reserve Bank of Chicago, pp 22-31.

Mamdough Alkhatib Alkswani, *The Twin Deficits Phenomenon in Petroleum Economy: Evidence from Saudi Arabia*, (King Saud University, Department of Economics), 2000.

Michael R. Pakko, *The U.S. Trade Deficits and the "New Economy"*, Federal Reserve Bank of St. Louis, Review, September-October, 1999

Michel Normandian, *Budget Deficit Persistence and the Twin Deficits Hypothesis*, University of Quebec at Montreal, Canada, Working Paper No-31, December 1994.

Ministry of Finance, *Economic Survey*, Mid July 1996 and 2002, His Majesty's Government (HMG/N), Kathmandu, Nepal.

Mushin Kar and Eric J. Pentecost, *Financial Development and Economic Growth in Turkey: Further Evidence on the Causality Isue*, Loughborough University, Department of Economics, UK, Economic Research Paper No. 00/27, December 2000.

Nepal Development Forum, *Economic Update, 2002*, The World Bank, January 30, 2002, Report No. 23978.

Nepal Rastra Bank *Quarterly Economic Bulletin*, Nepal Rastra Bank, Research Department, Kathmandu. Mid July 2002.

Nepal Rastra Bank, *WTO and Nepal*, Research Department, International Finance Division, April 2002.

Olga Vyshnyank, *Twin Deficit Hypothesis: The Case of Ukraine*, National University "Kyiv-Mohyla Academy", Ukraine, 2000.

Paul D. McNelis and Anjum Siddiqui, *Debt and Deficit Dynamics in New Zealand: Did Financial Liberalization Matter?*, International Economic Journal, Volume 8, Number 3, Autumn 1994.

Pedro Nuno Teixeira, *Do Economists Take Empirical Testing Seriously? The Case of the Human Capital Theory*, INEM - Vancouver, Canada, June 2000.

P. Geoffrey Allen (University of Massachusetts, USA) and Robert Fields (University of Lancaster, UK), *Econometric Forecasting Principles and Doubts: Unit Root Testing First, Last or Never?*, allen@resecon.umass.edu Department of Resource Economics, UM, MA 01002, USA & R.Fildes@lancaster.ac.uk Department of Management Science, UL, LA1 4YX, UK.

Peter Bernstein, *What did We Gain from Zapping the Deficits? (Budget and Trade Deficits of the U.S.)*, Copy Right 1998 M.E., Sharpe, Inc., Copy Right 2000 Gale Group, USA, May-June 1998.

Richard A. Musgrave and Peggy B. Musgrave, *Theory of Public Finance*, McGraw Hill International Editions, Finance Series 1989.

R.A. Stanford, *Deficits and Surpluses*, Working Paper, USA, 2001.

R. S. Pindyck and D. L. Rubinfeld, *Econometric Models and Econometric Forecasts*, International Student Edition, McGraw-Hill International Book Company, 1997.

Stilianos Funtas and Christopher Tsoukis, *Twin Deficits, Real Interest Rates and International Capital Mobility*, (Department of Economics, National University of Ireland, Galway), Working Paper No-49, September 2000. (JEL Classification: F36, F41).

Thomas I. Palley, *The Case Against Budget Surpluses: Why Government Debt is Good and Moderate Budget Deficits are Needed in a Growing Economy*, (Public Policy, AFL-CIO, Washington DC), Paper presented at the meetings of the Canadian Economics Association, McGill University, Montreal, Quebec, May 31-June 3, 2001.

USF Economics Homepage, *Interpreting the Regression results*, Downloaded Material at *www.thecoo.edu/academic/business/economies/eco320/Results.html*

Usha Nair - Reuchert (Gergia Institute of Technology) and Diana Weinhots (London School of Economics) *Causality Tests for Cross-country Panels: New Look at FDI and Economics Growth in Developing Countries*, JEL Classification: F12, F14, F10 January 2000.

Xiankun Gai and Ji Nan, *Testing for Unit Roots in Macroeconomic Time Series of China*, Shan Don Province Statistical Bureau, Quan Cheng Road 221, China.

Chandan Kumar Mukhopadhyay & Kanchan Dutta

12

TWIN DEFICITS PHENOMENON IN MALDIVES AN ECONOMETRIC ENQUIRY

INTRODUCTION

Issues relating to budget deficit, trade deficit and public debt etc. have been an intense area of research studies among economists for last three decades .The dramatic escalations in both the budget and trade deficits,widely known as the twin deficits phenomenon, have led many scholars to test the possibility of a relation between these two deficits .In economic literature two different theories exist in regard to the relation of these two variables, viz.

1. *Twin Deficits Hypothesis* (TDH), which argues that budget deficit causes trade deficit and hence the two deficits are twin. Therefore, this theory advocates for regulating Government deficits to achieve balance in the external sector.
2. The other one is the *Ricardian Equivalence Hypothesis* (REH), which contradicts the TDH and claims that increase in Government expenditure is absorbed by rise in private savings (to meet the future tax burden) causing no external sector deficit. Hence the two deficits are not systematically related to each other.

HOW BD AND TD ARE TWIN DEFICITS

The national income identity is

$$Y=C+I+G+X-M \qquad (i)$$

and

Y=C+S+T (*ii*)

Substituting (*ii*) in (*i*) we get

C+I+G+X-M = C+S+T (*iii*)

Or,

(X-M) = (T-G)+ (S-T) (*iv*)

where the symbols have their usual meaning.

i.e.
Y = national income
C = consumption
I = investment
G = govt. expenditure
X = export
M = import
S = savings
T = tax

The last expression in equation (iv) shows budget deficit and trade deficit always behave as twins implying budget deficit being the source of financing trade deficit where private investment and savings gaps remain stable over time. Although the relation between the two deficits is embodied in the national income identity, these two deficits also have economic linkages, established through the behaviour of economic variables like interest rate, exchange rate etc.

Theoretically, two types of mechanisms connect the two deficits. In the conventional Mundell-Fleming type of economy characterized by high capital mobility, an expansionary fiscal policy will raise the aggregate demand and will put an upward pressure on domestic interest rates. The high interest rate, in turn, will attract foreign capital in the economy and an appreciation of exchange rate takes place under flexible exchange rate regime. Export declines, imports rise and trade balance deteriorates. Thus the two deficits become twins. Even if the central bank does not allow the nominal exchange rate of the domestic currency to appreciate by absorbing excess supply of foreign currency under fixed exchange rate regime, there will be price rise on account of real value of domestic currency. This reduces export and raises imports causing trade deficit.

The other mechanism of the twin deficit relationship works through the *Keynesian income absorption* theory. According to this theory, an increase in budget deficit induces domestic absorbsion and thereby raises domestic income. Higher income will trigger more imports and worsen the external balance. However, if savings or investment adjusts to the changes in budget deficit fully, trade balance will not respond to fluctuations in the govt. deficits and the economy will have neutral deficits.

RESEARCH STUDIES ON TWIN DEFICITS

The twin deficit hypothesis (TDH) had specially been made more popular and gone through series of empirical investigations after the emergence of secular nature of simultaneous movement of twins in the United States from the early 1980s. In economic literature, researches focused on inter-link between twin deficits.

SEVERAL RESEARCH STUDIES

Table 1
A summary of research studies on twin deficits has given in table 1 and 2

Researcher/s	*Sample countries*	*Findings*
Darrat (1988)	USA	Bi-directional-causality, between-BD and TD
Bahmani-Oskooee (1989), & Latif- Zaman & Do Costa (1990)	USA	Uni-directional causality from BD to CAD
Enders and Lee (1990), Dewald and Ulan (1990)	USA	No causal link between the two deficits
Miller and Russek (1989), (1990) and Bachman (1992)	USA	Uni-directional A b e l l causality from BD to CAD.

The empirical studies on twin deficits in the context of other countries also produced mixed results. These results are also shown in the table below.

Table2

Researcher/s	*Sample countries*	*Findings*
Khalid & Guan (1999)	10 countries	Uni-directional causality from BD to CAD in USA, France &Canada. No causality between Bd and CAD in UK & Australia.Weaker support for bi-directionalcausality too in Canada. TwoWay causality for India. Causality from CAD to BD in Pakistanand Indonesia.Unidirectional causality from BD to CAD for Egypt and Mexico
Vamvoukas (1999)	Greece	One way causality from BD to TD
Kearney &Monadjemi (1990)		8 countries Causality from CAD to BD in Germany, Australia and France.
Laney (1984)	58 countries	Causality from BD to CAD indeveloping countries. Amongstthe world's largest economies,Canada & Italy only demonstrate a statistically significantpositive relationship between BDand CAD.
Bernheim (1988)	6 countries	Surplus for USA, UK, CANADA and West Germany, but deficit in CAMexico. No effect on CA for Japan.
Islam (1998)	Brazil	Bilateral causality betweentrade deficit and budget deficits.
Ali-salman-saleh, Mahendhiran Nair &Tikiri Agalewatte (2005)	Sri Lanka	Causality from budget deficit tocurrent account deficit.
Olga vyshnyak (2001)	Ukraine	BD Granger causes to CAD
Akbostanci and Tunc (2002)	Turkey	Twin deficit hypothesis holdsand RicardianEquivalence Hypothesisis not validated both in long runand short run.
Alkswani (2000)	Saudi Arabia	Causality from trade deficitto budget deficit.

From the above tables it is clear that, there have been numerous empirical studies examining the twin deficit problem in developed countries. However, the number of empirical studies examining the long run relationship between budget deficit and trade deficit for developing countries are scarce. The present study is devoted to address this issue. An attempt has been made in this study to investigate into the relationship between BD and TD for one of the member countries of SAARC namely—*'MALDIVES'*.

AN OUTLINE OF THE ECONOMY OF MALDIVES

The Maldivian archipelago, located 300 miles south-west of the southern tip of India and 450 miles west of Srilanka, is a beautiful string of 1192 coral islands scattered across the equator in the vast expanse of the Indian ocean.

The Maldivian economy is based on tourism and fishing .Out of 1192, only 200 are in habitat. The population is scattered through out the country. Development has been centered upon the tourism industry and its complimentary service sectors, transport, distribution, real estate, and Government taxes on the tourist industry have been ploughed into infrastructure and used to improve technology in the agricultural sector. Tourism, Transport and communications, Government Investment, Manufacturing, Real estate, Fishing, Construction, and agriculture account for 32.9, 15.4, 12.6, 7.8, 6.9, 6.2, 3.6 and 2.5 percent of GDP respectively.

Poor soil and scarce arable land have historically been limited to agricultural of a few crops, such as coconut, banana, papayas, mangoes, taro, betel, chilies, sweet potatoes, and onions. Almost all food, including staple, have to be imported.

In the industrial sector which provides 8% (approx) of GDP, consists of traditional boat building and handicraft, while modern industry is limited to a few tuna canneries, a bottling plant and a few enterprises producing PVC pipe, soap, furniture and food products. In recent years, Maldives has successfully marketed for tourism its natural assets, beautiful un-polluted beaches on small coral islands, diving in blue waters abundant with tropical fish and glorious sunsets.

Recently some experts commend Maldives for its impressive growth and success in improving general living standards. Inflation and unemployment are relatively low and steady growth since 1980, has lifted Maldives to a lower middle-income countries. As far as trade policy is concerned, tariffs are the main trade policy instrument. Tariff barriers are few. Import licensing is mainly automatic and import quotas apply only to rice, flour and sugar. However, Maldives has a plan for a more diversified export- oriented economy and sought clarifications for emerging as a regional free trade hub by 2020.

DATA AND METHODOLOGY OF THE STUDY

The sample data of BD (budget deficit) and TD (trade deficit) used in our study hold for the period 1979 to 2003 of the annual observations. The data have been collected from various issues of International Financial Statistics (IFS), a publication of IMF.

As far as methodology is concerned, the *Augmented Dickey Fuller test* and *Phillips -Perron* test have been done for testing the presence of unit root, and then test of co-integration is performed and it is followed by the estimation of the vector error correction model. Granger causality tests have been performed in order to identify the direction of causal relation between the variables concerned.

UNIT ROOT TEST

Stationarity of the time series data on TD and BD has been enquired into through 'Unit Root Tests. These tests includes ADF (Augmented Dickey Fuller Test) and Phillips –Perron test. The results of the ADF test have been presented through the Table 3

From the above table it is clear that, TD is nonstationary at levels with both fixed lag 1 and max lag 8 based on (SIC) but becomes stationary upon the 1st difference with fixed lag 1 and with maximum lag length 8 it becomes stationary in 2nd difference. On the other hand, BD is also stationary in the 1st difference with max lag length 8 based on SIC as well as with fixed lag 1 (with 10% level of significance). These findings have further been confirmed through the Phillips-Perron test. The results of the test have been presented through Table 4.

Table 3
Results of the ADF Test (UNIT ROOT TEST)

Variable	*Order*	*ADF statistic*	*Lag length*	*Test critical values* 1%	5%	10%
TD	Level	-1.585625	1(fixed)	-3.752946	-2.998064	-2.638752
TD	1st difference	-5.720087	1(fixed)	-3.769597	-3.004861	-2.642242
TD	Level	-0.669360	8(SIC)	-3.886751	-3.052189	-2.666593
TD	1st difference	-1.542703	8(SIC)	-3.920350	-3.065585	-2.673459
TD	2nd difference	-5.025350	8(SIC)	-3.886751	-3.052169	-2.666593
BD	Level	-1.447886	1(FIXED)	-3.752946	-2.998064	-2.638752
BD	1st difference	-2.968411	1(fixed)	-3.769597	-3.004861	-2.642242
BD	Level	-1.547296	8(sic)	-3.737853	-2.991878	-2.635542
BD	1st difference	-4.674093	8(sic)	-3.752946	-2.998064	-2.638752

Table 4
Results Of Phillips-peron Unit Root Test

Variable	*Order*	*P-P test statistic*	*Test critical values* 1%	5%	10%
TD	Level	0.838218 prob. (0.9926)	-3.737853	-2.991878	-2.635542
TD	1st difference	-5.839028 Prob (0.0001)	-3.752946	-2.998064	-2.638752
BD	Level	-1.58885 Prob (0.4727)	-3.737853	-2.991878	-2.635542
BD	1st difference	-4.674093 Prob (0.0012)	-3.752946	-2.998064	-2.638752

From the above table it is clear that BD and TD are stationary at 1% level of significance upon 1st difference.

COINTEGRATION (ENGLE- GRANGER METHODOGTY)

If TD and BD were twin deficits, then one could expect a long run relationship between these two variables. Before estimating such relation, it is pertinent for us to know if such relation really existed. This involves test of co-integration. The co-integrating equation is

$$TD_t = \alpha + \beta\, BD_t + \upsilon_t \qquad (v)$$

where υ_t is the error term and υ_t is also termed as the linear combination of TD_t and BDt since,

$$\upsilon_t = TD_t - \alpha - \beta BD_t \qquad (vi)$$

If υ_t, the residual, does not contain unit root and is stationary, the series TDt and BDt are said to be integrated. In such case a long run stable relationship between these two variables is expected to exist. The results of the estimation of the equation (vi) are given in the Table 5.

Table 5
Results of the co-integration tests

Variable	*Order*	*ADF test statistic of* u_t	*Lag length*	*Test critical values* 1%	5%	10%
U_t	Level	-5.068964	8 (SIC)	-3.737853	-2.991878	-2.635542
U_t	Level	-2.742371	1 (FIXED)	-3.752946	-2.998064	-2.638752

It is observed that the error term is stationary at 1, 5, and 10 % level of significance taking maximum lag length 8 based on SIC and υ_t is also stationary at 10 % level of significance for fixed lag 1. It proves that the two variables are co-integrated *i.e* there is long run relationship between these two variables.

FURTHER TEST FOR COINTEGRATION

Although the Engle and Granger procedure is easy to perform yet the estimation of the long run equilibrium regression equation requires that we place one variable on the left hand side and use the other as regressor. However, in practice it is possible to find a situation where one regression indicates the variables are co integrated, whereas reversing the order of the variables indicates no co-integration. In our case, we may write the co integrating equation in reverse order such that

$$BD_t = \alpha + \beta TD_t + \upsilon_t, \qquad (vii)$$

The test statistic, in this case indicates that there exists no co-integration at 1% level of significance (though there exists co-integration at both 5 and 10 % level of significance).

In order to avoid such problem *Johansen methodology* has been adopted to test the long run relationship between BD and TD. The results of the test are being presented through the Table 6

Table 6
Results of the test of Co-integration adopting Johansen 's methodology

Trend assumption: Linear deterministic trend

Null hypothesis	*Alternative hypothesis*	*Lag intervals*	*Trace statistic*	*Maximum Eigen statistic*
NONE	AT MOST 1	(1,1)	Null: 10.15558 Alt: 2.377141	Null: 7.778436 Alt.: 2.377141
NONE	AT MOST 1	(2,2)	Null: 21.63223 Alt: 1.772180	Null: 19.86005 Alt.: 1.772180
NONE	AT MOST 1	(3,3)	Null: 14.58106 Alt: 3.618716	Null: 10.96235 Alt.: 3.618716
NONE	AT MOST 1	(4,4)	Null: 15.62983 Alt: 0.556394	Null: 15.07344 Alt.: 0.556394
NONE	AT MOST 1	(5,5)	Null: 19.69778 Alt: 3.258836	Null: 16.43895 Alt.: 3.258836
NONE	AT MOST 1	(6,6)	Null: 16.32665 Alt2.097026	Null: 14.22963 Alt.: 2.097026

FINDINGS AND EXPLANATIONS

The findings from the test results as given in the table 6 are being given in tabular form through the table 7

Table 7
Findings from the test results

Lag intervals	*Trace statistic*	*Max.Eigen value test Stistic*
(1,1)	No cointegration at both 5 and 1% levels	No cointegration at both 5% and 1% levels
(2,2)	1 cointegrating equation at both 5 and1% levels	1 cointegrating equation at both 5-and1% level.
3,3)	No cointegration	No cointegration
(4,4)	1 cointegrating equation at 5% level but no cointegration at 1% level.	1 cointegrating equation at 5% level but no cointegration at 1% level.
(5,5)	Same as (4,4)	Same as (4,4)
(6,6)	Same as (4,4)	Same as (4,4)

It is, therefore, observed that for lag intervals (2,2) the two variables are co integrated. It implies that exists a long run relationship between the variables.

SHORT-RUN RELATIONSHIP (VECTOR-ERROR CORRECTION MODEL)

In the short run, there may be disequilibria even when long-run equilibrium stable relationship exists. This motivates the study of short run relationship between the variables concerned. Consequently, a model that combines both long run and short run behaviors of the variables are examined through the estimation of the Error Correction Model (ECM). In this section we have estimated vector error correction model which consists of the following equations.

$$\Delta TD_t = \gamma_1 + \rho_1 e^{\wedge}_{t-1} + \alpha_1 \Delta TD_{t-1} + \alpha_2 \Delta TD_{t-2} + \alpha_3 \Delta BD_{t-1} + \alpha_4 \Delta BD_{t-2} + \varepsilon_{1t} \quad (viii)$$

and

$$\Delta BD_t = \tilde{a}_2 + \rho_2 e^{\wedge}_{t-1} + \beta_1 \Delta TD_{t-1} + \beta_2 \Delta TD_{t-2} + \beta_3 \Delta BD_{t-1} + \beta_4 \Delta BD_{t-2} + \varepsilon_{2t} \quad (ix)$$

The results of the estimation of these equations are given in the Table-8

Table 8

Results Of Estimation Of The Vector Error Correction Model

Dependent variable	*Explanatory variables*	*Coefficients*	*Standard errors*	*t-statistics*
ΔTD_t	Constant (γ_1)	-262.3149	249.783	-1.05017
		-.332981	0.29350	-1.13453
	ΔTD_{t-1}	-0.494771 (*)	0.29341	-1.68626
	ΔTD_{t-2}	-0.3.48093 (*)	0.22529	-1.54509
	ΔBD_{t-1}	4.054712	3.66286	1.10698
	ΔBD_{t-2}	-5.007952 (*)	3.18253	-1.57357
ΔBD_t	Constant (γ_2)	-11.08013	21.3055	-0.52006
	$e^{\wedge}_{t-1}$	0.037817 (*)	0.02503	1.51063
	ΔBD_{t-1}	0.247158	0.31243	0.79109
	ΔBD_{t-2}	0.197267	0.27146	0.72669
	ΔTD_{t-1}	-.021082	0.02503	-0.84237
	ΔTD_{t-2}	-0.021870	0.01922	-1.13811

* Implies significant at 10% level of significance.

FINDINGS

From the above result, it appears that there exists a short run relationship between BD and TD, since the coefficient of $e\hat{}_{t-1}$ in equation (ix) is significant at 10% level. The estimates of the model also indicates the Granger causality between BD and TD. In the present case BD Granger causes TD since one of the lagged values of BD in equation (viii) is statistically significant, and side by side the lagged values of TD are not statistically significant in equation (ix). However, the following section has been devoted to enquire into the Granger causality between these two variables.

Table 9
Results Of The Granger Causality Test

Null hypothesis	*Alternative hypothesis*	*Lag length*	*Degree of freedom*	*F statistic*	*Probability*
BD does not Granger cause TD	TD does not Granger cause BD	1	(1,23)	Null= 7.31496 (**)	0.01327
				Alt = 0.60866	0.44400
BD does not Granger cause TD	TD does not Granger cause BD	2	(2,21)	Null=2.84819 (*)	0.08420
				Alt =0.39264	0.68091
BD does not Granger cause TD	TD does not Granger cause BD	3	(3,19)	Null= 2.84692 (*)	0.07282
				Alt =0.29843	0.82599
BD does not Granger cause TD	TD does not Granger cause BD	4	(4,17)	Null= 2.16014	0.13561
				Alt=0.47860	0.75107
BD does not Granger cause TD	TD does not Granger cause BD	5	(5,15)	Null=4.94989 (***)	0.01870
				Alt=1.11718	0.41585
BD does not Granger cause TD	TD does not Granger cause BD	6	(6,13)	Null=4.87636 (***)	0.03756
				Alt=0.27562	0.92899
BD does not Granger cause TD	TD does not Granger cause BD	7	(7,11)	Null=7.82534 (***)	0.05941
				Alt=0.13724	0.98527

***, **, * Implies level of significance at 10 %, 5% and 1% respectively.

GRANGER CAUSALITY TEST

The Granger Causality Test has been performed with the estimation of the equations

$$TD_t = \theta_1 + \alpha_1 TD_{t-i} + \alpha_2 BD_{t-i} + \varepsilon_{1t} \quad (x)$$

$$BD_t = \theta_2 + \beta_1 BD_{t-i} + \beta 2 TD_{t-i} + \varepsilon_{2t} \quad (xi)$$

with different lags of the independent variables. where i = 0, 1, ..., K. In our case the lags of the independent variable range from 1 to 7. The Table 9 presents the results of estimation.

FINDINGS

The Table 9 shows that there is a uni-directional causality from BD to TD, i.e. budget deficits Granger causes trade deficit considering the time period 1979 to 2003 with lag length 1 to 7. However, there exists an exception at lag length 4 in which the F value is not significant. In this case Trade deficit is not found to Granger cause budget deficit.

SUMMARY AND CONCLUSION

This study presents a few important findings, which are being stated below.

1. Time series data on TD and BD are non-stationary at levels but these attain stationarity upon first differencing.
2. BD and TD are co-integrated. So there exists a long run stable equilibrium relationship between these two variables.
3. BD Granger causes TD, but TD fails to Granger cause BD. Consequently; there exist a unidirectional causality from BD to TD.

The finding on causality has an important policy implication. Trade deficit in Maldives appears to be the outcome of budget deficit. The transmission mechanism has not been enquired into. Nevertheless, the findings tootify for the fact that a rise in aggregate demand following liberal fiscal policy may end up with frustrating current account deficit. Consequently, prudent management of the budget deficit may be of an important help for ensuring desired decline in trade deficit.

REFERENCES

Abel, Andrew B.and Ben S.Bernanke (2003), *Macro Economics,* New Delhi: Pearson Education.

Abdul Nasser Hatemi- J and Ghazi Shukur,: *Multivariate Based Causality Tests of Twin Deficits in the U.S, International Business School,* Jonkoping University, post box 1026, Sweden.

Akbostanici, Elif and Gul Ipek Tunk (2002), *Turkish Twin Deficits: An Error Correction Model of Trade Balance,* Turkey, Middle East Technical University, Departments of Economics.

Ahmet Zengin: *The Twin Deficit Hypothesis (the Turkish case),* Zonguldak Karaelmas University, Zonguldak, Turkey.

Ali Salman Saleh, Mahendhiran Nair, &Tikiri Agalewatte: The Twin Deficit Problem in Srilanka: An Econometric Analysis, South Asia Economic Journal (2005), Sage Publications.

Arjun Kumar Baral & Shankar Prasad Acharya: "Twin Deficit Hypothesis: An Empirical Investigation on Nepalese Time Series (1964—2000)": *The Journal of Economic Society,* Vol. 7, 2006, page no. 53-68.

Burnside, Carig Martin, Eichenbaum and Sergio Rebelo (2001), *On The Fiscal Implications of Twin Crises,* NBER working paper no. w 8277

Carlos Fonseca Marinheiro, Ricardian Equivalence: *An Empirical Application to the Portuguese Economy,* Faculty of Economics of the University of Coimbria and Katholieke Universities, Leuven, Portugal, March 2001.

Anil Bhuimali & Anil Kumar Biswas

13 TOURISM DEVELOPMENT IN BHUTAN: ITS IMPACT ON THE ECONOMY

INTRODUCTION

Tourism industry has become a significant field of activity all over the world. Developed countries were the pioneers for encouraging tourism development due to their strong economic and natural resource base. For the time being, the developing countries have also entered the industry. Now it is a major source of revenue, foreign exchange and employment opportunities. The countries differ regarding their tourism infrastructure and tourist products. Bhutan, a land-locked small country located in the Eastern Himalayas, possesses huge potentialities for tourism development. Its dense forests, mountainous beauty, traditional cultural value systems all are attractive to the foreign tourists. However, the tourism industry in Bhutan was opened as late as in 1974. Although few numbers of tourists visited that year, it has increased gradually. Since then, Bhutan's tourism industry is playing a vibrant role in the earning of revenue, foreign exchange and employment opportunities. In 2005, Bhutan's tourism industry earned 18.5 million US dollars from 13,643 tourists. Unemployment is a newly emerged issue of Bhutan. This problem can be tackled through the development of tourism industry. Bhutan's tourism industry was initially promoted by the government initiatives. However, the planned development process is putting an increased priority for the development of private sector. Therefore, tourism industry was privatized in 1991. Bhutan's tourism industry confronts several constraints. However, tourism development poses most serious problem in the sustainability of the development process. So, Bhutan approached very cautiously in the matters of tourism development. It is followings a restricted tourism policy for the sustainability of development.

A very few economists have shown their interests in the studies of tourism industry unlike the in other branches of economics viz. industry, agriculture, trade and public finance. In this paper, an approach has been made for the study of economic significance of tourism development in Bhutan. Our study is based on the secondary data available to the Royal Government Bhutan (RGOB) as well as some other national and international agencies. Statistical tables have often been used for showing the trends of important variables. Relationship between the variables has been discussed analytically without any causal test due to nonavailability of reliable statistical data

TOURISM POTENTIALITIES: A GLOBAL PERSPECTIVE

Tourism industry is a fast growing industry. International tourist arrival all over the world increased from 25 million in 1950 to 693 million in 2001, an increase of 28 times. World Tourism Organization (WTO) projected that by 2020 tourism industry will appear as the world's primary industry generating more than $ 2 trillion of global revenue. There is widespread disparities over the world either in terms of tourist arrival or tourist earnings. Europe ranks first in terms of tourist arrival following America. Between 1950-1990, about 65 percent of international tourist visited Europe. In 2005, France ranked first with international tourist arrival of 75.3 millions. Tourist arrival in the same year was only 49.5 million in the USA. In fact developed countries are the tourist hotspots due to their developed infrastructure and quality tourist products. Developed countries together attracted 65 percent of world tourist arrivals and 72 percent of all receipts from tourism while the developing countries attracting 21 percent of international tourists and 26 per cent of the tourists receipts.[1] Belated involvement of the less developed countries as well as their insufficient tourism products and carrying capacity is responsible for this type of unequal tourist trends. For example, Bhutan entered the tourism industry as late as in 1974 and there is still a single air service Druk Air in the whole country. In general, the share of South Asia in total international tourist arrival is less than 1 percent. India is dominant in tourist arrival within South Asia. Its share increased from 49 percent in 1985 to 60 percent in 1989 in terms of the region's total arrival. Despite the widespread disparity within South Asia, it is significant that between 1995 and 2003, tourist arrival in South Asia grows at 7.1 percent in average.

The economic impact of international tourism is a matter of great concern. It generates revenue, provides with foreign exchange and contributes substantially by generating direct, indirect or induced employment opportunities. In 1999, international tourism contributed 11.7 percent of world GDP, 8 percent of world exports and 12 percent of global employment. However, the magnitude of contributions differs between the regions and countries. Tourism accounted for 60.1 percent of exports for Barbados and 29.8 percent of GDP in 1988. The share of tourism in exports and GDP both are also high for Bahamas, Jamaica, India and some other countries. Dependence on tourism is significant for the countries where the share of exports is substantial in its GDP. Even in India, tourism contributed 10.3 percent of its exports in 1988. Average annual growth rate of tourism earnings for South Asia Sub-regional Economic Co-operation (SASEC) countries consisting of Bangladesh, Bhutan, India and Nepal was 1.9 percent between the period 1995-2002. Tourism income- multiplier was calculated for some selected countries where the values varied from 1.96 (Turkey) to 0.39 (Western Samoa).[2] Since tourism is a major source of foreign exchange. It is especially significant for the countries where the 'foreign exchange- gap' is dominant than the 'savings- gap' for the receipt of foreign aid.

The assessment of international tourism in employment generation reveals that in 1996 international tourism industry provided with employment opportunities for 225 million people. Direct employment arises in case of hotels and tourist guides while indirect employment arises from transportation and other services. It is surprising to note that despite all these economic impacts of tourism, tourism industry has been largely ignored either in economic development literature or in international trade theory.

At the end of this section, we are interested to point out some adverse impact of tourism. Overexploitation of tourist resources is a major threat to sustainable development. It may lead to environmental and cultural degradation. For example, tourism development in Nepal is attributable to deforestation, pollution and degradation of natural habitat. Economically, international tourism may lead to income inequalities. In Thailand, tourism development has serious implication for the breakdown of family life and mental health.[3] Therefore, sustainable tourism development policies should be implemented since the very beginning of tourism development.

TOURISTS PATTERN IN BHUTAN

The beginning of tourism industry in Bhutan is of recent origin. For the first time, tourists arrived in 1974 during the coronation of the King Jigme Singye Wangchuck.[4] However, there arrived a mere 287 tourists by that year. This least number of tourist arrival is significant for the fact that it signaled the breaking of long isolation of the country and the development of a viable tourism industry. Since then, there has been a 20 percent average increase in the number of tourist arrival. During the period 1995-2003, an average of 5,000 tourists visited Bhutan annually. Due to the lack of tourist infrastructure and carrying capacity, numbers of tourist arrivals were restricted to a certain limit. Bhutan has followed a 'high value-low volume' tourism policy. Bhutanese generally advocate the tourists who not only bring considerable money but also have experience and respect for Bhutan's divine culture and pristine environment.[5] These are the major rationale for less tourist arrivals in Bhutan.

Tourist arrival in Bhutan has increased steadily since 1990. In 2000, tourist arrival increased to 7,559. This increase was caused due to the emergence of Bhutan as a quality destination and additional licensing for the tour operators.[6] The increase in the number of tourists over the period 1998-2003 as well as the seasonal fluctuations of tourists arrivals within the years have been shown in Table 1.

Table 1
Number of Tourist Arrivals Between 1998-2003

Period	*1998 Number*	*1999 Number*	*2000 Number*	*2001 Number*	*2002 Number*	*2003 Number*
Jan	96	148	65	185	55	192
Feb	154	322	223	355	269	98
Mar	542	1145	1066	553	862	654
Apr	1167	604	995	1632	683	1219
May	267	395	415	276	296	397
Jun	97	108	187	146	79	178
Jul	152	132	162	129	114	112
Aug	340	348	307	252	213	198
Sep	1107	1069	683	868	760	613
Oct	1329	1856	2247	1308	1474	
Nov	678	841	996	517	643	
Dec	274	190	213	172	151	
Total	6203	7158	7559	6393	5599	3661

Source: Department of tourism, (Adapted from *Selected Economic Indicators* 2003, Royal Monetary Authority of Bhutan, Vol. 17, No. 3, September).

Table 1 shows that there is substantial seasonal variation in Tourist arrivals. Tourist visit increases only in the peak seasons of six months consisting of March, April and May. September, October and November. About 84 percent of tourists arrived during these six months. Over the rest of the year, the tourist arrivals sharply fall due either to extreme cold or heavy rain.

Developed countries of the world are basically source markets for Bhutan tourism. As the country is becoming well acquainted with the developed countries, their interests in Bhutan are also increasing leading to an increase in tourist arrivals from those countries. Table 2 shows the pattern of change in the member of tourists from selected developed countries between the period 1996-2008.

Table 2
Number of Tourist Arrivals in Bhutan by Nationality, 1996-2003

Nationality	*1996*	*1997*	*1998*	*1999*	*2000*	*2001*	*2002*	*2003*	*Change 2002/03 (%)*
United States	963	910	1471	2122	2754	2149	1913	1806	5.6
Japan	1211	1173	1032	1102	875	1038	892	952	6.7
Germany	722	533	520	574	662	414	346	496	43.4
United Kingdom	358	642	686	646	595	681	519	605	16.6
France	331	229	366	236	399	287	192	288	50.0
Netherlands	131	234	370	362	359	180	197	179	9.1
Canada	57	89	82	149	194	197	166	121	27.1
Australia	71	121	64	131	179	138	214	165	22.9
Taipei, China	32	83	135	179	175	44	40	90	125.0
Italy	242	186	218	276	156	192	177	331	87.0
Spain	49	33	109	118	141	73	68	77	13.2
Switzerland	161	186	170	296	137	170	164	177	7.9
Austria	156	156	270	197	131	128	92	152	65.2
Belgium	77	75	95	107	95	76	22	104	372.7
Thailand	181	140	19	71	92	36	46	66	43.5
Others	396	573	596	592	615	590	546	658	20.5
Total	5138	5363	6203	7158	7559	6393	5599	6267	12.0

Source: Asian Development Bank, *Technical Assistance for the South Asian Subregional Economic Cooperation: Tourism Development Plan*, November 2003.

From table 2, it is clear that the USA, Japan, Germany, the U.K. and Italy are the six most important markets for Bhutan tourism. It also shows that the USA and the U.K. have increasing trends in the number of people visiting Bhutan while Japan and Germany registers a decreasing trend.

The average length of stay for the tourists in Bhutan is very short. In 2000, it was 8.13 days. However, the length of stay varies based on the nature of tourist activities. For example, trekkers on average stay 7.4 days while cultural tourists averaged 8.3 days.[7] The highest length was achieved in case of some special tours such as bird watching and religious studies. Repeated visits are very rare in Bhutan.

MAJOR TOURIST ATTRACTIONS IN BHUTAN

Bhutan's mountainous sceneries, pristine environment, religious-cultural value system, secular and religious music, dances, festivals, historic monuments, traditional arts, crafts and huge botanical-zoological resources are the most important tourist attractions. National Day commemorates the establishment of the hereditary monarchy on 17 December 1907 by the first king Ugyen Wangchuk. However, the existing King's Birth Day and His Coronation Day are the most important secular festivals, which are celebrated through the parades and dances by the school children. The most important religious festival is Tshechu, a festival in honour of Guru Rinpoche for his great deeds.[8] It is to be noted that tourists are permitted inside the courtyards of the Dzongs (fortresses) exclusively during the festivals. Some festivals are celebrated as 'New Year' at different times and places. These are halfway between religious and secular festivals.[9] Bhutanese arts and paintings are unique. These arts are not concerned with abstract concept of 'beauty'. These are rather concerned with interpretation of Buddhist values and beliefs. Bhutanese craftsmen excels in their images on metals, deities, bells, swords, pillars, Jewelleries and so on. Original paintings of Bhutan since the beginning of the 16 century have been preserved in the temple Tanshing in Bamthang. Other historical interests include Bhutan's National Library in Thinphu, National Textile Museum, Folk Heritage Museum and Simtokha Dzong.

Adventure tourism like river-running, mountain-biking, rock climbing are common tourism practices in Bhutan. The most important adventure tourism in Bhutan is trekking. There are thirteen tourist treks in Bhutan some of which involve long journeys. Thus, trekking adventure in Bhutan is a real adventure.

Rare 770 species of birds are observed in Bhutan. Fishing (Catch and release system due to prohibition) is becoming favourite tourist activity. Bhutanese forests cover more than 73 percent of its total land area. 165 species of animals as well as over 300 species of medicinal plants make Bhutan potentially important tourist destination. Jigme Dorji National Park, Black Mountain National Park and Royal Manas National Parks are major tourist destinations. Eco-tourism is becoming viable and popular with these biological resources combined with the involvement of the local peoples. Very recently, the Black-Necked Crane Festivals for the protection of black-necked cranes (were being killed by the farmers) are being organized by the Royal Society for the Protection of Nature (RSPN), an NGO.[10]

TOURISM AND DEVELOPMENT PLANS OF BHUTAN

In the initial stage of tourism development, tourism industry in Bhutan was under the Ministry of Finance. It was reorganized in 1980 as the Tourism Commercial Organization under the Ministry of Communications and Tourism. It was further reorganized by forming Bhutan Tourism Corporation in 1983 under the Ministry of Trade and Industry. However, tourism industry was privatized in October 1991 in conformity with the greater development plans of Bhutan. Since then, the Tourism Authority of Bhutan (TAB), a regulatory division of the Ministry of Trade and Industry, overseas the tourism activities. It complies 33 private tour operators with the government's tourism policies.

Thus, in the initial stage, the government owned entire tourism infrastructure. The government invested Nu. 15.2 million for the development of tourism facilities including Nu. 12.2 million in hotel infrastructure. In the Ninth Five-Year Plan of Bhutan (2002-2007), total expenditure in the tourism sector was Nu. 183.672 million. Out of this total expenditure, Nu. 58.163 million is recurring expenditure while Nu. 125.509 is capital expenditure.[11] Foreign aid has often been used for the development of tourism industry. In July 1997, a training project for the tour operators with the estimated cost of Nu. 24.5 million was proposed to be set up. The Austrian Government agreed to advance required external aid of Nu. 17.5 million for the same project.[12] A hotel cum tourism management institute, funded by the Austrian government, will be established by 2008.[13] With the ongoing globalization process, Bhutan is welcoming Foreign Direct Investment (FDI) for tourism development, especially the development of hotel infrastructure. In 2004, tourism sector was boosted up because of the opening up of a luxury hotel with the help of FDI.[12] Other high-end projects financed by FDI are also underway.

There have been major policy changes for the tourism development in the Ninth Plan of Bhutan. The main goals of the policy changes in the Ninth Plan include:

- Promoting and maintaining Bhutan as a high quality tourist destination.
- Generating tourism related employment opportunities, especially for the rural people.
- Developing innovative tourist products in order to meet the interests of the visitors.
- Reduction of seasonality of tourist arrivals.
- Enhancement of knowledge of the tourist guides regarding local history and culture.
- Preservation of historical sites, domestic environment and culture.
- Promoting the quality of hospitality services.

The Royal Government's development philosophy is guided by the "Gross National Happiness" rather than the Gross National Product. Thus, RGOB judges development not by mere income growth; instead the Government affirmed the importance of less quantifiable values such as happiness, contentment, spiritual and emotional well-being of the people. Bhutan's tourism policy is reflective of this larger development philosophy.[17] With all these views and the mistakes other developing countries committed, the RGOB has followed a sustainable tourism policy, which should be environment friendly, socio-culturally desirable and economically viable.

Since the beginning, therefore, the RGOB is following a restricted tourism policy with a quota of 200 tourists per year. Later on, it was raised to 4000 per year. However, at present there is no upper limit. Rather, tourist arrivals are restricted indirectly through the pricing policies.[15] Bhutan is following the policy of 'high-value low-volume' tourism policy for minimizing the adverse effects. At the beginning, the cost was set at US $ 130 per day per person. It has been subsequently raised to US $ 165 per day and further to US $ 200 per day per person. 10 percent of this revenue goes to the external foreign travel agent, 35 percent to the government as the royalty and the rest to one of the 33 private tour operators. Despite this dearer prices, the wealthy tourists tolerate due to the benevolent social activities of the Royal Government such as provision of free education and medical services and taking a good deal of care of its people.[16] However, according to our recent tour into Bluton, no costs are charged from the Indian Nationals.

IMPACT OF TOURISM ON THE BHUTANESE ECONOMY

Bhutan's tourism industry is making a good contribution to the generation of revenue, earning of foreign exchange and provision of employment opportunities. Today, tourism industry is the sixth largest producer of revenue and third largest foreign exchange earner of the country. Bhutan's tourism industry earned US $ 7.98 million in 2002. Between the period 1995-2002, the average earnings from tourism have grown at 5.1 percent annually. Despite the significant contribution tourism industry is making in the revenue generation, tourism earnings are growing at a slower rate vis-à-vis its overall economic growth of 8 percent per annum. In 2002, average earning per tourist was 1,425 dollar. Table- 3 gives a clear picture of changes in the tourist earnings over the period 1998-2003.

Table 3
Bhutan's Tourist Revenue in Millions of US Dollar

Period	*1998 Revenue*	*1999 Revenue*	*2000 Revenue*	*2001 Revenue*	*2002 Revenue*	*2003 Revenue*
Jan	0.1	0.1	0.1	0.2	0.1	0.2
Feb	0.1	0.3	0.2	0.4	0.2	0.1
Mar	0.7	1.4	1.3	0.8	1.1	0.8
Apr	1.5	0.8	1.4	2.3	1.1	1.7
May	0.3	0.4	0.6	0.4	0.4	0.5
Jun	0.1	0.1	0.2	0.1	0.1	0.2
Jul	0.2	0.1	0.2	0.1	0.1	0.1
Aug	0.4	0.3	0.3	0.2	0.2	0.2
Sep	1.5	1.4	1.0	1.5	1.2	0.9
Oct	1.9	2.7	3.7	2.1	2.4	
Nov	1.0	1.1	1.5	0.8	0.9	
Dec	0.3	0.1	0.2	0.2	0.1	
Total	8.0	8.9	10.5	9.2	8.0	4.6

Source: Department of Tourism, (Adapted from *Selected Economic Indicators* 2003, Royal Monetary Authority of Bhutan, Vol.17, No. 3, September).

Table 3 shows that there is substantial fluctuation of tourist earnings. It increases rapidly during the high season while falls sharply during the slack season. Tourism accounts for about 5 percent of Bhutan's national revenue and 15 to 20 percent of its total exports.

Tourism is a major source of foreign exchange earning essential for ever growing imports. In the early phase of development, the demand for foreign exchange was low. However, with the ongoing economic diversification and social upliftment, the number of development projects increased substantially. It is to be noted that since the current account deficit of Bhutan is met by the acceptance of foreign aid, balance of payment has been favourable. However, the major goal of Bhutan's planned development process is to achieve self reliance by taking least possible foreign aid.[18] Under the circumstances, increased foreign exchange from tourism is a good complement to the growth of exports.

The problem of unemployment in Bhutan is an emerging issue. The educated Bhutanese are opting for white-collar jobs and tend to migrate towards the urban areas. Bhutan's tourism industry is offering direct, indirect as well as induced employment opportunities which would obviously mitigate the unemployment problems. Tour operators and tourist guides are getting direct employment in the tourism industry. For a long time, licenses were limited to 33 tour operators. However, by 2001, 89 tour operators had been registered. In September 2001, there were 224 cultural guides and 87 trekking guides. While some guides are permanently employed by the tour operators, others are employed on a temporary basis. Hotel staff and transport operators are availing indirect employment opportunities.

A total of 32 hotels and guest houses were approved for tourists' accommodation by 1996. In 2001, the number increased to 57 with 1013 rooms at different places of Bhutan. These hotels are employing 1000 staff. In case of transportation, Druk Air, the only air service of Bhutan is playing a significant role. When the service was established in 1982, there were only 20 persons employed. However, the total employment figure increased to

200 by 2002. Induced employment opportunities are the most significant for the Bhutanese people. Derived demand for the craftmen's products for meeting the tourist requirements as well as the demand originated from the development of tourism infrastructure are the key elements of induced employment. Although statistical data is very difficult to collect for these type of employment, it is fact that rising tourist arrivals would tend to raise employment opportunities.

Since decentralization and people's participation in the development process was the long charished contexts of development in Bhutan,[19] it was reflected in the tourism industry through the promotion of rural and culture based tourism. Local peoples involve in these tourism activities and earn income. It will also blockade the trends of rural urban migration.

PROBLEMS: THE QUESTIONS OF SUSTAINABILITY

The problems of tourism industry in Bhutan are twofold-structural problems which include lack of tourist infrastructure, limited diversification of tourist products, seasonality of tour activities, regional imbalance etc. and the spatial problems such as the sustainability of tourism development. Tourist infrastructure is limited to fewer number of hotels, tour operators and tourist guides. The ownership of private tourist activities is highly skewed. Out of 89 tour-operators, 6 operators were reported to have handled 80 percent of tourist arrivals in 1993. However, because small tour operators are becoming operational, the inequality is decreasing. In 2000, the top 6 tour operators handled 60 percent of the foreign tourists. Most of the tourist guides are Thimphu based and rural involvement is still very low. In order to avoid the inequality of involvement of rural and urban people in the tourism industry, the government is emphasizing alternative tourism activities like cultural tourism, ecotourism etc. Inter regional inequality is another problem. Most tourist activities are concentrated in Thimphu and Paro. Haa and Gasa have low level of tourist activity while Zhemgang and Lhuetse have not tourist activities at all. However, these regions have huge potentialities such as trekking, bird watching, medical tours, adventure tourism as well as cultural tourist activities. The problem of seasonality is imposed by the geographical and climatic nature of the country. March-April and October-November are the periods of high tourist activity. Tourist activities in monsoon and winter is limited by heavy rain and extreme cold. The seasonal nature of tourism leads to inequal arrivals of visitors over the year. It also imposes heavy pressure on the limited tourist infrastructure during the peak seasons. Revenue earned from tourism also fluctuates substantially. 84 percent of tourist arrive during the peak six months (March-May / September-November). The average length of stay is also very short. It was 8.13 days in 2000. The average length of stay varies between the tourist activities. 22 days, the greatest length of stay was achieved for some special interest tourism such as bird watching and religious studies. Although price subsidies are offered for the slack season tourists, alternative tourism development strategies are drawing special attentions.

Product diversification in tourism is insufficient for Bhutan. Tourism in Bhutan has so far been mostly limited to cultural tourists, sightseers and trekkers. In 1999, out of a total of 7,158 tourists, 6,328 were cultural tourists and 830 sightseers.[20] However, other forms of tourism such as ecotourism, adventure tourism, health tourism and domestic tourism have good prospects. The Tourism Authority of Bhutan is giving top most priority in the quality of tourist products by promoting tourist infrastructure, cleaning of tour treks, providing training to the tourist guides and improving hospitality services.

The department of tourism lacks both manpower and finance for managing the tourism industry effectively. Due to the rising competition between the tour operators, few of them are giving rebates to the foreign tourists. Breaking of this pricing integrity is contradictory to the Royal Government's "High value-Low volume' tourism policy. It is significant to note that collection of data and intensive research is essential for the sound tourism policies and correct decision-making.

Sustainability of tourism is a key element of tourism development. Nepal's tourism industry was given importance since the early 1960s. Over a long period of time it has adversely affected the environmental and socio-cultural balance of the country. De-forestation due to wood harvest for supplying fuelwood to the tourists affected is landscape. Use of plastic, tin and other non-degradable materials turned some popular treks into 'garbage trails'. Tourism is blamed for commercialization of art, culture and religion rather than reviving them.[21] Indian tourism industry is also accused of degrading its natural environment. Overcrowding, congestion, environmental pollution etc. emerged where ever full-fledged tourist centres had been set up. Environmental injury was observed in Garwal Himalayas where ecological balance was long preserved.[22]

However, since the very beginning, Bhutan's tourism industry was strictly controlled for preserving the traditional culture and environment. Thus, it has minimum adverse effects. The Fifth Five- Year Plan document of Bhutan pointed out that tourism has not created in Bhutan the cultural and environmental problems like many other tourism oriented countries.[23] In a few years, tourism related environmental and cultural problems emerged in Bhutan. Destruction of vegetation, creation of garbage trails etc. have grown. Government's recent policies pinpoint these problems for sustainability of development. Besides, in this initial stage, it did not reach critical level because 73 percent of Bhutan's land is covered with forests. There remains 13 percent excess forests for further exploitation by maintaining 60 percent for preservation.

Govt's policy now recognizes eco-tourism for sustainable tourism development. Bhutan is rich in resources for ecotourism. However, eco-tourism must be compatible with effective conservation and must operate within the area's natural capacity and future sustainability. The development of eco-tourism should be limited to development of trails and access routes as well as visitors centres. Several seminars on eco-tourism have been conducted. Phobjikha Valley programme was the first such real attempt for developing eco-tourism conserving endangered black-necked cranes.

CONCLUSION

Discussions made so far indicates that tourism industry have growing significance in the economic development world over. However, the developing countries are getting less benefits from tourism vis-à-vis the developed countries. Bhutan is a late comer in tourism industry. Bhutan has exclusive tourist attractions. The numbers of tourist arrivals have considerably increased overtime. Earnings from tourism industry is growing at a moderate rate. Bhutan's tourism industry is a suitable vehicle for the solution of its emerging unemployment problems and the problems of urban migration. Although tourism development was a government venture since its beginning, it was privatized in 1991 in conformity with the larger planned development approaches of the RGOB. Bhutan has been following a restricted tourism policy since the very beginning. Initially restrictions were imposed in terms of the number of tourist arrivals while pricing policies have been used thereafter. These restrictions were imposed due to the shortage of tourist infrastructure as well as for the preservation of traditional environmental and cultural values. The main problems of the tourism industry in Bhutan are seasonality, regional imbalance, institutional backwardness so on. Bhutan is following sustainable tourism policies keeping in view the pitfalls of the neighbouring countries. If the approach of the country is cautious as it is at present, Bhutan can substantially benefit from tourism industry even with its substantiality.

REFERENCE

Harrison, David (1992), "International tourism and the less developed countries: the background" in David Harrison (ed.) *Tourism and the Less Developed Countries*, Belhaven Press, London, p. 8.

Ibid 1, p. 16.

Op. cit.

Interview between Billi Bierling and Dr. Martin Uitz, *Mountain Forum Bulletin*, January 2006, p. 13.

Ibid. 4.

The Planning Commission, *Ninth Five-Year Plan* (2002-2007), Main Document, RGOB, pp. 120-124.

Ibid. 6

Pomaret, Francoise (1994), *Bhutan*, The Guide Book Company Limited, Hong Kong, pp. 102-103.

Ibid. 8.

Reinfeld, Marti Ann (2003), "Tourism and the Politics of Cultural Preservation: A Case Study of Bhutan", *Journal of Public and International Affairs*, Vol. 14, Spring.

Ibid. 6.

The Planning Commission, *Eight Five-Year Plan* (1997-2002), Project Profile, RGOB, Vol. 2.

Kuensel (2006), January 4.

Asian Development Bank, *Asian Development Outlook* 2005, Hong Kong, pp. 138-139.

Brunet, Sandra et. al (2001), "Tourism Development in Bhutan: Tensions between Tradition and Modernity", *Journal of Sustainable Tourism*, Vol. 9, No. 3, pp. 252-261.

Ibid 4.

Tobgay, Mr. Sonam (2006), "Overview of tourism in Bhutan and how it fits into the general development plans of Bhutan", Programme Officer, Tourism Authority of Bhutan, Thimphu, Bhutan, June 12.

Basu, G.K. (1998), *Bhutan: The Political Economy of Development*, South Asian Publishers, New Delhi, pp. 46-60.

Rizal, Dhurba P. (2001), *Bhutan: Decentralization and Good Governance*, Adroit Publishers, Delhi.

Dorji, Tandi (2001), "Sustainability of Tourism in Bhutan", *Journal of Bhutan Studies*, Vol. 3, No. 1, pp. 84-104.

Gurung, Harka "Sustainability and Development in Mountain Tourism", ICIMOD.

Singh, Tej Vir (1993), "Development of Tourism in the Himalayan Environment: The Problem of Sustainability" in MSS Rawat (ed.), *Himalayas : A Regional Perspective*, Daya Publishing House, Delhi, pp. 63-77.

The Planning Commission, *Fifth Five-Year Plan* (1982-1987), Main Document, RGOB, Thimphu, Bhutan.

INDEX

P